CANDLESTICK DECORATED IN HIGH RELIEF
With name of maker, William Grainger, and dated 1616
(*Victoria and Albert Museum*)

CHATS ON
OLD PEWTER

H. J. L. J. Massé

Edited and revised by
Ronald F. Michaelis

With a new section,
"American Pewter in the Eighteenth and Nineteenth Centuries," by

Henry J. Kauffman

THIRD REVISED EDITION

DOVER PUBLICATIONS, INC.

NEW YORK

Published in Canada by General Publishing Company, Ltd., 30 Lesmill Road, Don Mills, Toronto, Ontario.

Published in the United Kingdom by Constable and Company, Ltd., 10 Orange Street, London WC 2.

This Dover edition, first published in 1971, consists of:

(1) An unabridged republication, with minor revisions, of the second revised edition of *Chats on Old Pewter* as published by Ernest Benn, London, in 1949 (original edition: Benn, 1911). The present edition, published by special arrangement with Ernest Benn Limited, contains a new Foreword by Ronald F. Michaelis.

(2) A completely new section, "American Pewter in the Eighteenth and Nineteenth Centuries," written specially for the present edition by Henry J. Kauffman.

International Standard Book Number: 0-486-22129-6
Library of Congress Catalog Card Number: 72-138803

Manufactured in the United States of America
Dover Publications, Inc.
180 Varick Street
New York, N.Y. 10014

FOREWORD TO THE DOVER EDITION

SINCE 1949, the year in which the revised edition of this work was published, the number of pewter collectors in the British Isles must have increased tenfold (since 1911, the year of initial publication, perhaps about a hundred-fold), and knowledge of the subject has become correspondingly more widespread. It is thus all the more remarkable that this book, in its present form, is virtually as up-to-date as it was twenty years ago. For that reason it is not proposed to alter the text in any way, except to correct the few minor errors that have been noticed.

Some thought was given to the question of amending the chapter on prices, but it was concluded that little would be gained by quoting some of the very high prices which have been paid for fine examples of early and rare pewterware in recent years. It was only to be expected that, with the amplification of the number of collectors and the extended distribution of available pieces, prices would have risen dramatically; this is a tendency which has affected collectors in every field, and one can see little chance of amelioration in the future.

Devotees who in the past were able to form collections at the prices then obtaining (or perhaps their descendants) will be elated at the great increase in value of the items they possess. But this state of affairs acts to the detriment of newcomers to the hobby, who, unless they are fortunate enough to afford purchases at today's level, will have to be content with far less voluminous collections, or will have to include items which were formerly not considered

5

old enough or exciting enough. This is an inevitable process of change as the years progress. In my own earlier days as a collector I seldom retained a piece of pewterware of date later than, say, 1750, but today, if one is to continue to add to such a display, one must acquire examples ranging well into the nineteenth century. It was then a case of "familiarity breeds contempt," for in a day's search in almost any locality in England one could find literally dozens, or even hundreds, of examples of late eighteenth or early nineteenth-century pewterware in the form of plates, dishes, lidless tavern mugs and other objects. But this is no longer the case, and what was once offered (and refused) for a few shillings is today sold readily—when available—for as many pounds.

The greater interest in British pewterware, in both England and the United States, has come near to denuding the home market of this class of material, and has also been largely responsible for forcing up the prices. It is probable that the greater amount of publicity given to high prices realized in the auction rooms is causing those few who still own an item or two of old and "collectable" pewter to bring it out of storage and sell it whilst the going is good; this could account for the fact that every so often a completely unknown, though very good, piece not previously recorded as having graced one of the older collections, is offered and eagerly purchased. One wonders when the bottom of the barrel will be reached.

In contemplation of the merits of the present book, I was struck with the great wisdom and foresight of the original writer, who, besides being one of the most knowledgeable of the older pewter devotees at a time when only a handful of collectors thought the subject worthy of consideration, was himself an able amateur craftsman in the repair and care of antique pewterware. It is worth

recording that, in the course of some forty years of collecting on my own account, I have come across several examples
of Massé's amazing skill—specimens of collectable pieces
which he repaired by the insertion of a section of new
metal here, or with a newly soldered seam there, or from
which he had to remove the traces of some earlier "botched
up" repair to bring the item back to a state very closely
approximating its original perfection. Whenever he
manipulated the piece in any way, he stamped the specimen with his initials "H.J.L.J.M." in minute letter
punches on the underside or inside of the repair, so that
posterity should be aware that, despite its apparent
perfection and original condition, the object had had some
treatment by a later hand. What a lesson this points to
present-day "restorers" of old furniture, china, ivories
and other beautiful things which sometimes contain only
about half of their original construction, and are passed
off as "original" by dealers and collectors alike, who,
it would be kinder to say, are perhaps rather more
unknowledgeable than unscrupulous!

A repair made to an object, which at the time may have
been readily apparent, can, with years of exposure to the
elements, be disguised completely by the overall oxidation
or patination of the object, but modern scientific methods
of detection, such as the use of ultraviolet light, under
which the fluorescence of different materials may be
clearly seen, reveal alterations much more readily. In
fact, the use of ultraviolet light in relation to antique
pewterware is a field still largely unexplored, but this
subject is too technical and too lengthy to be discussed
here. This book is—and undoubtedly will remain—one
of the most useful references for the younger collector,
and a mine of information for the student. For that
reason one would not wish to complicate the joys of

collecting by the inclusion of such technical and scientific data.

Those who wish to pursue the study of antique pewterware generally are advised to read all the specialized literature upon which they can lay their hands, and to meet with as many other collectors as possible for the purpose of discussing and mutually exhibiting specimens of all strata of interest. The collector of today is far more fortunate than those of Massé's time in that there are now in existence societies and clubs devoted entirely to this study, such as the Pewter Society (formerly the Society of Pewter Collectors, founded in 1918) in England, and the Pewter Collectors' Club of America. Membership in either is open to all serious students and collectors.

Mention of America is pertinent; whereas at the time of Massé's original version of this volume it is doubtful if there were more than a dozen or so collectors there, the position is very different today. In the United States there is undoubtedly as much interest in old English pewterware as ever there was in England itself, and certainly a vast interest in the productions of the American pewterers. Many of the early American craftsmen had, of course, emigrated from England or obtained their moulds from there in order to commence a trade in which they later came to be eminently proficient. I am gratified that the publishers of this edition are adding a new section devoted entirely to American pewter—this is all the book lacked. The resultant publication should have universal appeal.

R. F. MICHAELIS

Sussex, England
August 1971

FOREWORD TO THE 1949 EDITION

WHEN this volume was originally published in 1911 it was intended to be somewhat in the nature of a supplement to Mr. Massé's earlier book *Pewter Plate*, the first edition of which was published in 1904, very shortly after the first exhibition of old pewter which he staged at Clifford's Inn Hall.

For that reason much of the pewter he illustrated and described was that which had recently been on view, and which was still fresh in the minds of many of the readers of his later book. This all happened some forty-odd years ago, and much of the pewter has now changed hands, and many of those who had helped in the display, by loaning pieces from their collections, have now passed on.

In addition, many of the articles which, in the days when the study of pewter was in its infancy, were looked upon as desirable additions to a collection are now more or less disregarded by collectors who have learned more of their subject.

So far as the history of the Pewterers' Guilds, and the manufacture, care and repair of old pewter, is concerned there is little that can be added to what Mr. Massé has already said and, beyond a few necessary amendments in the light of present-day knowledge, his chapters on these subjects have remained substantially as he wrote them.

Mr. Massé was one of the pioneers in pewter-collecting and an authority on his subject; the early work he put in is recognized and appreciated even to-day.

The late Mr. Howard H. Cotterell later came to be

acknowledged as the expert *par excellence* in this particular field, and his monumental work *Old Pewter, its Makers and Marks*, published by Batsford in 1929, is still accepted as the standard work on the subject of English (or British) pewter.

Mr. Cotterell was able to go very much farther than had hitherto been possible in attributing many of the doubtful touches on the London touch-plates to their rightful owners.

The present writer has been able to go even farther in this respect, and it is hoped that the lists of pewterers given at the end of this volume will be found of use to students of pewter history.

It is always a difficult task to decide just how much to include in a book of this size, and how much to exclude, and yet still ensure that the resultant volume shall serve the maximum of usefulness within its scope; for example, it could obviously not now give anything like a comprehensive list of known pewterers or their marks, for the very good reason that there are some 5000 references to separate pewterers in Cotterell's book alone, plus many hundreds of marks which have not been definitely attributed to any known pewterers, and since the publication of his book a tremendous amount of additional material has come to hand which is even now being collated, sifted and checked with the ultimate object of being published as a supplement to Cotterell's work. This will include as many more references again as are already contained in his book, besides attributing many of the unknown marks to pewterers yet to be listed.

The chapter in this volume of "Chats", which at the time of its original publication in 1911 included all known pewterers, has now been amended to include only those pewterers who are known to have struck their touches on the existing London or Edinburgh touch-plates. Their dates of obtaining Freedom have been given in all cases.

An additional list is here given of the touches in the order in which they were struck upon the plates.

The chapter on Prices, which is one of the features of this series of books, has been retained but, instead of a long list of prices for articles—some of which are of only limited interest—being given, a few representative prices have been selected for pewter of more general appeal.

It might be considered that to quote prices for items of pewter ware, many of which are probably unique, cannot, in any event, be of much help to the uninitiated. The value of any article of purely æsthetic interest is that which the buyer places upon it.

It is pointed out that prices are, at the time of writing, beginning to find a steadier level than was the case immediately following the second world war, in common with most other articles, collectable and otherwise.

Printed prices should, therefore, not be taken too literally, either by collectors or dealers, but should be looked upon as an indication of the trend of collecting interest in pewter at various periods rather than as any hard and fast "price-list" upon which to base future transactions.

In conclusion I would like to thank the many private collectors and museum authorities who have so kindly allowed me to reproduce specimens from their collections.

R. F. M.

TWO DISHES WITH CAST ORNAMENT (EDELZINN)

(Victoria and Albert Museum)

CONTENTS

ENGLISH PEWTER SPOONS
Attractively displayed on an oak spoon-rack
(*Collection of the late A. V. Sutherland Graeme*)

LIST OF ILLUSTRATIONS

CHATS ON OLD PEWTER

LIST OF ILLUSTRATIONS

17

CHATS ON
OLD PEWTER

PAIR OF PRICKET CANDLESTICKS AND A CHRISMATORY
(*Victoria and Albert Museum*)

PEWTER AND OLD OAK
(*Collection of the late A. V. Sutherland Graeme*)

CHAPTER ONE

ADVICE TO COLLECTORS

IT is not easy to advise a prospective collector of pewter as to what objects he should chiefly devote his attention. In the case of silver, we know how comparatively rare are pre-Reformation specimens, and in the case of pewter it is almost as unusual an occurrence to light upon a piece earlier than the seventeenth century. When such specimens are met with the price is apt to discourage even the most enthusiastic. However, as long as there is any old pewter left, and as long as there is any pewter even of doubtful antecedence forthcoming, there will be many ready to buy the pieces and place them on their shelves and dressers.

In forming a collection the wiser course will be to specialize in a predetermined group of pewter—either British or foreign. Whichever group is chosen it is certain that the collector will find ample scope for expression of his individuality, and it is more than probable that he will later confine his activities to a narrower field than that implied in the broad terms used above.

No one can hope to form a representative collection of pewter produced in both Britain and other countries and, whilst it is very likely that the collector will, in his early days, acquire a mixture of odd pieces, merely because they are made of pewter, he will, doubtless, eventually "weed out" and base his future plans on the specimens which appeal most to his æsthetic sense.

21

Foreign pewter, of course, will appeal to the lover of more ornate forms, but the genuineness of the specimens is very often open to question. Frequently, too, quite good old pewter is manipulated so as to appeal to the tourist by the addition of absurd coats-of-arms, worked roughly in *repoussé*, or to enhance the price a legend accompanies the object, and the dealer guarantees that it was formerly in a monastery or a nunnery, or else in a nobleman's house till quite recently. This is common in the case of pewter in Bavaria and in Tyrol.

So, then, *caveat emptor*, and let him not buy recklessly everything that he sees in the shop-windows, not even in those of the countryside, covered with a dust like that on some bottles of old port wine.

Any one with unlimited time and means may mark down remote country districts and explore them for himself, but it is not often that finds are made in this way. The dealers' agents have already worked the whole country fairly well and bought for a few pence, and by the sack, what was regarded as lumber by the descendants of former possessors.

Much good pewter has disappeared for ever, having been sold to travelling tinkers for use as solder.

There is such a thing as Roman pewter, but it is so rare that a collector could never hope to fill even one small case. The quest would be keen, no doubt, but with long intervals between the acquisitions. Such pewter is more suitably placed in museums, where county enterprise has provided them, or in a central building such as the British Museum, or the Victoria and Albert Museum at South Kensington.

A collector who wished to specialize within very narrow limits might confine himself to Elizabethan or, better, to Jacobean pewter.

ADVICE TO COLLECTORS

The wider term — seventeenth - century — can better express the favourite period of most serious collectors of British pewter, and includes all Jacobean, and many of the William and Mary pieces.

Pewter of the first half of the century is hard to find and the collector may consider himself fortunate indeed if he can count even one or two treasures of date earlier than 1650 among his collection.

As suggestions for collectors, it may be noted that spoons form an interesting subsection of the subject of pewter.

Practically all that can be said about them is to be found in the late Mr. F. G. Hilton Price's monograph *Old Base Metal Spoons*, published in 1908, but still regarded as the standard work on the subject.

This is a very thorough manual, containing illustrations, from drawings to scale, of most of the marks to be found on English spoons.

The earliest spoons are rare and price will prohibit the collector from acquiring more than a representative collection, but their charm is everlasting and, provided they are displayed in a manner where they can be seen to advantage, such as on an old oak spoon-rack, perhaps with the spice-box which was a frequent adjunct to these fixtures, they will be a source of delight to the collector and his friends.

Early tankards, again, may be suggested, and with them may be included measures. Of these, infinite variety is to be had, for they are with or without lids, of various nationalities, shapes and sizes. Moreover, there is always the chance of a *trouvaille*. A collector may not be lucky enough to pick up a William and Mary tankard for 4s. 6d. but it has been done and may be done again.

Church plate attracts many collectors, and specimens

of flagons, chalices, patens (both footed and otherwise), collection plates, or baptismal bowls may be found.

Much church pewter must have left its original home by improper means, and it is well to mention here that none of the articles which can rightly be called the the property of the Church should have been sold or disposed of without a "faculty".

The bent of other collectors may lie in the direction of what the Germans call *Edelzinn* (see page 12). Here again the chances are but small of meeting with invariably genuine pieces, and would-be collectors may have to content themselves with Herr Demiani's book and the wonderfully clear reproductions of the pieces in his and other collections.

Another work, which gives very fine illustrations, with descriptions of decorative German pewter, is Erwin Hintze's *Nürnberger Zinn*.

Salts, usually wrongly called salt-cellars, can form an interesting class on their own.

They followed, as did pewter spoons, the fashions of their counterparts in silver, and can, therefore, be dated fairly accurately. Some salts, such as the large Master Salts used in early Stuart days, may be difficult to find, but later specimens dating between, say, 1675 and 1750 may still be picked up for reasonable sums.

Candlesticks of the seventeenth or of the early eighteenth centuries, which again were modelled largely on silver patterns, are particularly popular with collectors, but genuine early examples are rare and, consequently, prices will keep them out of the reach of the younger collector.

Candlesticks made in the late eighteenth and early nineteenth centuries are fairly easy to find and the collector who has a leaning in this direction might commence his collection with these, weeding out by degrees as his collection, or his knowledge, increases.

The collector will be sure to have offered to him specimens of "tokens". These were metal—frequently pewter—disks or tablets, with initials and sometimes a date upon them, that were issued to intending communicants some time before the proposed celebration, and collected in church on the day appointed, under proper supervision. They were generally cast, but in some cases were stamped, more or less roughly, on pieces of pewter of the size required.

For a Scotsman such tokens will have an interest that the Southron will perhaps hardly appreciate. The competition is keen and the supply is limited, so the unwary must be doubly on their guard.

These articles, with other articles of Church use, such as Communion Plate, seem rather more suitable for museums than for individuals. Those interested in them will find several excellent illustrations in the late Mr. Ingleby Wood's book *Scottish Pewterware and Pewterers*, and for the traveller in Scotland the collection in the Smith Institute, Stirling, will certainly repay careful inspection.

Plates and dishes in themselves, unless of early type or by early makers, with clearly marked touches, are not of surpassing interest. Plates and dishes, if in good condition, may be used as backgrounds, or in the equipment of a dresser, or in the reconstituting of a "garnish", but plates collected with no definite aim or object would soon pall on the most ardent collector.

To collect pewter which has been marked by a recognized maker would be interesting, but there is this difficulty: much excellent pewter was unmarked by the maker or has a mark that is not now legible; and much, again, was made by pewterers whose marks are not on the touch-plates now in existence.

A collection of such marked plates, dishes, and vessels would be of more value to the student of touches than to an ordinary collector.

Some collectors have had an eye solely to the shapes of pewter ware, and ignoring the place of origin, and in many cases the quality, have chosen pieces for the beauty of their lines, and for nothing else.

One has heard of enthusiasts who began to collect pewter merely because a friend had done the same. This does not betray much originality, but the feeling of very keen rivalry that might arise could produce one or perhaps two very good collections. If, however, neither of the two knew anything about pewter, the earlier moves in the game—for it is more like that than serious collecting—would be apt to verge on the ridiculous.

Cases have been known in which the desire to have a dinner-service in pewter of a certain number of pieces has been the prime cause of the collection being made, and, the step once taken, the collector has added wisely later on, and then, weeding out the less desirable pieces, has passed them on to delight others less fortunate than himself.

It was once suggested by a connoisseur to a friend that he should make a collection of faked pieces and offer them to a certain well-known museum as a warning to the authorities of the institution in question and as a guide to future collectors. There is really something in the idea, and a good collection of *bona-fide* fakes would be extremely interesting for many reasons. The thing, too, has been done in another department of archæology, and in one of our provincial museums there is a wonderful array of faked flint weapons and tools, which have deceived even the elect who know everything.

ADVICE TO COLLECTORS

The beginner in collecting pewter will be faced with the difficulty of determining the difference between pewter and Britannia metal.

It has been said by some writers that Britannia metal contains no lead whereas pewter contains as much as 25 per cent., with its other component parts, and that pewter will, in consequence, leave a blackish mark if a corner or sharp edge of the article be drawn across a sheet of paper, whilst Britannia metal will leave no mark at all. This is not true, in fact, and the results may still leave the collector in a state of bewilderment. A surer method will be to know what was made in Britannia metal, and also to know some of its makers.

Avoid anything bearing the names I. Vickers, Broadhead and Atkin, "Ashberry" or "Colsman's Improved Compost", also anything with the word "Sheffield" or "J. Dixon" or "Dixon and Sons", or bearing a catalogue number impressed on the bottom. It has been commonly thought that James Dixon and Sons of Sheffield also made pewter, but they have themselves definitely stated otherwise in a letter published in a well-known collectors' journal in which they said that pewter had not been made by them within the living memory of their oldest employee, who (in 1918) had been with them sixty-four years. They were able to trace no tools or remains of tools used in pewter-making and the succinct paragraph quoted from their letter as follows surely clinches the matter: "We have often come across pieces of our own Britannia metal which has erroneously been included amongst well-known collections of pewter. . . ." The firm has since confirmed the information quoted then and, it is hoped, has laid this ghost for ever.

Articles which were frequently made in Britannia metal are tea-pots, coffee-pots, hot-water jugs, candlesticks, snuff-boxes, small bait- and fishing-tackle boxes, sandwich-boxes, salts and pepper-castors.

Britannia metal came into use only at the end of the eighteenth century and articles produced in that metal are, in any case, too late in date to interest the serious collector, so that the question of the metal should not cause any real difficulty.

The test in the old time for pewter was mainly that of the quality of the alloy, for there was no opposition alloy, such as Britannia metal. All through Welch's *History of the Pewterers' Company* mention is made of the seizing of pewter on the ground that it was "so many grains or penny-weights less than 'fine'."

In our own time we can fall back on the analytical chemist, who for a fee will tell us to a certainty the composition of the alloy submitted to him. We may feel inclined, if we have the requisite scientific knowledge and the necessary apparatus, to do it ourselves, but the accumulated experience of the expert is a thing well worth the fee in any important case.

The main difficulty in following the suggestion above, however, is that it will entail shaving or scraping a small portion of the metal from the piece in question, and few will feel inclined to damage the piece to this extent.

The late Mr. W. J. Englefield, of the pewtering firm which has continued in business since the year 1700, still used the test of comparison by weight of a disk of the metal to be assayed, with a disk of pure tin, cast in the same mould.

This is a time-honoured method and it is by this means that the assay was taken of the metal in pewterers' work-shops. "Fine" metal contained the proportion of lead allowed by the Pewterers' Company's edicts, metal to which too large a quantity of lead had been added being dubbed so many grains "less than fine ".

A collection once formed, it becomes necessary to display it, so as to make the most of it, both from the collector's point of view and also from that of the student.

It may be shown on a dresser, but the average dresser is overloaded with countless little trifling objects, which literally crowd out the others and mar the effect. The less the dresser has upon it, over and above its due complement, the better will it look.

Failing a dresser, a recess with strong shelves — for pewter in the aggregate is somewhat heavy — may be utilized. If it be in a dark corner, the shelves may be painted white and the recess itself papered with white lining paper. If, again, the recess is light enough, the lining of the walls may be of brown paper of a suitable tone, or it may be green or red. The latter harmonizes well with the white paint of the woodwork and the soft colour of the pewter. One collector known to the writer has his dining-room enamelled entirely in white, and the effect is charming. The pewter looks dazzling when it has been recently cleaned, and still better, if anything, just before the cleaning time, which is as regular as a Church feast, comes round.

Small objects look best under glass, and the same applies to spoons, the latter in particular being too delicate to stand handling, and now too valuable to be allowed to lie about in an unprotected condition.

If both foreign and English pewter be collected, each kind in common justice should be kept so separate and distinct that no comparison may suggest itself. It is only fair to the foreign, and it is the due of the British, ware.

At an exhibition of pewter in 1904, a collector, in his ignorance, bewailed that there was no art shown in the

English pewter, because there was so little ornament. This same person waxed wildly eloquent over the foreign pewter (some of it at least of doubtful authenticity) which was grouped in a special corner. Collectors such as these often develop into critics, and then woe to the uninitiate who blindly follow those who cannot, or who will not, see.

In some country museums an attempt has been made to reconstruct an early kitchen with brass, copper, iron and pewter utensils brought from various sources.

Such a collection can be of great interest, and the idea may be welcome to a collector with the necessary room at his disposal. A little care will be required in selecting objects of a date that will synchronize with the rest, for anachronisms would completely spoil the effect. If the kitchen were lofty enough, all the doubtful specimens could be "skied."

Pewter should not be mixed up indiscriminately with other things. Nothing is in worse taste, apart from the aggravating distraction, than a dresser littered up with china, firearms, daggers from Italy and the Levant, bead necklaces from the South Sea Islands, watch-keys, snuffers, and cloisonné enamels from China or Japan. All or any of these things may be collected if the mania is over-powering, but most of them should be kept where the dust cannot settle on them.

English pewter had of old a good reputation on the Continent for quality, and English tin was also much sought after by foreign pewterers. Harrison, who is so often quoted, wrote that "in some places beyond the sea a garnish of good flat English pewter, of an ordinarie making (I saie that, because dishes and platters in my time begin to be made deep like basins, and are indeed more convenient both for sauce, *i.e.*, broth, and keeping the meat warme), is esteemed almost so pretious as the like number of vessels that are made of fine silver, and in manner no less desired among the great estates, whose workmen are nothing so skilful in that trade as ours, neither their mettall so good, nor plentie so great, as we have here in England."

Mr. Ingleby Wood wrote in his *Scottish Pewterware and Pewterers* that "There is one vessel peculiar to Scotland alone, the exact counterpart of which is not to be found in any other country, and that is the '*quaigh*', '*quaich*', '*queych*', or '*quegh*', as it is variously styled. This article was a vessel of a flat, deep saucer-shape, and furnished with two 'lugs' or ears by which to hold it: it was used for the purpose of a drinking-vessel for liquors such as spirits, wine, and ale, but the larger ones were also used for broths, porridge, and the like." The name may be Scottish enough, but the vessel was common in France, even with the distinguishing characteristic of perfectly plain ears.

The word is said to be derived from the Gaelic *cuach*— *cf.* quaff—and the vessel was a shallow drinking-cup made of small staves hooped together with wooden or metal bands. The size varied from the diminutive pocket quaich $3\frac{1}{2}$ in. in diameter to the largest size with a diameter of 9 or 10 inches. The shape varied, too, from the bowl pattern with a graceful curve to the stiffer, almost rectilineal type, with straight sides. Most quaichs were left quite simple and unadorned, and as a rule are more solidly made than the porringers with which they are often confused.

Primarily for domestic use, they were used also in church for various uses. Mention is made in *Old Scottish Communion Plate* that two pewter "quechs" were to be bought to hold "the tokens and collections at the Communion tables".

Scottish quaichs are among the greatest rarities in pewter, and only about half a dozen *genuine* examples are known to-day.

Scottish pewter was, as Mr. Ingleby Wood explains, not made in that country to any great extent before the end of the fifteenth century. Before that time it was looked upon as a luxury, and whatever was used was imported, probably from France, with which country the connection was very intimate, and also from the Low Countries.

Mr. Wood ascribes the rarity of pewter in Scotland, as compared with its plentifulness elsewhere, to the poverty of the nation as a whole.

Rubbings of pewter marks should always be taken with great care. There seems to be an idea that a rubbing on thick paper done with heelball is all that is necessary for the expert. Of course, it is sometimes possible to detect even from such rough specimens a maker's device; but it is not quite fair on the expert. Compare such a rubbing with one taken with an FF pencil on fine bank-post, and heelball will not be used henceforth.

Fine-grained foreign letter paper is good, but it is sometimes *too* thin. Cigarette paper, also, is too thin and shows up the ribs in the "laid" paper as darker lines. This makes it difficult to separate the rubbing from the background of the paper.

Tinfoil can be used with advantage. That used for cigarette packets and chocolate is good but is sometimes too thin. Rubbings can be obtained by pressing the foil into the mark with the tips of the fingers.

Another method of obtaining a record of the impressed mark, particularly from inside a flagon or tankard, is by the use of a ball of plasticine, to which has been added a little fine plaster to stiffen it. An impression thus obtained can be superimposed on smooth paper if a smear of blacklead is lightly rubbed over the surface of the plasticine where the mark is impressed.

If the marks on a piece of pewter submitted to a collector are incomplete or almost indecipherable, at any rate at first sight, patience is necessary, and by means of a rubbing, carefully made, more may be gathered than from the pewter itself. It is an excellent plan to keep notes of all marks that present themselves either by drawings or by rubbings. The latter are to be preferred, as the eye of the artist may see things that are not there, and in pewter marks this is undesirable. In rubbings though it may be a case of *dum mortale perit*, yet *litera scripta manet*.

Never attempt to force a mark by jumping at conclusions, and always try to confirm any possible solution by reference to the small marks or "hall-marks". Some years ago a mark was printed as LEX SERVE. Whatever that may have been thought to mean does not appear; but the LEX was quite clear, and also the . . E . VE.

Had the investigator thought of looking through the list of pewterers who struck their touches on the London touch-plates he would have been given a clue, for the only two that satisfy the conditions were ALEX. CLEEVE —father and son. Then, as one obtained his freedom in 1688 and the other in 1715, the piece itself would probably have helped to settle the question of date.

Looking at pewter marks for long is very tiring work, and a good magnifying-glass is absolutely necessary. For those who can accustom themselves to it, a watchmaker's eye-glass is one of the most convenient, though the magnification often leaves something to be desired.

Difficulty may be experienced in examining a mark placed inside, at the base, of some tall objects such as tankards and flagons, and here it will be found of advantage to keep a magnifying-glass mounted at an angle of 90 degrees to the stem, which would be about 6–7 inches long. A wooden skewer or some similar object may be used for this purpose.

Photographic reproductions of the London touch-plates in possession of the Pewterers' Company have been given in both Welch's *History of the Pewterers' Company* and H. H. Cotterell's *Old Pewter, its Makers and Marks*. The Edinburgh touch-plates have been reproduced in Cotterell's book and in Ingleby Wood's *Scottish Pewterware and Pewterers*.

CHAPTER TWO

DEALERS' AND MAKERS' DODGES AND DEVICES—FAKES

DEALERS, and collectors for profit, often try to induce customers to buy pewter as being "Silver pewter". What does the adjective mean?—for the two names are contradictory in every way. The one is a precious, and the other a more or less base metal. Silver melts at a temperature of 1830° F. (or 950° C.), while tin melts at 442° F. (230° C.), and at a less temperature when alloyed. The two would not combine, and the baser metal would to a large extent volatilize before the silver melted to combine with it. The melting-point would be lower than that of silver, but still too high for the making of a satisfactory tin alloy. It is also stated that through imperfect combination of the two metals the silver would have a tendency to collect in patches, which, as silver tarnishes or oxidizes very quickly, would show up as blackish spots on the less black surface, when tarnished, of the pewter.

In old times, when tin was alloyed with lead, and the latter was not as pure as it should have been, the other metals present in the lead naturally went with it into the melting-pot. As old lead sometimes contained several pennyweights or even ounces per ton of impurities, silver being one of them, pewter made with such lead might be termed silver pewter; but it must be taken for granted that the silver was not knowingly added by the old pewter-founder. He took his lead, or his peak as he called it, in all good faith and added it to his tin. If he had known that he was presenting his customers with silver to any extent he would have tried to alter matters, for he would not have approved of a practice by which anybody got something for nothing. If the practice had been known at all it would have cropped up at court meetings of the Pewterers' Company and been officially recorded in the minutes.

What, then, is meant by "Silver pewter"? It can mean that the metal is of exceedingly good quality, and takes a high polish on its hard even surface. Such good quality was a feature of the York pewterers, and their metal most nearly deserves the appellation.

The craze to make a pewter vessel look like one of silver is no new thing. One Sebaldus Ruprecht as early as the fourteenth century found out a method of doing it, and for a while he reaped the benefit. Later, another German artist went a little farther and proclaimed to the world that he could give his wares the appearance of having been gilded with pure gold. He died in 1567 and his secret with him, no doubt to the great delight of the goldsmiths of that time. Yet another, according to Bapst, claimed that he could make pewter as soft and pliable as wax and, after working at his will upon it, could give it a hardness quite alien to the ordinary metal. This ingenious process has not come down to us, nor are there specimens in the German museums.

English pewterers have tried their hands at the same thing, and one Major Purling (Welch, ii. 116, 117) brought out in 1652 an alloy intended to imitate silver and called *Silvorum*. The Pewterers' Company nipped this new invention in the bud by prohibiting one of their members, Thomas Allen, from working for Major Purling, and in the following year by fining Lawrence Dyer for making "faulce plat called silvorum", and by confiscating what he had made.   Later on Dyer became Warden of the Company, 1669, and Master in 1675. His pewter is of excellent quality.

An alloy termed *Melchior*, which looked very like silver, was popular in France in the early twentieth century. It contained:

Copper	.	.	.	55 parts
Nickel	.	.	.	23 ,,
Zinc .	.	.	.	17 ,,
Iron .	.	.	.	3 ,,
Tin .	.	.	.	2 ,,

A French pewterer of the seventeenth century claimed [1] that he could make pewter of such excellent quality that he could use his vessels as melting-pots for other makers' silver. The result was that his refined pewter, which looked like silver, was as beautiful in appearance, as light, and as brilliant, was in great request. His price for plain ware was 100 sols the pound, with higher prices for decorated pieces.

Another statement which was current with some collectors and dealers, who said they had seen it vouched for in print, was that the X with a crown above it was the excise mark, and showed conclusively that the Government duty on pewter had been paid.

Statements such as this are merely misleading and have no foundation in fact. The crowned "X" was originally a mark permitted to be struck only on work of good quality, and was allowed to be struck twice on exceptionally good pieces. It seems to have come into use about the end of the seventeenth century and was frequent, in its qualifying sense, for about one hundred years.

[1] *Journal d'un Voyage à Paris* (1657).

It later came to be used indiscriminately on tavern pots and measures, and its significance has gone.

Yet another statement which has, sad to say, gone the rounds of some pewter circles, from the fact that it appeared in print, is that the Gloucester candlestick now in the Victoria and Albert Museum, South Kensington, is made of pewter. It is nothing of the sort. It is of pale bronze, cast by the *cire perdue* process, and richly gilt and decorated. The stem is divided into two parts by bosses, ornamented with the emblems of the Evangelists, supporting a cup at the top. The base is triangular. There are altogether over forty monsters represented in grotesque attitudes, wrestling and struggling with nine human beings. It is considered to have been Hildesheim work of the early twelfth century, *c.* 1110. It is figured in Mr. Lethaby's *Mediæval Art*, p. 125. If it had been made in pewter it would hardly have lasted a tenth of the time that has elapsed since it was given by Abbot Peter to the Abbey at Gloucester.

Just as we have in our midst those clever fabricators of mediæval armour, and horse trappings, complete to the smallest detail—and there are quite as clever workmen doing it quite openly abroad—so there are to be found pewterers with more ingenuity than morality, and the collector must take the risks—in other words, buy his experience.

It is no good trying to formulate a list of "Don'ts" for his benefit. Human nature is always the same everywhere, and he would resent it with a mind made up to buy, at the first opportunity, the thing as to which he is warned.

Faked pewter is not by any means as uncommon as one might suppose. During the last forty years or so some clever and dishonest craftsmen have been at work, and some of the results of their handiwork are to be seen in not a few collections and museums where (let it be proclaimed to the shame of their owners or custodians) they are looked upon as genuine and desirable pieces.

The prevalence of a large amount of faked pewter is due, to some extent, to the fact that some dealers know very little about it and consequently pass on, as genuine, pieces which should have been dishonoured.

If a dealer does not know—and admittedly a dealer cannot be an expert in everything which passes through his hands—he should be prepared to return the purchase money to the buyer in the event of an article proving wrong. If a high price is paid for a supposedly genuine piece the dealer should, similarly, be prepared to guarantee it as such, and give a written invoice accordingly.

The passing of fakes may net a nice profit for unscrupulous dealers at the time, but will eventually lead to their being boycotted by collectors of experience, for news of good (or, for that matter, bad) pieces soon travels among connoisseurs.

For obvious reasons it would not be wise to describe the methods by which fakes may be detected, but it is stressed that, unless an obvious bargain is offered from a reliable source, very great care should be exercised by the buyer, who should endeavour to take the advice of a knowledgeable friend before paying a stiff price for a "rare" piece.

The beginner is recommended to form contacts with other collectors, and to join study circles on the subject, if such can be found to exist in the locality. Sometimes a local museum curator can place collectors in contact with one another.

Travellers in Holland and Belgium and elsewhere have no doubt experienced the glib tongues and the guile of the touts attached to the bric-a-brac shops and possibly have been persuaded into buying some new "old pewter"!

It is a curious thing that if a collector advertises for any unusual piece of pewter which he knows from description only, or from hearsay, the piece will be heard of in a remarkably short time.

A collector wishing to have a complete set of table pewter advertised for a pair of asparagus tongs. It will hardly be believed, but it is a fact, that the article was quickly provided, to the collector's great delight. Her collection was now perfect. Disillusionment was, however, soon to follow. An expert was invited to see, and to value, this perfect collection, but among the articles he put on one side as spurious and as anachronisms was the pair of asparagus tongs.

It is within the bounds of probability that an advertisement asking for specimens of spoons of the time of Alfred the Great, pepper-pots of the time of William Rufus, or a processional cross of the time of Lady Jane Grey would be promptly answered by the same enterprising manufacturer who has supplied other interesting *objets d'art* in pewter within the last forty years.

To track down such fakers is not within the scope of the present volume, but collectors are invited to be careful and cautioned against supplying sketches and drawings of their requirements. If they do this they will have themselves to thank when counterfeits or made-up pieces of pewter, good enough in their way, are submitted for their consideration.

The demand for old pewter has been met very much in the same way that the demand for old oak has been satisfied. The pieces come either "from the countryside"— with a vague indication of a neighbourhood to give local colour—or else "from a source not available to the general

A RARE BALUSTER WINE MEASURE
Sixteenth-century. Dug up in Westminster in 1903
(*Pleydell-Bouverie Bequest, Victoria and Albert Museum*)

A GROUP OF THREE TAPPIT-HEN MEASURES

L. to R. Unlidded (1 pint Imperial Standard) ; crested chopin (1½ Imperial pints) ; Scots pint (3 Imperial pints) with uncrested lid

(Michaelis Collection)

SCOTTISH "POT-BELLIED" FLAGON OR MEASURE   A FINE TALL TANKARD OR FLAGON

c. 1700   *c.* 1690

(*Victoria and Albert Museum*)

SCOTTISH TAPPIT-HEN MEASURE   A NORMANDY FLAGON

(Collection of the late Frederick Jaeger)

public"—or again "from a collection the owner of which does not wish his name to be made public property".

Some of the most common articles of Continental pewter being reproduced and faked are Dutch spoons, two-eared dishes or porringers with embossed Tudor Rose design in the base, or massive plates and dishes with heraldic designs cast in high relief.

The spoons are frequently of the round-bowl variety, with round or octagonal stems, known as "slipped-in-the-stalk", and, although known in their genuine form, it is not feasible that so many could have come down to us in the fine condition in which they are found. It is probable that there are more round-bowl spoons in existence to-day than there were when they were a household necessity of everyday life in the Low Countries.

Beware when you are offered the Tudor Rose porringers. When a dealer tries to sell these as bleeding-bowls or quaichs the buyer should be on his guard—the more so when a choice of a dozen or more is offered, all with the same design pierced in the ears, and the same initials, or maker's mark, punched on the ears.

The heraldic dishes already mentioned frequently bear the same makers' marks, perhaps a crowned rose with initials N.D. in the upper part of the crown, or a beaded circle with St. George or St. Michael and a dragon, with the letters A.I.C.

Plates with these marks have been going the rounds and may be bought abroad for a few francs. The probability is that they are being reproduced somewhere at the present time to satisfy the demand for "art" pewter. The following are the schemes of ornamentation:—

1. Arms of Louis, eldest son of Louis XIV and Marie Thérèse of Austria, d. 1711. The coat of arms is surmounted

by a royal crown, surrounded by the Ordre du Saint-Esprit, with two dolphins as supporters.

2. Arms of Philip V, King of Spain, son of the Dauphin Louis and Marie of Bavaria (1700–41), with the arms of France on an escutcheon of pretence. The coat of arms is on a shield surmounted by a royal crown, with the Order of the Golden Fleece suspended from it.

3. A cinque-foiled plate with a moulded edge. In each foil there is a fleur-de-lis, and in the centre of the plate a salamander with a large crown above it. The field is *semé* with fleurs-de-lis.

4. A many-foiled plate with a moulded edge, but no rim—with the field *semé* with fleurs-de-lis. In the centre a lion rampant; above all, a crown.

5. An oval dish with the arms of a French marquis—name unknown.

It would be interesting to know how many plates there are going the round of the shops and occasionally getting into collections with the arms of Lord Marcus Hill, and purporting to have been used in the Peninsular War. The engraving is very roughly and badly done as a rule, and seems to have been added long after the fancy date ascribed to the plates. Some specimens, with a variation in the arms, are said to be those of Viscount Hill, and to have been used by him in the Peninsular War. Lord Hill, however, did not become Viscount till 1842, and this fact helps to discount the genuineness of the engraving. In one case the plates were good plates with a dated mark 1675. It seems a pity that good old plates like this should be degraded by the addition of bad engraving. The engraver might have taken plates somewhat nearer the time of Lord Hill.

Mantelpiece ornaments of various design were formerly very commonly made in brass, and of later years there was a tendency to produce these in pewter. They are carelessly made, and seem to have been cast in plaster moulds (made from the brass originals), all in one piece. Many of the brass ones were cast in two pieces, viz., the figure portion, and the base, and the two parts were then screwed together. In the more shameless copies the screws are shown cast in position. The metal, too, in quality is more like that used in casting common squirts, toy cannon, and thin tin soldiers. Such reproductions must be avoided.

Another object to be viewed with great caution is a perfect *bénitier*. As a rule, the material being poor, and the lower half being too heavy for the upper portion, which is either pierced work or a slender cross, the two halves have come to pieces early in the lifetime of the *bénitier*, and repairs have been necessary. There are, no doubt, perfect specimens, which are undoubtedly genuine, but they are not met with every day, and must be regarded as suspect.

Forks, again, from their nature, and from the usage they received, had a short lifetime, and a collector should fight shy of a fork and spoon sold as a pair. There may be chance specimens of such pairs, but they are rare.

Modern pewter forks are like modern concrete, in that they are reinforced with steel wire in the stem of the handle and in the prongs. Without this they would be quite useless.

Another trick of dealers, or dealers' agents, is to have a legend engraved on a chalice, stating the church or chapel from which the vessel was obtained. This gives an added interest, no doubt, and enhances the value, but sometimes the faker goes too far, and adds an impossible inscription. An instance may be given: X sold Y a couple of chalices with a legend stating that they came from a meeting-house of the Society of Friends. As a matter of fact the

Society of Friends do not require chalices, their Eucharistic service being entirely spiritual.

Deep dishes are likely to prove a snare to the eager and the unwary. They are often faked up from one of the halves of a bed-pan. These halves are made in deep dish moulds, but that is no valid reason why a novice should be asked a big price for a deep dish which is so faked, with a fictitious mark, from a damaged article of humbler use, picked up at the old-metal price of, say, 1s. 6d. per lb.

Caveat emptor again applies to the "tappit-hens" that hail from some canny workman's bench in that artistic centre, to wit, Glasgow. They are cleverly made, and look genuine enough—but they are not what they seem.

On the unwary the ignorant shopman may try and palm off a Normandy flagon as a real "tappit-hen", but the collector of British pewter should know better. Although there is some similarity in shape there is a distinct difference between them, and the reader is advised to familiarize himself with each by a glance at the illustration facing page 41. The lower section of the tappit-hen *never* slopes inwards towards the base as does the Normandy flagon, but may even slope slightly outwards.

Fancy prices have been asked of late years for certain articles and in certain centres only. For this the collectors themselves have mainly been responsible. They place an inquiry for a certain *objet d'art* with one or perhaps two dealers. The dealer and his agents, here, there, and everywhere, inquire and offer a price. Someone keeps back the required object, knowing that the keener the competition, the more willing the dealer will be to pay more, for of course he will get it quite easily from his client. Eventually it changes hands at a considerable premium, and the customer who placed his inquiry, with perhaps a limit of price, has to increase this before he secures the thing so keenly coveted.

The writer has been told, quite sadly by some, that the holding of the first exhibition in 1904, simultaneously with the appearance of *Pewter Plate*, caused a craze and forced up prices at once. To this it may be replied that it may have made it expensive just then for anyone who began to collect for no special reason at that particular time. There were, however, keen collectors of pewter twenty years before that, and they had the real fun, for they collected from their own instinctive appreciation of the ware, without any help from any available source— for none such was then in existence.

It may be true that the exhibition caused a demand for certain everyday articles, such as porringers and spoons, and that for a time, as there was a shortage of these, prices went higher, but the supply with a little effort soon met the increased demand.

CHAPTER THREE

PEWTER PRICES

IT is by no means easy to write on the subject of the prices of pewter dispassionately, for there is the feeling that when once the prices recently paid in an auction-room or shop are entered in a formal list, dated and so authenticated, as it were, dealers who may happen to have similar articles in stock will take advantage of the prices paid, and alter their prices so as to bring them into line.

Much as this is to be regretted, it cannot be helped. It is part and parcel of the methodical system under which this series of books is being produced, that prices should be chronicled with care and accuracy for the information of collectors.

The prices paid for pewter have not, however, been as systematically recorded as of silver, china, and other articles of *vertu*, and to supplement this deficiency, information from various private sources has been collected and tabulated chronologically.

Those who began to collect fifty or sixty years ago, for the pleasure of collecting, were able to pick up for very little, practically next to nothing, articles that nowadays cannot be found in the ordinary way. It is a most interesting study to compare the prices that these real collectors paid with those offered, and sometimes refused, in the dealers' shops to-day.

Good and genuine pewter, with a bona-fide mark upon

it, is practically certain to find an appreciative buyer, willing, even if it be offered privately, to pay a reasonably liberal price. The number of pieces of good ware must be, from the nature of things, limited, and though there may still be future finds hidden away in lofts and garrets, they cannot be so numerous as to cause any fear of a general slump in prices.

The list has been compiled from various sources, but all names, whether those of dealers or collectors, have been suppressed, for it would have been a free advertisement for the former and a breach of confidence in the case of the latter.

The following prices will show how the price, even for such everyday articles as plates, has steadily increased, especially when the maker has been a man of some reputation.

It must not for a moment be supposed that some of the articles, intrinsically, are worth the amounts which have been paid for them. If sold again to-morrow most of them might fetch very much less, while some (and there is no need to specify these) would sell at much higher prices because of the demand for such just at the present time.

Several collectors who were asked to contribute lists of prices, dates, and places regretted that they had kept no systematic record as to any of these matters. Their one point of agreement, however, was that they as beginners had happened upon pieces at a third or a fourth of the prices charged to-day.

To mention but a few special instances. Spoons used to be found in excavations, usually in Thames Street or in Bermondsey, and passed years ago into collectors' hands for a few pence. Now it requires the outlay of as many pounds sterling before the desired article is acquired.

There must have been collectors with hawk-eyed agents always on the alert for any chance of the ground in the streets, or in private property, being opened.

Snuff-boxes, too, used to be picked up for a few pence, now the price is more often asked in shillings.

Plates have been bought for 4d., and the sellers seemed glad to get rid of them at the price. On one occasion the writer saw a miserable specimen, 18 in. in diameter, all pit-marked and cracked, which had been bought for 18s. 6d. It was unmarked, very poor in quality, and even when put in proper repair, scaled, cleaned and buffed, it would not be worth half the price paid for it, plus the cost of repairs.

In the following list the pewter has been grouped in types so that the reader may gain some idea of the trend of prices over a period of years.

			£	s.	d.
1906	Porringer, D. 5¾ in. . . .	Birmingham	2	0	0
1907	Porringer (Flemish), 4 1/16 in. . .	London	0	17	6
1908	Porringer, 18th-century (by John Home)	—	1	10	0
1919	Porringer, 18th-century, 4¾ in. .	Auction, London	1	15	0
	Porringer, 18th-century, 6½ in. . .	Auction, London	2	10	0
1929	A Bleeding-bowl, dated 1679, and 2 others	London	8	0	0
1929	3 Cup Salts	Auction, London	4	0	0
1946	2 large Salts, 2 smaller do. and a pair of late Taper Sticks . . .	Auction, London	7	10	0
1947	An early Triangular Salt, and an early Capstan Salt	Auction, London	11	0	0
1923	Baluster Measure, quart, Bud thumb-piece	—	4	15	0
	Baluster Measure, pint, Bud thumb-piece	—	3	17	6
	Baluster Measure, ½ pint, Bud thumb-piece	—	3	5	0
	Baluster Measure, gill, Bud thumb-piece	—	2	0	0
1930	Baluster Measure, gallon, double volute	London	20	0	0

		£	s.	d.
1945	Baluster Measure, quart, and six others, smaller . . . . London	25	0	0
	Baluster Measure, gallon, hammer-head, and a quart ditto, double volute . . . . . London	70	0	0
1900–10	Plates, 18th-century . (each) —	⌠0	4	0
		⌡0	10	0
1929	4 Plates, 18th-century 9¾ in. (by Durand) . . . . —	4	10	0
	4 Plates, 18th-century 9¾ in. (various makers) . . . . . —	2	10	0
1938	Plates 9 in. and 9¾ in. . (each) London	⌠0	10	0
		⌡0	15	0
1945	Plates, 9 in and 9¾ in. . („) London	⌠0	10	0
		⌡0	15	0
1929	Dish, 21¼ in. Reeded rim, inscribed . London	4	10	0
1938	A pair of 18½ in. Chargers . . London	11	0	0
1943	A broad-rim reeded Dish, 16½ in. . London	1	10	0
1944	A pair of 18 in. reeded Dishes (by John French) . . . . London	6	0	0
1946	A broad-rim Paten, D. 9 in. . . London	4	10	0
1907	Jacobean Candlestick . . . Auction, London	15	0	0
	Pair Altar Candlesticks . . . Auction, London	2	5	0
1908	Pair Queen Anne Candlesticks . Rugby	0	18	0
1910	Jacobean Candlestick . . . Monmouth	0	10	6
1919	Pair Queen Anne Candlesticks . . —	2	0	0
1929	Late Stuart Candlestick, horizontal fluting . . . . . London	26	0	0
	Pair late Georgian Baluster Candle-sticks . . . . . . London	3	0	0
	Pair Italian Altar Candlesticks . Auction, London	7	10	0
1939	A rare early Stuart Candlestick . Auction, London	10	0	0
1946	A Trumpet-based Candlestick, c. 1670 Auction, London	22	0	0
1946	Octagonal-based Candlestick, c. 1690 Auction, London	12	0	0
1892	Tappit-hen, uncrested . . . Edinburgh	0	6	6
	Tappit-hen, chopin size, uncrested . Glasgow	0	6	0
1898	Tappit-hen, crested . . Auction, Glasgow	0	7	0
1902	Tappit-hen, uncrested, mutchkin . —	2	10	0
	Tappit-hen, uncrested, mutchkin . —	1	15	0
1904	Tappit-hen, height 11 in. . . —	3	17	6
	Tappit-hen, height 12 in. . . Auction, Glasgow	4	0	0
1919	Tappit-hen, crested . . . Auction, Glasgow	13	0	0
1929–36	Tappit-hens (various) . . —	⌠3	10	0
		⌡13	10	0
1936	Tappit-hen, 11½ in., uncrested . . London	10	0	0

			£	s.	d.
1946	Tappit-hen, mutchkin, crested . .	London	12	10	0
1902	Set of 6 Motto Plates (by John Home)	Auction, London	15	10	0
1946	Set of 6 Motto Plates (by John Trout)	Auction, London	44	0	0
1902	Communion Chalice . . .	Glasgow	1	15	0
1919	Church Chalice	Auction, Glasgow	3	0	0
	2 Communion Cups, late 19th-century	Auction, Glasgow	6	10	0
1929	Bell-shaped Chalice, 8¼ in. . .	Auction, London	3	15	0
1938	A "York" acorn-shaped Flagon *c.* 1735	Auction, London	15	0	0
1910	Late 18th-century Tankard by Carpenter and Hamberger . .	London	1	0	0
1919	18th-century Tankard, domed lid .	Auction, London	7	5	0
1929	18th-century Tankard, domed lid .	Auction, London	6	10	0
1938	Various late Stuart Tankards, flat lids	Auction, London	⎰16 ⎱20	0 0	0 0
1945–48	Various late Stuart Tankards, flat lids (some engraved) . .	—	⎰38 ⎱75	0 0	0 0

CHAPTER FOUR

WHAT IS PEWTER?

WHAT is pewter? A simple question but one which is capable of many very different replies. The simplest, however, is that pewter is an alloy of the tin group, to which other metals are added according to the purpose for which the resulting alloy is to be used.

Fine pewter consisted of tin 112 lb. and 26 lb. of copper, this amount of copper being apparently the maximum that the tin could take up into itself. Sometimes brass (as Harrison calls it, "kettle brass") was used instead of copper. The proportion is very roughly 4 : 1, really 4 $\frac{4}{13}$: 1, and the alloy was that used for écuelles, salts, platters, chargers, square pitchers, cruets, chrismatories, and for other articles that were made either square, ribbed, or fluted. Tin and temper consisted of tin 100 and antimony 1·6.

Another superior kind of pewter was composed of tin and antimony in the proportion of 100 : 17. This gives a fine, hard, resonant pewter. Closely allied to this is the alloy known as Pemberton's alloy, which is tin and antimony 9 : 1.

Trifle, or common pewter, was made of 83 tin to 17 antimony, or, with but a slight variation, 82 tin to 18 antimony.

The above are the chief alloys of tin and copper or tin and antimony. They are fairly hard and durable, white in colour, are easily burnished and retain their polish.

Where antimony was not used, its place was taken by lead, and in this direction we find most abuse, even in the earliest times: in some Roman pewter of the fourth century as much as 30 lead to 70 tin, a very high proportion indeed.

English pewter as specified for vessels of tin had the same proportion of lead as fine pewter had of copper, viz., 26 lb. to the hundredweight.

Ley, or lay, or common pewter, with the quality reduced by alloying, was composed of tin 80 to lead 20, or in some cases of tin 70 to lead 22·5. From this common metal it is easy to descend to what is known as black-metal—of which the cheapest public-house pewters were made—a compound of tin and lead about 60:40. The proportion of 112 tin to 26 lead varied from 112 to 16 or to 22, or as given, to 26, and the alloy was used for articles that were circular in shape, such as bowls, pots, cruets, and candlesticks—the circular form giving them a certain amount of strength.

By the addition of bismuth, or tin-glass, a further range of alloys was obtained. It was added, as a rule, to plate pewter, and helped, with the antimony, to give it the necessary degree of hardness. One alloy was tin 100, antimony 8, copper 4, and bismuth 4. Another was tin 90, antimony 7, copper 2, bismuth 2, and another was tin 89·3, antimony 7·1, copper 1·8, and bismuth 1·8.

Foreign pewterers, as far as can be ascertained, did not use much antimony, if at all, in their alloys. Fioravanti specifies 88 tin to 12 lead for dishes and porringers. The pewterers of Limoges, who were famous, used only 4 lead to 100 of tin; while those of Montpellier in the fifteenth century used pewter of two qualities: 96 tin to 4 lead for dishes and porringers, and 90 tin to 10 lead for ewers and salts.

WHAT IS PEWTER?

Modern French pewter used to be made of a certain standard, and practically the same as the trifle quoted above, 83 tin to 17, or in reality $83.5 : 16.5$, this having been found safe for use even with acid ferments. About forty years ago the limit of lead was fixed at 10 per cent. Ordinary French pewter plates were formerly made of tin 92 to lead 8, an alloy of high quality, that would cast well and work up satisfactorily. Much early eighteenth-century French pewter had no lead in it at all, being composed of tin 100, copper 5; or as in another analysis, tin 100, copper 3, bismuth 1. Towards the end of the century the best French pewter was made of tin 100 to lead 15, and if the tin was new and pure the lead was increased to 20 lb.

At different times the above alloys have been varied in their proportions and in their combinations. Zinc has been added, and the result was an alloy called Ashberry metal, composed of tin 77.8, antimony 19.4, and zinc 2.8. It casts very cleanly and readily, is hard to the touch, and in consequence wears well. In many respects it resembles Britannia metal, which was invented about the middle of the eighteenth century.

In England, in 1907, the standard of pewter for tankards and measures came within the purview of the Board of Trade, and this body insists, with all the force of a Governmental Department, on a relatively high standard, viz., 80 per cent. of tin and not more than 10 per cent. of lead in such articles. Also the measures are to be stamped by the maker. This regulation deals a death-blow to the black-metal tankards, etc., with 40 per cent. of lead, and the pewter of this Board of Trade standard will be able to be collected by posterity as pewter.

Britannia metal is a special kind of pewter, of good quality, and should contain no lead. A good quality is composed of tin 150, antimony 10, copper 3. For B.M. castings the proportions may vary as much as shown in the following table:—

Tin	Antimony	Copper	Zinc
140	5	2	—
90	8	2	—
85·7	10·4	1	2·9
81·9	16·2	—	1·9

There are countless other variations.

Zinc, if added even in a small quantity to pewter, will prevent the characteristic *cri* being heard when the object is bent. Lead has the same effect, but to a lesser degree.

As it was found that Britannia metal could be fashioned on the lathe by the process called "spinning" more readily than could pewter, the new alloy began at once to oust the other, and the ousting became more complete when, later on, it was found that Britannia metal could be electro-plated.

Here was the chance for the manufacturers to make in the new metal, with a view to future electro-plating, all the articles that had hitherto been made in silver for the upper classes, or in pewter for the rest, and they were not slow to come forward. The facility with which the new alloy could be worked led to all kinds of eccentric shapes and designs. Like all new things it caught the popular taste, which was not then at a very high artistic level, and the result, in a few years, was that the pewter trade, which was in a languishing state, gave up the hopeless struggle for existence. It lingered on because the bar industry, always a conservative trade, had not seen fit then to abolish pewter tankards and mugs in favour of earthenware or glass, and because bar-fitters adopted the metal for counter tops and other fittings. There was a certain demand, too, for hospital appliances (mainly for export) in the way of syringes, etc., and these are to the present day made of pewter because they are less liable to breakage, and are more easy to keep in an absolutely aseptic condition.

Can the art of the pewterers be revived? To this the answer must be: Only within certain limits. We have seen attempted revivals in the German Kayserzinn, quite good pewter as far as the alloy was concerned, and sold over here under another name, with the German name only partially obliterated. This attempted revival came at an ill-chosen time, for the world was writhing in the snaky coils of *l'art nouveau*, and all and sundry went mad in the worship of the meaningless curves and the broken lines, which, starting from nowhere, tried to return there by the most circuitous paths.

As soon as the Kayserzinn epidemic was over, the same thing appeared again under another name, and the world that would be artistic was invited to buy vessels of strange design, some with insets of weirdly coloured enamel, chunks of sham turquoise, slabs of pearl, and calling itself Urania metal. It had a short spell of success with a certain class, because it was advertised as "old silver fashion," and certainly looked like electro-plate.

In our churches, alms-dishes of pewter with a broad rim, bearing the arms of the diocese and the emblems of the Saint to whom the church might be dedicated, would be found far more dignified than the stamped brass horrors with sham jewels that are in use at the present time. So, too, with the font ewers, which, as a rule, are as ugly to look at as they are awkward to hold.

Altar candlesticks of pewter, simple in form, might well be reintroduced, as far superior to the ordinary type now in common use.

CHAPTER FIVE

HOW IS PEWTER MADE?

THE next question that presents itself is, "*How is Pewter made?*" To this the answer is simple, "*By the traditional methods.*" These methods are (1) by melting the alloy and casting it in moulds; (2) by hammering the metal previously reduced to plate form; (3) a combination of both these methods; (4) by turning on a lathe, a process usually followed by that of burnishing; (5) by spinning —this latter a modern method only possible on power-lathes, and used generally for the alloy known as Britannia metal.

The methods of manufacture being traditional, it is not surprising to find that the tools themselves are the same. Compared with the tools of some crafts, those used by the pewterer are but few and simple to make and to keep in proper working order.

One of the most important hand tools is the hammer, and for this reason it was chosen as the mark *par excellence* of a pewterer, and would account for the importance of the class of workmen known in Scotland as "hammermen." The representations of the hammer in marks or touches give it as with a shortish handle, like the modern sculptors' hammers. The most important part of the hammer was the hitting-face, or pane. If that were scratched, it would imprint scratches on the pewter; therefore the panes are kept bright, clean, and smooth. In the same way the surfaces of anvils and swages have to

TWO SCOTTISH CHALICES OR COMMUNION CUPS

(*Collection of the late Lewis Clapperton, Esq.*)

A RARE PEWTER QUAICH

Scottish, c. 1670

(Collection of the late Lewis Clapperton, Esq.)

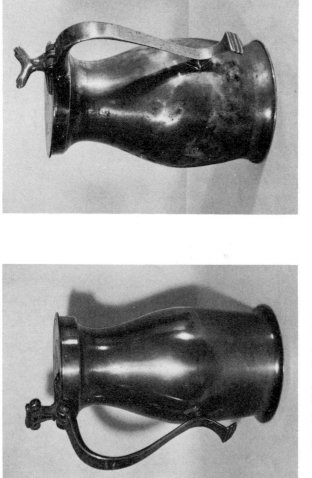

"Double-Volute" thumbpiece
c. 1760

"Bud" thumbpiece
c. 1680

ENGLISH BALUSTER WINE MEASURES

Gallon capacity (Old Wine Standard)

(*Michaelis Collection*)

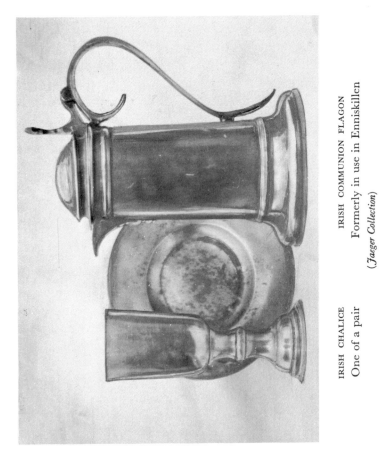

IRISH CHALICE
One of a pair

IRISH COMMUNION FLAGON
Formerly in use in Enniskillen
(*Jaeger Collection*)

be kept brightly polished. With a swage of suitable shape placed in contact with the booge of a plate, and the proper-shaped hammer used on the inside, the plates of the best quality were, and still are, finished. There are hammers of various patterns, each with its special use.

The moulds for the casting of pewter were formerly made, as a rule, of bell-metal or bronze, and, from the fact that they were expensive to make in the first instance, belonged to the craft guild or fellowship, and were loaned as required to qualified masters of the craft. Sometimes they were the joint property of several pewterers, and were valuable trade possessions. Mr. Welch gives a list of fifteen moulds bought in 1425 from Hugh Swan, Thomas Parys, and some other pewterers, four in number. These moulds were for the casting of dishes and bowls, and the total weight of the moulds was over 118 lb., each mould being composed of four parts, for the greater convenience of removing the pewter after being cast.

Before using a mould for casting, the inside has to be moistened with red ochre moistened with white of egg, or else dusted with powdered pumice-stone or gum sandarac. The casting when removed from the mould will show quite clearly the markings caused by the bristles of the brush with which the egg and ochre was applied. It goes without saying that the finer and smoother the interior surface of the mould, the better will be the resulting casting. If a mould is bright in any part of the inside, or the ochre and egg has worn away, the pewter when poured in will refuse to flow over or to remain on that spot, and a hole or a crack in the casting is the result. This may lead to disaster later if any hammering is to be done.

The moulds must be thoroughly well warmed, so that

the metal when it is poured in does not become chilled and refuse to run in consequence, and the metal must be just the right heat. A knowledge of these two temperatures cannot be learned from a book, but must come from experience.

Another point is that the scum that forms in the melting-pot must not be allowed to go into the mould. Pewterers sometimes use a mechanical device so as to prevent the scum from leaving the ladle. The writer, for small castings, makes use of a self-skimming solder-ladle with a fine nozzle. With this a clean stream of pewter is ensured with absolutely no trouble.

Pewter can be cast in plaster, iron, stone, steel, or sand moulds, but, of course, where hundreds of dozens of castings or more were required, a massive gunmetal mould was the best, and in the end the cheapest that could be procured. For one or two castings a wooden mould can be used, or for a simple shape such as that of a thumb-piece of a tankard, a piece of waste metal, such as a piece of an ordinary canister bent to the required shape and lined with paper to prevent adhesion, will serve for a mould. In either case, the casting will require subsequent working up and finishing.

In the Guildhall Museum are some moulds for casting pilgrims' badges, made of some close-grained stone similar to lithographic stone, and some are of schist. These badges are usually found to be of lead, but in some cases they were pewter.

Wherever it was possible, the makers cast the pewter object in one piece, and then finished it afterwards by scraping or grating, and by hammering in the case of spoons, by turning in the case of good plates, followed by planishing, or hammering, on a swage or special anvil with a highly polished hammer.

HOW IS PEWTER MADE?

Moulds being expensive, it will not be found surprising that part of one mould did duty as a common factor for several different objects, *e.g.*, the base portion of a candle-stick might be identical with a large salt, the top part being added after the rest was complete.

For some circular objects the moulds were made to come into three pieces with a vertical section, and the practised eye will detect the line of juncture of the sections of the mould. Salts with moulded rims and moulded feet are often cast in this way, though sometimes they are built up from separate castings.

Plates and dishes are finished by hammering with special hammers with rather short handles, the blow being directed on the inside of the part known as the booge. These marks left by the pane of the hammer can be seen on the under side in a series of concentric rings. In trenchers that have been entirely wrought by hand from a circular disk, the centre point from which the circle was struck can be easily distinguished, and so also in the case of many plates.

In pewter finished in the lathe the marks of the tool can frequently be discerned, especially on the under side of the bottoms of tankards and large flagons. Though the lathe was a necessary piece of apparatus in a pewterer's workshop, it was looked upon in the light of a special tool, rather than as a tool for general use. For this reason its use was subject to restrictions. A man, for instance, who had an order for tankards would be within his right in using it, while if detected in making saucers on the lathe he was liable to have them all forfeited. To-day it is, perhaps, the chief tool of all. In old work the marks left by the lathe will be found in many cases to be in a spiral, best seen on the outside of the bottom of a tankard or similar vessel. This was the result of the careless use of the tool. Sometimes, again, the marks are very irregular; this may be due to the fact that the lathe was turned by hand-power, the boy who supplied the power being known as a "turn-wheel."

Early in the eighteenth century the lathe began to be developed, and has by degrees since 1740–50 become what it is now—a tool of precision with a capacity many times greater than the types of lathe which is superseded.

Many articles in pewter owe their graceful lines and the fine detail on their mouldings to the precision of the lathe on which they were turned.

A small bowl fresh from the mould is a much clumsier object than it will appear when it has gone through the hands of the turner and has received its final polish. In some cases the mouldings are just indicated and the body is comparatively thick. In the process of turning the mouldings will be quite clearly defined and the thickness of the body reduced by about one-half.

Small defects are made good before turning; large defects necessitate the return of the castings to the melting-pot.

Soldering must be done with extreme care. All edges to be joined must be scrupulously clean, and no dust, dirt, or grit allowed to settle on the surfaces to be joined. If defects exist, or there are pieces missing along the line where junction is to be made by solder, they may be left till afterwards, provided that they will be then equally accessible.

The golden rule in soldering is, have the edges clean and carefully adjusted, so that they touch quite closely. Apply the flux, use as little solder as possible, and, most important of all, do not use more heat than is necessary to cause the solder to flow where it is required.

Pewter may be repaired with pewter, and no solder,

if the right amount of heat can be brought to play on the joint, and the other side of the metal is kept cool.

Various solders are used for various purposes, but one of the most satisfactory for pewter is known as mercurial solder. It melts at a temperature suitable for the majority of pewter articles, flows well, and is easily removed if too much has been applied. The addition of the mercury causes the melting-point to be low, but of course the mercury is volatilised by the heat applied to melt the solder.

Soldering-irons may be used, but many experts prefer to use a blow-pipe. If the article to be soldered is circular, it is placed on a rotating table of iron (similar to the small iron stands used by sculptors and modellers), called a "gentleman." Where the solder is to run all round, as at the bottom seam in a flagon, the convenience of the rotating table is great.

Burnishing is done in the lathe. While the piece to be burnished is rotating at a considerable speed, a burnisher of bloodstone, agate, or polished steel, with soap and water as a lubricant, is held firmly, by means of a long handle, against the rotating pewter. In a short time the burnishing process is finished. The surface thus obtained is only suited for wares before sale, and soon disappears when the article is subjected to daily use.

Burnishers vary in shape, some being made of a tapering piece of steel, round in section and bent round into a crook, others being somewhat T-shaped, the cross-piece, however, being set obliquely to the shank. Everything on the burnisher is smoothed and made round, and the part of the tool that burnishes must be absolutely bright.

All the lathe tools of the pewterer have much longer handles than the ordinary turner's tools, even than those used for soft wood. This is due to the peculiar way the tool is held under the arm of the turner.

The rest for the tools is an iron bar the same length as that of the lathe bed, with holes at intervals for the insertion of spurs, against which the tools are occasionally rested when required.

In most of his work the turner of pewter holds his tool *under* the rest and not *on* it, as in ordinary lathe practice. He seems by so doing to be able to follow the outline of any piece of irregular shape, even if it be an oval. This he could not do if he rested his turning-tool on the rest.

By the courtesy of Mr. W. J. Englefield the writer was enabled to inspect his range of workshops, and to see a most interesting collection of tools that had survived from a bygone day, all old pewterers' tools. The chief point about them was the large size of some of them, verging almost upon cumbersomeness. Of this the explanation given was that for a large dish of 20 or 22 inches diameter, revolving in a lathe, a large-sized tool would be necessary.

In the inventory of a Rouen pewterer, dated 1402, quoted by Bapst, the actual tools of the workman were as follows:—

    A lathe.
    A set of fourquettes.
 14 turning tools.
  2 square tools.
  4 brushes.
  1 burnisher for two hands.
  2 hooks.
  2 scrapers.
  1 file.
  1 pair pincers.
  7 cores, or mandrels.
  1 chinole for turning.
 Moulds.
  3 casting-ladles.
  3 small hammers.
  1 pair snips.
  1 small chisel.
  1 mould for low salt-cellars, with lid.

HOW IS PEWTER MADE?

1 mould for salt-cellars on a foot, also with lid.
1 mould for salt-cellars, *en façon de gallice*, with lid.
1 mould for casting lead cups.
2 moulds (different sizes) for casting acorn hinges.
2 moulds for casting knobs (pommettes) for salt-cellar lids.
1 pair of small scales.
1 pair of small compasses.
1 little bunch of iron wire.
1 piercer, or borer.
2 pair bellows.
1 hone.

It will be noticed in the above list that the lathe comes first, as the most important tool for the pewterer, and the tools for use with it are practically 22 out of 33, or just two-thirds—a very high total.

The author of *Le Potier d'Etain* (1909 edition) says quite truly of pewterers in France that the trade seems to have been modernised but very little and that it has kept to the old processes of the Middle Ages. The same may be said of our English pewterers. Conditions have changed, but methods are practically the same. If the Rouen pewterer of 1402, and Bosetus, the first pewterer known by name, were to revisit a pewterer's workshop of to-day they would see many things being done, if not most, that were matters of common daily experience to them over five centuries ago. They would appreciate the power lathe, though it would be no easy task to explain to them a steam engine, a gas engine, or a dynamo. They would welcome the greater convenience and the handiness of modern tools, taken as a whole, but they would in the main recognise them as developments of their older implements.

The modern pewter-worker uses gouges, chisels, hooks of various shapes and sizes, point-tools, side-tools (right and left). Some tools, such as spear graters, are spade-like pieces of steel, about $\frac{5}{16}$ of an inch thick, mounted in a

63

strong and long handle. In this way the cutting edge, when blunt by use, could be replaced by merely turning the tool on the rest.

A pewterer's gouge is a round-nosed tool rather than a gouge proper, and the chisels are bars of steel, rectangular in section, ground so as to give a bevelled cutting edge. These tools may vary in thickness and in width. By grinding down either of the respective angles of the cutting face a *side-tool* is obtained.

Some of the tools used in France at the present time are similar to those used in England. A *gouge plate* is like our *point-tool* but slightly broader. A *gouge ronde* is like our *round-nosed* tool. For mouldings they use a kind of templet in hard steel, which produces the moulding automatically and very mechanically. Another tool is a *frisoir*, of various shapes, either with a straight edge like a chisel, but with corners rounded off, or pointed like a point-tool, but yet with no sharp angles. The *frisoir* is usually made of thin plates of steel screwed or riveted on to a thicker piece as a handle. Often they are used without any handle at all, like our steel scrapers. They are used to make the surface ready for the *brunissoirs*, or burnishers. These, like ours, may be pieces of steel of various shapes, *e.g.*, with long handles or merely thinnish plates of steel with a smoothly rounded edge. Or again, they may be of bloodstone, agate, or flint. The latter is said to wear excellently.

The French tool called *plane* is rather like a wide chisel with its cutting angle rather obtuse. Another tool in common use is the *outil plat*, which is like our firmer chisels with bevelled edges, but its cutting edge is on the skew.

An interesting point in the turning of dishes or plates is the way in which a dish is made to form a chuck to hold another. A dish or plate (number 1) is secured to a carefully made wooden core by the process known as "springing-on." When securely fixed the plate is finished on the exposed side, then another from the same mould is superimposed, adjusted so as to run true, and then soldered at three points of its circumference to the under plate. Plate 2 is then turned, and forms in its turn a chuck for another. When the workman has as many as he can conveniently keep on the core he takes off the pile and, with a different core as chuck, repeats the process. This time, however, he pares down the waste edge of the rim and releases the plates, one by one as finished, from the pile.

CHAPTER SIX

THE CARE AND REPAIR OF PEWTER

IT will have been gathered from remarks made elsewhere in this book that carelessness and neglect have
been responsible for the disappearance of much pewter
of worth and of beauty. This being so, there is the more
reason for looking after and treating with respect pewter
that has been in existence, say, for a couple of centuries
or more, with a view to its living quite as long again;
for if it has survived so long there is surely no reason now
for any decay to begin to show itself. Any inherent weak-
ness would have developed in infancy or youth, and not
waited to come out in the respectable old age of two
hundred years.

Our forefathers who had pewter were in all probability
rather harsh but certainly thorough, for we read of
pewter being "scoured," and when we realize that the
process involved the use of Calais sand applied with elm
leaves we may, perhaps, tremble for the pewter. There
were other ways of cleaning. The plant *Equisetum hiemale*
is also, or rather was, known in country places as pewter-
wort. It contains a large quantity of silica in its cane-like
shoots, and for this reason was used in the same way as
the sand with the elm leaves.

For very dirty plates the following may be tried. Take
1 lb. of the finest silver sand and mix with it 1 oz. of salts
of tartar. Add water and apply this with friction, but on a
soft woollen rag. When the pewter is clean, wash the sand

THE CARE AND REPAIR OF PEWTER

all off, and polish with a soft cloth dipped at intervals as required into sifted whitening or precipitated chalk.

Another method is to get some very fine ash, such as that which occasionally collects in flues, or between fire-bricks in a kitchener and the plate of the oven. If sifted carefully through fine muslin a very clean and inexpensive abrasive will be obtained. It may be employed with vinegar and a rag, or by means of a half-lemon.

Any of the cleansing soaps which contain kieselguhr, or infusorial earth, will clean pewter well and effectively, but as a rule there is no need for such rough methods. Very fine emery-flour—knife-powder in fact—or crocus powder are much finer in themselves, and applied with a rag are excellent.

Rotten-stone, a fine argillaceous or siliceous limestone, disintegrated by long weathering, is a splendid abrasive for such soft metal as pewter. It may be mixed with soft soap and turpentine. The polishing may be finished by rubbing with dry rotten-stone on a soft cloth. Sweet oil and whitening may also be used.

For cleaning very dull pewter, or pewter that has been painted, boiling is the best method, and Mrs. Gerald Walker told the writer that protracted boiling in water with hay will clean the most obstinate pieces and make them look as though new. Care must be taken to keep a proper amount of water in the vessel in which the boiling takes place, to prevent in any case the pewter articles from any chance of burning or melting.

Scraping is not of much use unless done by an expert with the proper scraper, though light scratches can be erased with even strokes of a cutting instrument, such as a piece of broken glass or the disused blade of a safety-razor.

Burnishing will often remove the slight scratches caused by ordinary wear and tear, though not the gashes caused by knife-cuts on plates or platters. When burnishing is done in the lathe, the workman lubricates the work, which is revolving rapidly between centres, by directing on to it a jet or slow stream of soap and water. This has the effect of preventing heating and consequently of preventing the metal from sticking to the burnisher. Burnishers vary in pattern according to their special use.

Buffing is often done on pewter to give it a brilliant surface, but such a polish as can be got in this way seems quite out of place on any pewter that was intended for use in a household.

There are many polishing pastes and fluids, and most of them are good, but the best for use on pewter will be that which contains no acid and the least abrasive substance.

In Welch (ii. 130) we read of the oiling of pewter, and that the Pewterers' Company paid 19s. 6d. per annum for such oiling to their pewter. Nothing is said as to the oil used at the time this was done (1661), but the object, no doubt, was to prevent the oxidisation of the various pieces of pewter ware at the Company's Hall. It is an excellent thing to oil pewter wherever gas is the illuminant, or where the pewter is exposed to the vapours of town atmosphere. Nowadays we have our choice of oils, but perhaps thick vaseline is even better, as a very little spreads over a considerable surface, and, moreover, is easily removed if the pewter be required. Oils like linseed are quite unsuitable, as they dry on the surface. Sperm oil is not pleasant to handle. An American oil can be got for preventing rust on tools and bicycles, and is very thin and spreads well. It may be rubbed off and will still, like vaseline, leave a protective film on the surface.

Paraffin oil is an excellent cleansing medium for pewter, provided there is no hurry. It has the one disadvantage that it soaks through if the metal be at all porous, and the odour will remain long after the oil has disappeared from the surface, unless all traces of the oil be removed by means of benzine.

Some pewter plates, otherwise perfect, show signs of an efflorescence, either over the whole surface or in some cases only in places. Various explanations are given of this defect. It may be due to chemical decomposition in the antimony, caused by overheating the plate, or it may develop after lapse of time.

It is an unsightly defect and there is but one satisfactory remedy, and that is by treating the decay after the manner of decay in a tooth, and having it filled. The decayed portions must be carefully excavated and the cavity filled with good pewter, melted with care and the help of a suitable flux into its place.

A plate that is riddled with holes, like a sieve, can be restored in this way and made quite perfect. But it should certainly be stamped by the repairer or by the collector as a restored plate. If not, it is unmistakably a faked piece.

Sometimes pieces of pewter have been found to separate into their component parts, owing to the decomposition of the solder. This frequently happens in the case of the older church flagons, in which the bottom portion, comprising the moulded foot and the bottom of the flagon, becomes unsoldered from the cylindrical body. It may have been caused by carelessness on the part of the person responsible for the proper ablution of the vessel, and the wine, having been left in the vessel and having become acid, has acted to the detriment of the solder.

Some of the Apostel-teller and Kaiser-teller in museums seem to have been rescued just in time, as they are on the point of dropping to pieces. Specimens in private hands should be reinforced either with pewter carefully applied, or by layers of some quick-drying, hard-setting cement. The writer has seen a thirteenth-century sepulchral chalice treated quite successfully in this way, and made capable of being handled.

Plates and dishes are apt to crack where the rim joins the booge. The cracking is due to careless handling or the bending back of the rim when the plate is allowed to fall on a hard surface, and the rim is dislocated in consequence. To straighten out such bent rims the plate should be put face downwards on a hard level substance, such as a slab of marble or stone, if smooth enough, and hammered with a hammer, some substance, such as thick rubber sheeting or leather, being interposed to act as a buffer.

A crack can be mended by being soldered as soon as it is detected, with half the trouble that a crack of some years' standing will involve—the new crack being in most cases quite free from dirt.

The black scale that is found on old pewter is difficult to remove. It comes off sometimes in flakes, at others it seems to bring the pewter with it, and at others again it refuses to desert the surface from which it derives its own existence. It often drops off if the surface where it has formed has been hammered or bent, and it often scales off in the neighbourhood of any part that is being repaired by means of solder and a blow-pipe. There is no simple and safe means which will act like a charm universally.

Occasionally it may be scraped off dry, and the rough surface left underneath can soon be restored to good condition by rubbing or burnishing. There may be some few traces of pitting; for these there is no remedy but filling.

Another cause of decay in or damage to pewter is that

sand, in itself an excellent scouring medium, may, if it is allowed to get in between the knuckles of a hinge, work untold damage, both to the knuckles and also to the pin. The only remedy is to have the hinge entirely, or partially, repaired. There is no difficulty in inserting a pin of larger diameter, or in restoring the whole or part of the worn-out hinge, but it needs care in the doing.

One of the commonest causes of decay or ruin in the case of tankards is the addition of ball feet, or lions couchant as feet, to the bases of Continental tankards which were not originally made strong enough to bear these additions. These tankards or flagons would have lasted for years if they had been kept as the maker left them, viz., with a broad, flat base. The added feet caused the weight to be supported at three or four points only, and the weight of the vessel, especially when full of liquid, pressing on the feet, brought on an indentation in the bottom. After a time this was noticed, and the readjusting of the feet would crack the pewter round the place of juncture of the feet.

Wherever a tankard or large flagon was intended to have feet as part of the original design, it will be found that the body and the bottom are more than usually substantial. There is a very massive specimen in the Victoria and Albert Museum, South Kensington, which is well worth studying in every way. Its construction is excellent, so is the ornament, and the proportions are perfect. The feet are just as secure as they were when the vessel was first finished in 1635.

Dents in plates are common defects, but can be removed easily enough with a suitable hammer, or mallet. A flat-iron with a well-polished surface will make a good anvil for the purpose, and the force of the blows can be more evenly distributed if a thin plate of steel, such as the blade of a cabinet-maker's scraper, be interposed between the hammer and the soft pewter. The face of the plate should rest on the anvil and the blows be directed on the required spot on the under side.

For treating dents in flagons, and hollow ware generally, a fairly rigid piece of steel or iron will be required. One end should be secured in a vice, and the other should be inserted underneath the bulge or dent that is required to be removed. A series of gentle blows should then be given to the part of the vessel where the dent occurs. The exterior surface will require smoothing and levelling after being raised to its former level, with a fine file, and finally burnishing.

Specimens of pewter are often found in which the spout or the handle has been soldered in, apparently, by a travelling tinker or by a novice. In the one case the idea was to make the vessel watertight, in the other to mend it somehow, even if three times the necessary amount of solder were used in the process. All this careless and ignorant mending is an insult to the pewter and, since the advent of blowpipes, quite unnecessary. If a workman cannot mend pewter so that the join is barely visible, he had better not advertise himself as a repairer.

It is not every piece of pewter that is so carefully made as to withstand the wear and tear of daily life, and some, especially in later times, has been made, or at any rate finished, quite carelessly. Tankards and flagons are often found in which the handle has parted company with the body. The reason of this is that the body has been turned after manufacture and made too thin to stand the inward thrust of the lower part of the handle, especially when the tankard was filled with liquid. The writer has seen a German flagon in which the handle had come away from the body, which had been turned down in the lathe till

ROMANO-BRITISH PEWTER
Found in the Roman Baths at Bath
(*By permission of the Spa Committee of Bath Corporation*)

ROMAN PEWTER
(*British Museum*)

A SEPULCHRAL CHALICE

Fourteenth-century. From the grave of an ecclesiastic at
Witham-on-the-Hill, Lincs

(*Collection of the late Lewis Clapperton, Esq.*)

A RARE ENGLISH BEAKER, C. 1670–80
With wriggled-work decoration typical of the late Stuart period
(*Michaelis Collection*)

A RARE STUART TANKARD

c. 1675.   With wriggled-work decoration, by Peter
Duffield of London

(*Collection of Cyril C. Minchin, Esq.*)

A GROUP OF SEVENTEENTH-CENTURY FLAT-LIDDED TANKARDS

(*From a collection now dispersed*)

it was no thicker than a visiting-card. When the owner tried to get it repaired, various artificers declined to handle it, so after a time it was packed off to Munich. It came back to all appearances neatly and strongly mended—but it was found to leak. The explanation was not hard to find. The repairer had cut out a round hole in the body and cut out a tightly-fitting disk of the same size with a **V**-shaped rim, in slightly thicker metal. To this disk he had soldered the loose end of the handle, and then, inserting the disk in the round hole prepared for it, had hammered the disk round the edge and made an apparently good job of the repair.

As it leaked it was sent to an expert repairer, and it was found necessary to cut out a piece about three inches by two inches from the body and fill the space with new pewter. fixing the handle in position at the same time in the new piece, which was at least five times as thick as the original.

When a handle is thus parted from the body and levered outwards, it generally dislocates the upper rim and causes the rim to crack on both sides near the point where the handle joins the body. Where this takes place it is merely a question of time for the handle to come out bodily.

CHAPTER SEVEN

OLD PEWTER AND THE PEWTERERS

O LD pewter, with all its charm of colour, with all its antiquity, and with all its historical association, cannot be discussed in the same way that china, earthenware, or old furniture have been treated. If we take a specimen of Roman pewter and compare it with an eighteenth-century piece we shall find that though the alloy when analysed is somewhat different, yet the workmanship, as far as can be ascertained, is practically the same. It is not possible to stop at a certain date and say that from that time onwards this, that, or another method was introduced, to the exclusion of those that had been used before. There is no question of glazes and painting, underglaze, or peculiar methods of firing, and so forth. The craft of the pewterer when we first come upon authentic specimens seems to have reached a high point of practical development, and in later specimens any inferiority will be found to be due to deliberate wrong-doing by a particular workman, and is not to be put down to the time at which the retrograde workmanship is encountered. Some Roman pewter found at Icklingham, in Suffolk, in 1852, and some more found at Wangford in 1877, was of beautiful technique, and some of it rang as musically as any piece of the sixteenth century. In fact, as a whole, these specimens of Roman work were more ornate than our English forebears cared to make. One of the pieces was a cup with an octagonal rim, showing traces of inlaid ornament, and another had its sides fluted, probably to give it strength, for it was very thin, and the rim was decorated on the flat with tiny raised heads. Compared with these little delicate vessels the ugly pint-pots of William IV and Victoria are nowhere, either in quality of metal or in beauty of design.

The Romano-British pewter shown facing page 72 will give the reader some idea of the fine utilitarian shapes adopted for pitchers and ewers. It is doubtful if anything has since been made in pewter which combines usefulness and beauty to such a degree.

The small deep bowl to the left of the British Museum group deserves special mention on account of the diagonal fluting, which serves the purpose of strengthening what would otherwise have been a very frail object.

This type of ornamentation was adopted by the Swiss some fifteen centuries later.

Another fact worthy of comment is the remarkably fine condition of the pewter found in the Roman Baths at Bath, Somerset.

Its immersion in the celebrated waters seems to have been its very salvation.

These pieces can be seen in the Pump Room at Bath, and are illustrated by permission of the Spa Committee.

Pewter was made practically all over Europe, as may be gathered from a study of Bapst. It was made to suit local needs, and the pewterers flourished, or the reverse, just as did their artistic brothers, the goldsmiths, with whom, in fact, on the Continent they worked more in unison than was the case in our own country. Everybody required drinking-vessels, plates, and salts, and where wood was out of the question, and pottery was scarce, pewter was in requisition.

Scarcely any of the very early ware has survived, for

from the nature of the material it was bound to suffer considerably, and as the users knew it could be recast at very little expense they probably took very little care of it, the more so as it was not costly in the first instance.

In our own country the chief places outside London where pewter wàs made were York, Newcastle-on-Tyne, later at Bristol, Exeter, Bideford, Barnstaple, Bewdley, Birmingham, Wigan, Gloucester, Norwich, Kingston-upon-Hull, Ludlow and Lynn. In Scotland, Edinburgh, Perth, and Glasgow were most important as centres of production and distribution; in Ireland, Dublin, Cork, Youghal, and later Galway. Mention is also made in seventeenth-century records of pewterers in Kinsale and Clonmel.

In France, with tin obtained mainly from England, the chief centres were Paris and Lyons, Limoges, Rouen, Poitiers, Laon, Amiens, Tournay, Troyes, Tours, Reims, Dijon, and Saumur, also at Chartres and Le Mans, and further south at Nîmes, Avignon, Montpellier, Angoulême, Angers, Chinon, Bordeaux, and Toulouse.

In Spain, Barcelona was the chief emporium, and in Italy Bologna was an important centre. So, too, from its position, Venice.

The Lowlands had its headquarters at Bruges and Liége, and important centres at Ghent, Mons, Namur, Brussels, and Antwerp. Further afield there were Amsterdam, Breda, Maestricht.

In Germany, Augsburg, Nuremberg, and Salzburg were most important, and in the north Breslau and Hamburg.

In England there were always travelling workmen, whom the Pewterers' Company viewed with disfavour. They were classed with the "deceivable hawkers," specially so described in various Acts of Parliament. No doubt many of them were dishonest when and where they could be so with impunity, but under the able supervision of a farmer's wife in the north country no doubt they had to turn out honest, if not first-class, work. They had their rounds, and whatever their faults satisfied the requirements of their time.

The same kind of thing was done in Italy, and the men who went round were called *stagnarini*. They were far more common than the stationary pewterers.

At what date exactly these itinerant pewterers ceased to go round to the farm-houses recasting the pewter it is impossible to say. The necessity for them ceased when stronger spoons came into being, and when crockery, with its cheapness and its gaudy decoration, superseded the metal plates and dishes.

It may be noted, however, that up to about the end of the nineteenth century such itinerant workmen used to go round in the country districts of the Ardennes of France, recasting the spoons as required, retinning coffee-pots and other vessels of copper or of brass, and repairing plate and tinned articles generally.

As a rule they seem to have gone on annual rounds, and to have timed their visits, which lasted several days, so that all repairs and recastings should be finished before the date of the village fête. They recast the spoons in a mould, scraped them, and to some extent surfaced them by burnishing, partly to improve their appearance and partly to remove the scratches and other marks incidental to their manufacture. They do not seem to have hardened them very much by hammering.

The men who wrought in pewter were members of a guild with very careful organisation, but we do not find, in England at any rate, that it received any official recognition before the twenty-second year of Edward III, *i.e.*, the year 1348 (*vide* Riley's *Memorials of London and London Life*).

In that year the pewterers petitioned the Lord Mayor to give his sanction to certain rules, regulations, and ordinances that they had made for the protection of their trade. The petition was obviously made with a view to the protection of the pewterers from dishonest dealers and unscrupulous persons who tried to undersell them, and from a desire to get the better of those who sold inferior manufactures.

The better to do this, restrictions were to be put on the making of the alloy, and inspectors or overseers were to be selected from those who were most skilful in the trade. To facilitate this supervision, and to restrain the incompetent, it was proposed that no one who was not a lawful workman or who had not been properly apprenticed should work at the trade. More than this, there was to be no secret working, and at unlawful houses.

The men who made the pewter in our own and foreign countries were men who knew their business thoroughly in all its details—there were working men in those days and working masters too, which was of greater importance, for the apprentices, limited in number, had to be thoroughly well taught and trained. There were then no gentlemen pewterers—for all alike were under the eagle eye of their Guild, or later the Company. We must remember, too, that in the Guild there was a religious bond, that of fellowship, which united the members in a way that is quite unknown to the workmen of our times. There was a kind of freemasonry which caused them to club together and relieve distress among their fellow-workmen and, though we may smile, it was a religious feeling that was the *raison-d'être* of the solemn meal in the hall of the craft which was given after the Guild

78

had attended the funeral of a newly deceased brother-craftsman.

In those days of bonded brotherhood the guild feeling flourished exceedingly. No master could order a lock-out, and the workmen did not, or rather could not, go out on strike. The brotherliness of the men and masters, and the fatherliness of the masters to the apprentices, were strong points in the system. It was the sympathy of those in the craft, together with efficient and reasonable control, that made for contented workmen and, as a corollary, work of the highest excellence.

From their jealousy for the quality of the workmanship, standards were established, and every attempt made by the authorities to keep possible delinquents up to the mark. Searchers were empowered to make surprise visits to the workshops, within reasonable limits as to time—and as night-working was not allowed there was no hardship in the search in the case of a genuine pewterer doing normal work. "The first time those of the trade who were found working otherwise than as before set forth, and upon assay shall be found guilty; upon the first default let them lose the material so wrought; upon the second default let them lose the material and suffer punishment at the discretion of the mayor and alderman; and if a third time they shall be found offending, let them forswear the craft for evermore." This is the rule quoted from Riley's *Memorials of London and London Life*, pp. 241 *et sqq.*, where he gives the ordinances of the Pewterers' Company in 1348, 22 Edward III.

The practice of the Guild in England was the same in all essential points as that of the workers in pewter in Paris, Limoges, Rouen, or elsewhere, not that the rules were copied bodily, but because practical rules made by practical men working under similar conditions would have a natural tendency to crystallise into the same resulting regulations.

French pewterers were for many years called *batteurs d'étain—i.e.*, hammermen—as they were regularly called in Scotland. At an early date we find branches of them called *pintiers*, and by the end of the sixteenth century the *potiers* were differentiated into *les potiers dits de rond, les potiers maîtres de forge*, and *les potiers menuisiers.*

Having standardised the workmen as far as it was possible to do so, and the quality of the metal by the inspection of workshops and the confiscation of inferior work, the next step was to fix the standards of weights for the various articles made in pewter. The list of these, with the weights, will be found on pages 86–87, so that there is no necessity to quote them here.

The next step was for the Company of the Pewterers to try and appropriate the control over the tin trade between Cornwall and London. In this there was a partial success, and the Company reached the zenith of its power when the Crown gave it the right of search over the whole of England. This was given in 1473, and confirmed a few years later in the same reign.

This right of search was costly to enforce and troublesome to maintain, but it ensured a very high standard for English-made pewter.

In 1503, a most important year for the trade, the marking of pewter was made compulsory, and prohibitions were made as to its sale except on the premises of a pewterer, or in open fair and market. The whole Act of Parliament is most interesting, describing as it does the "knowing thieves and other pickers that steal as well pewter as brass . . . and bring such stolen vessels . . . to sell, and sell it for little or nought," and again, "have deceivable and false beams and scales, that one of them

PRICKET CANDLESTICK
Temp. Charles I
Dug up in London

TRUMPET-BASED CANDLESTICK
Temp. Charles II

(Collection of the late Lewis Clapperton, Esq.)

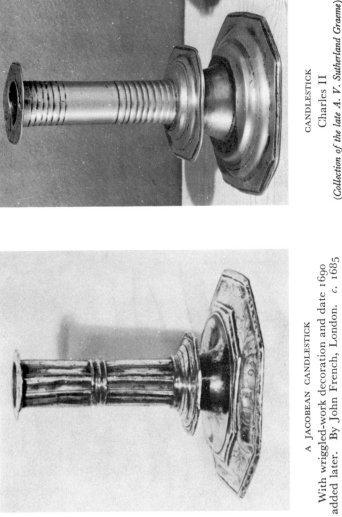

A JACOBEAN CANDLESTICK

With wriggled-work decoration and date 1690
added later. By John French, London. *c.* 1685

(*Jaeger Collection*)

CANDLESTICK

Charles II

(*Collection of the late A. V. Sutherland Graeme*)

will stand even with a 12 lb. weight at the one end against a ¼ lb. at the other to the singular advantage of themselves."

In this Act "London quality" was made the standard for both pewter and brass, under penalty of forfeiture.

The "deceivable hawkers," in spite of Acts of Parliament, still continued to deceive, and the Company tried to have them "suppressed."

Working in the public view was forbidden, under penalty of a fine, in 1601, and so too the exportation of English moulds abroad. This was part of the prohibitive restrictions against foreign work and workmen.

All through the history of the craft the keynote is protection of the most rigidly selfish kind. The London pewterers were very jealous as to the preservation of trade secrets, and were always on the watch by means of searchers to find out delinquents in London, and also in the country. An open shop where a passer-by could see for himself some of the processes of manufacture was forbidden. Casual help in the workshop, such as that given by a turn-wheel other than his prescribed work, would be a punishable offence for the master if detected. Foreign workmen were more odious to the pewterers than they seem to have been to the goldsmiths. An English pewterer was not to settle abroad, under penalty of being deprived of his rights as an Englishman. Other trades, too, were harassed when they produced wares that promised to enter seriously into competition with the pewterers' wares—as, for instance, the petty complaint that stone pots, i.e., earthenware beer measures, could not contain the amount prescribed by law.

The practice of one maker laying sworn information against another for bad workmanship may show righteous anger at any lowering of the standard, but it savours somewhat of pharisaical righteousness, and it is a relief to find (in Welch) that the pious informer of one year was the miserable sinner, and heavily fined at that, of a month or two later.

Foreign pewter ware, whether French or Dutch, was always being impounded for being below the proper standard, but the English pewterers resented their own pewter being excluded from other countries. They professed the policy of the open door as long as English pewter, and that only, might be received by its means.

This dog-in-the-manger policy in the end brought about the ruin of the trade. In the first half of the seventeenth century the control of the all-powerful Company of Pewterers began to be weakened, for the competition of the country pewterers, whom the Company now refused to admit as freemen, began to increase till it grew too strong to be checked. By 1729 the Company, when bad pewter was reported to be made in Bristol, felt that they were not strong enough to insist on their right of search (which they had previously claimed) in a place so far from the metropolis. Here was the beginning of the end. By the dropping of the valuable right of search, the standard of quality became a matter for each man to settle for himself, and English pewter, which had been as highly esteemed abroad as at home, began slowly and surely to deteriorate.

In mediæval times pewter was the material for the table-ware of kings and nobles. Edward I is said to have had leaden vessels used (let us hope they were pewter) to cook the viands for his coronation banquet, and our George IV had pewter plate used on his tables, or some of them, at his coronation banquet in 1820. From 1272 to 1820 is a sufficiently long cry, and during that time pewter was in use, at first increasing in importance, and at the end of the time beginning to wane in popular favour by force of circumstances.

Edward I by 1290 is said to have possessed over three hundred pieces of pewter of various kinds—probably plates, porringers, and drinking-vessels—the real necessaries of the time. The pewter was plain, but there were attempts at decoration, probably made by goldsmiths rather than pewterers, as witness the so-called *salière* of Bosetus in the Cluny Museum, Paris. It is more probably a reliquary, as it has a sacred subject represented on it. One resembling it, with similar ornament, can be seen at the Victoria and Albert Museum, South Kensington.

In the fourteenth century pewter was being generally used by the nobility and gentry both here and abroad, and though the English pewter was good, the French was admitted to have more style. Everything seems to have been made of pewter. The price was high, however, in this and the next century, though pewter slowly began to come into favour with the middle classes.

The families which had not to consider economy too much had whole services, while others were able to have what they wanted on hire, for a season or by the year. This was a great convenience at a time when almost all household comforts were carted from the country to town or *vice versa*.

A full set or garnish of pewter consisted of twelve plates, twelve dishes or bowls, and twelve saucers or plates of small size. The width of the brim, and consequently the weight of the garnish, varied. Hence the price varied too, for price depended upon weight, from 6d. to 8d. per lb.

In 1534 the Pewterers' Company made a present to the King's Attorney of two dozen trenchers of pewter at 6d. a lb., as well as a complete "garnish of vessell" at 4¾d.

There was probably some difference in quality in these two lots of pewter. Harrison, in 1580, in his *Description of England* writes: "In some places beyond the sea a garnish of good flat pewter of an ordinary making is esteemed almost as precious as the like manner of vessels that are made of fine silver, and his manner no less desired among the great estates, whose workmen are nothing so skilful in that trade as ours."

The point he refers to in the word "flat," is that in his time plates were beginning to be made considerably deeper, a change which, as he says, made them "more convenient both for sauce, broth, and keeping the meat warm."

Pewter by the end of the fifteenth century had gradually superseded the use of treen, or wooden platters.

They were commonly made of sycamore wood, and the square platters had a circular receptacle in one corner for the salt. Pepys in 1663 wrote: "We had no napkins nor change of trenchers, and drank out of earthen pitchers and wooden dishes." He probably means bowls, as the word "dish" was loosely used till much later in the expression "a dish of tea."

In the sixteenth century pewter was probably in universal use, as may be seen in the inventories quoted by Bapst, of the Dukes of Burgundy, of our own ecclesiastics and nobles.

The *Ménagier de Paris* (sixteenth century) says that the bourgeois class were compelled to be satisfied with pewter on their dressers and sideboards, while their betters displayed their gold and silver plate. One consolation which the bourgeois had, for which, no doubt, they had to pay, was that they could call their pewter "à façon d'argent." Although earthenware and china began to be in general use in the seventeenth century, we still find the more durable material holding its own, at any rate, till well on into the eighteenth century. Certainly this was so in the kitchens of houses of any size and in the better middle-class houses. Its use overlapped the introduction of crockery, but the latter, with its colour and its patterns, won the day. Pewterers, like the monastic copyists after the introduction of printing, still continued to show what they could do, but their art was doomed, and it gradually went from bad to worse, till it was almost killed by the introduction of Britannia metal. By 1851 it was scheduled as a nearly extinct art, though in some departments of the trade a demand for certain objects caused a certain supply.

CHAPTER EIGHT

WHAT WAS MADE IN PEWTER

V ERY early in Welch's *History of the Pewterers' Company* a list is given (vol. i, p. 3) of what was, in 1348, usually made in pewter. He quotes from the Company's records. "First for as moche as the craft of peuterers is founded uppon certein maters and metales as of brasse, tyn, and lede, in pte of the wheche iij metals they make vessel, that is to saie pottes, salers, disshes, platers, and other things by good folke bespoken, whiche werkes aske certeine medles and alayes after the maner of the vessels bespoken which thinges cannot be made without goode avisement of the peuterere experte and kunnynge in the crafte."

Vessels—*i.e.*, dishes, saucers, plates, chargers, square pots, square cruets, chrismatories, cistils, and other things that were made square—were to be made of fine pewter, while other things such as round pots, such as were known later as hollow-ware, were of lay.

In the following list are enumerated the weights of the various things that were made of pewter for household use in the middle of the fifteenth century:

								Weight per dozen lb.
Chargers	.	.	.	.	.	largest size .	.	84
						next size .	.	60
						middle size .	.	39
						small hollow	.	33

WHAT WAS MADE IN PEWTER

			Weight per dozen lb.
Platters	. . . . . .	largest size .	. 30
		next size .	. 27
		middle size .	. 24
		small middle size .	22
Dishes	. . . . . .	largest size .	. 18
		middle size .	. 14
		King's dishes	. 15
		small size .	. 12
		hollow .	. 11
		small hollow	. 10
Saucers	. . . . . .	largest size .	. 9
		middle size .	. 7
		next size .	. 6
		small size .	. 4
Galley dishes and saucers	. . .	largest size .	. 12

The smaller sizes of these were slightly lighter.

		lb.
Cardinals' hats and saucers	. . . . .	. 15
Florentine dishes and saucers	. . . .	. 13
	next size .	. 12
Small bowls	. . . .	. 13

All these were made by casting from moulds by workmen who seem to have worked at that special branch of goods.

Of pots and measures for liquids made at that time, we are told of—

		lb.
Square pottles (2 quarts)	. . . . . .	. 4
quarts	. . . . . .	. 2½
pints	. . . .	. 1½

There were also made for drinking purposes—

Normandy pots.
Stope (stoup) pots.

Spoons and small salts were made by a humbler class of workmen.

In 1612 the Company sized several parcels of trifle, or, in other words, standardised the weights for double and for single bells (? salts) with pepper-boxes and balls—in various sizes, and other patterned salts, beakers, wrought or plain, and both for children and for their elders, beer bowls, French cups, wine cups, both high and cut short.

Candlesticks are described as ordinary high, great middle, small middle, and middle pillar. Some are expressly mentioned as "new fashion." There are also great bell and low bell, also great, middle and small writing candlesticks.

Spout pots varied in capacity from a pottle to half a pint. Ewers were either great or small, and were called hawksbills or ravensbills, great or small French, the weights of either description being the same. There were also thurndells or thurindales of a "new fashion" and in two sizes, some being "hooped," Winchester and other quarts and pints, with and without lids—some of these, too, were "hooped." Goddards (tankards) were also of two sizes, and some were upright, others round. The largest had "dolphin" ears.

Of the articles thus made in England out of pewter, it will be seen that there was an endless variety. From the lists, too, we find that several articles are entered as "new fashion," proving that the craft as a whole was quite alive to the importance of introducing occasional novelties.

Specimens of most of these articles are in existence. Some of them are known by name only, as, for instance, the "Ephraim pints" and "Danske pottes," and some of the dishes, but the date of manufacture, as a rule, will be found to be some time after 1600. Earlier pieces may be found, but they will necessarily be of rare occurrence.

English pieces will be for the most part plainly finished, very restrained, and dignified in form.

In foreign pewter there is more variety, and articles are found of a kind which apparently was not produced in England—Guild tankards, wine-bottles and pilgrim-bottles.

Beakers (Germ. *becher*) of various heights and diameters were in very general use. They were used by the Lutherans as Communion cups, and are often covered with a rudely engraved history of the life of Christ, with a few of the prototypes. Judging from the similarity of treatment they must have come from one workshop. They date about 1710–15.

They have been found engraved with busts of William and Mary, other spaces being filled in with carnations or sometimes with tulips. Others are engraved with shipping scenes, extremely well done.

One early one was exhibited at Clifford's Inn in 1908, and contained cast ornament referring obviously to Edward VI. It was much worn and very battered; the beaker was thin, but of metal of good quality and very strong. There were no maker's marks.

Early English beakers are rare. Beakers were more frequently made abroad than in England. The beaker developed into the beer cups, some of them quite simple and nice to handle, others very ugly and with no beauty of line whatever.

One hundred years or so ago some were given to Lord Bloomfield by the Emperor Francis Joseph of Austria, and they were stamped with a date 1840.

These Austrian and German beakers are made now of a hard alloy like type-metal, cast in piece moulds and turned down inside very thin, to serve as mementoes of various towns, Nuremberg, Dresden, Munich, Cologne, and so forth. They are cheap and they do not break, so they are beloved by a certain class of tourists.

Nineteenth-century English beakers, in proportion as they are later in date, developed horizontal mouldings at the foot, half-way up, and round the lip. These mouldings are quite meaningless and only serve to conceal the lines of juncture where they are made in two pieces. In fact, they only want handles and glass bottoms for their downfall to be complete. The weight of the added handle was the reason for widening the base of some of the modern tankards to have the base wider than the top, to give increased stability.

No one, except an inexperienced beginner, is likely to look twice at the nineteenth-century beer tankards, except that some of those of better quality may do to repair older pieces.

Boar's-head dishes. Such is the name given to circular chargers of large diameter, such as 25 or 26 inches or more. The finest specimen known to the writer (in 1911) had been in one family since 1650. Its diameter is $28\frac{1}{4}$ inches, with a $4\frac{1}{2}$-inch rim.

Another fine one is dated 1725, and is the property of the Mayor and Corporation of Abington, Berkshire. It is dated 1725. It is $25\frac{5}{8}$ inches in diameter with a $3\frac{1}{2}$-inch rim.

In connection with the Abington dish, it is curious to note that it has been at some time used upside down as a block for mincing up meat, to the detriment of its under surface.

Bowls of small size, rather shallow, with one or two handles (generally called porringers), vary in form and size just as they did in the design of the ears or handles. If we can picture a time when there was very little earthenware, and realise what this involved even in a humble private establishment, we shall at once recognise the importance of the porridge-pot or porringer in all countries.

It is simpler to group all these handled vessels as porringers, than to attempt to subdivide them according to their uses. They are found with one or two handles, and in some cases the handles are of different types, one being ornamented—the handle proper—the other being plain, with a hole in it for greater ease in hanging it on a hook. Some specimens, especially the larger and later French ones, have lids with ornament in low relief; and some of the German ones are more bowl-like and have lids with three feet, on which the vessel could stand when in use. The Dutch porringers of the eighteenth century have large roses at the bottom in many instances, and in the genuine old specimens the roses are good. In the pseudo-antiques, now turned out by the dozen, the roses are less satisfactory, and the handles, which are very roughly cast, are carelessly soldered to the bowls.

These handles were recognised as a decorative feature of the bowls, and the under side of the ear is sometimes the more ornamental, rather indicating that the decoration was to be viewed when the vessel was hanging on its hook, and not when it was in use.

Many of the best specimens have a wedge section forming the under part of the handle as a means of strengthening what was undoubtedly the weakest part of the porringer. Some of the bowls, however, were so thick, and the handles so stocky and strong, that no strengthening device was required.

One pattern is sometimes met with to-day, viz., "the great flower de luce," or fleur-de-lis. Another kind was that known as the " *Three-leafe-grasse ear*," which seems to suggest a plain trifoliate ear.

The so-called "wine-tasters" were, as a rule, thinner and slighter in make, and have but one handle. Sometimes they are no stronger than porringers from a toy set.

Blood-porringers, or bleeding-bowls, in some cases resembled the ordinary type, but they are generally found with graduation marks in ounces, on the inside. Bleeding-bowls made within the last fifty years are single-handled and are more like saucepans than the early type of porringers.

Porringers are found in France, of comparatively recent date, with plain and simple ears.

As a special form of bowl we find the barber's bowl, generally recognised by the space cut out to fit the neck, and in some cases by the little recessed cavity in the rim for the soap.

Biberons are of Swiss origin, and have rather pretty spouts. The lids, which fit very tightly, have peculiarly massive hinges. The continuation of the spout is carried down to the bottom of the vessel so that the contents, if very rich, could be drunk off without the grease or any scum on the surface.

Bowls on feet with swing handles and a lid are sometimes met with. They are known by various names, such as soup-tureens, broth-bowls. The latter seems the better title, as they hold about enough for one person.

The earliest type of English candlestick existing to-day is most likely the pricket type, a specimen of which is shown facing page 80. The example illustrated was formerly in the collection of the late F. G. Hilton Price and later passed to the late Lewis Clapperton, C.A., of Glasgow, and now reposes in a Scottish museum.

Following this type came the trumpet-based style (also shown facing page 80).

Contemporary with the trumpet-based were candlesticks with circular bases with depressions to catch the molten tallow, and a plain, or slightly knopped, stem finishing in a plain socket with everted rim. The amazing example, with raised cast decoration and cast-in name of its maker—William Grainger—and date 1616, is a variant of this type. This is reproduced by permission of the Victoria and Albert Museum authorities (see *frontispiece*).

This was followed, in the latter half of the seventeenth century, by the square base, with either square or round pillar.

A fairly large variety of types was produced in the last quarter of this century, from the round base with plain pillar, broken by a large ball-like knop, to the fine octagonal-based candlesticks with drip-tray placed above a broad, decorated base.

The bases of some of these were probably cast from the same moulds as the salts of the period. It is a strange fact that there are comparatively few eighteenth-century English pewter candlesticks to be found.

This is probably due to the fact that many households favoured the very beautiful silver examples produced in this period.

Most of the pewter candlesticks and taper-sticks found to-day, made in the style of the Queen Anne and early Georgian silver examples, are of Dutch manufacture or, at any rate, Continental in origin.

Some of the seventeenth-century Dutch bell-based candlesticks are exceedingly pleasing in style, and in quality and design are equal to any produced in this country.

The more ornate baluster candlesticks of the nineteenth century, usually made of a hard metal, are not of any particular interest to the serious collector, but can look very effective if kept bright and placed on a modern mantelpiece or sideboard.

Eighteenth-century church candlesticks are frequently, curiously enough, reversions to the earlier type known as prickets. They are very flimsy, especially in the bases, except when this latter part is cast in one piece. In the style of their ornament they are after the usual Church fashion of the period.

Cups, mugs, or goblets, the former with baluster handles, are occasionally found, and the earlier ones are of great beauty.

There come on the market occasionally genuine specimens of hanaps, or Guild cups, for the most part of the seventeenth and eighteenth centuries. (See illustration facing page 96.) They are usually 17, 18, or 20 inches in height, including the elaborate lids, on which there is, as a rule, some crest or emblematic figure giving some hint as to the nature of the Guild—*e.g.*, a lamb on the cup of a Clothworkers' Guild, a horse on that of a Blacksmiths', a mallet and square on that of a Masons', bones and cleavers on those of a Butchers'.

These hanaps were frequently decorated by lions' masks round the top of the body, from which medallions, or shields, or disks to receive names, were suspended. Many of these so-called Guild hanaps are quite fictitious articles.

Coffee-pots, or urns, on three feet, are often met with, and are generally of Flemish origin. The feet are, as a rule, of brass, so is the tap, pewter taps not being found quite satisfactory. These urns are found severely plain, or else very elaborately ornamented. One lent to the first Exhibition at Cliffords' Inn in 1904 had three brass taps, brass feet, and a brass knob on the lid. The body was engraved with three typical Dutch landscapes: (1) Canal scene; (2) Farm scene; (3) Lake with windmill.

Specimens are found painted all over with Watteau scenes, and evidently of French origin. Why they were painted if a hot beverage was to be brought in them to table will remain a mystery.

Ewers, in France at any rate, in the seventeenth century favoured the helmet pattern, and they, being massive, as a rule, have come down to our time, while the basins have gone to pieces. Fluted specimens, though a little stronger structurally than those left quite plain, have proved unable to stand rough usage and have in many cases cracked along the lines of the flutings.

Italian specimens are sometimes met with, very carefully made and finished, and of excellent pewter.

A rare find in perfect condition is a Posset-cup, in shape resembling the silver brandy-saucepans found in Irish silver of the eighteenth century.

Some fine specimens can be seen in the Victoria and Albert Museum, London.

There is a very handsome beaker with a lid, examples of which are found in various foreign museums, purporting to be the handiwork of Baron Von Trenck, and executed by him while in prison in Magdeburg in 1763. The beaker with its lid is covered all over with engraving, lettering, and stippled ornament, all of which is said to have been done with a sharpened nail. The Baron admits in his *Life* that his first attempts were rude, as may be well imagined, but that he grew more expert and spent a whole year in this employment. It is a pity that the sharpened nail has not been preserved, for the armorial bearings on the inside of the lid are most delicately worked, so much so that many professed engravers would be hard put to it to do such intricate work with all their gravers in first-rate condition.

Inkstands, again, were of various patterns. One of the

earliest known to the writer was a travelling inkbottle of the sixteenth century that belonged to the late Mr. F. G. Hilton Price. One is mentioned as early as 1411 by Bapst, made by one Goupil of Tours. It seems to have been large and quite round in form. The round form seems to have been the germ from which the other types developed. We get the round, low inkstand, and the same, slightly higher. To steady them a moulding is added at the foot, and to keep dust from the ink a lid is added. A couple of holes in the top serve as a place to put the pen or pens when not in use. Next, to secure the table or any papers from the chance of blots, the base is developed as a tray, and in the pictures by Rembrandt, and others of his time, of civic and private life, various patterns may be traced with ever-varying details.

The "Logger-head" type proper has a broad flange to steady it, but those made to-day for cheapness are without this feature.

As soon as the pounce-box was made as an accessory part of the inkstand, and a little box for wafers was added, the whole thing began to look important, and here, as always, the pewterers followed the lead given by the silversmiths. We get the oblong tray, in some cases of considerable size, with its various necessary adjuncts, later with a taper-holder. Then, to increase the dignity, ball feet or claws were added.

Of another type are the flat kind, with two flap-lids, beneath which everything is efficiently concealed and protected from dust. With ball feet they look well enough, but with half balls on slender supports the effect is weak-kneed and grotesque.

A similar type is used to-day and is usually known as a "treasury inkstand."

Some of the small circular and rhombic inkstands of the

THREE HANAPS, OR GERMAN GUILD CUPS
(*Victoria and Albert Museum*)

TWO CAPSTAN SALTS, ENGLISH
c. 1685
(Collection of the late Lewis Clapperton, Esq.)

MASTER SALT
c. 1675
(Victoria and Albert Museum)

Queen Anne type are so beautifully finished that they seem to have been made by silversmiths. There are, in fact, at the present time some inkstands in silver which have been made to order from pewter originals—an object-lesson to the silversmiths of our time.

The little Dutch specimens with one or more drawers are rarely perfect, the opening for the latter being a contributory cause to the decay.

The so-called synagogue lamps of the Jews are not so in reality. They were used, but were lamps lighted at sunset by the female head of the house, on Fridays and on the eves of the great festivals. These lamps consist of the hook, a weight, a crown or shade; the lamp usually stellate with seven wicks, a drip-tray or receiver, and a pendant. They are uncommon in pewter, and are very seldom perfect, as might be expected from lamps consisting of so many component parts.

Night-light lamps with a glass oil reservoir graduated in hours are sometimes to be bought. The earlier ones are of stronger construction and the glass portion is much thicker than in the modern replicas, which are more common.

Salts, or salers as they were called, from the French *salière*, are among the earliest pewter objects mentioned in Welch (vol. i, p. 3). They are merely described as salers, and nothing is known of their shape. In 1490, in the inventory of the goods belonging to the Pewterers' Company, there are entered "viij saltes of fyne metell" without coverings, weighing 6 lb., made of "such metalls as (has) been crossid upon the heed bifore in this boke." This does not tell us very much, but we know from early inventories that salts were generally made with lids. These were therefore unusual in this respect.

In 1551 the pewterers had to consider the question of

some salts which had been found made in lay instead of fine metal. These were ordered to be broken up, and the makers and the owners were to bear half the loss respectively, and the Court decided that "from hensforth whatsoever they be that makyth any salts other than iiij s. salts and iij s. salts and chopnets greate and small after the olde fashion that then they shall be forfeyted. And that no man make no Salts of any new fashion without yt be allowed and adjudged by the Master and Wardens. Except yt be of fyne mettell." The case was so serious that the names of the offending salt-cellar makers were entered on the minutes.

The importance of the passage just quoted is that it gives a clue to the meaning of chopnets or chapnuts as applied to salts. The list of salts in Welch, ii, p. 61, gives great double bells with pepper-boxes and balls, nine pounds weight the half-dozen.

Great double bells, plain .	.	.	6 lb. the half-dozen.
Middle double, with balls	.	.	6 lb. ,,
Middle double, plain	.	.	4 lb. ,,
Small double .	.	.	3 lb. ,,

There are also specified as follows :—

Great single .	.	.	6 lb. the half-dozen.
Middle single .	.	.	3 lb. ,,
Small single .	.	.	$2\frac{3}{4}$ lb. ,,
The wrought acorn salt .	.	.	4 lb. ,,
The great chapnut .	.	.	$1\frac{1}{2}$ lb. ,,
The small chapnut .	.	.	1 lb. ,,

If a conjecture may be hazarded, the word chapnet may be an anglicised version of the French *chapournet*, and the chapnet may have been either a very light (3 oz.) salt with a domed lid, or a shallow salt with a semicircular depression. The latter may be of the same form as that of the master-salt which is illustrated facing p. 97. The master-salt was the principal salt on the table, and it was used to show the place of the head of the table, rather than to contain the salt for the various courses of the meal. Next to each person was a trencher salt, a much smaller utensil.

Another seventeenth-century type is spool-shaped. On the flat rim of the upper part are three snail-like projections, which were used for preventing the linen napkin which was used as a cover from touching the salt. If necessary, too, the salt could be passed by means of these spars. Similar salts in plate are to be seen in the Tower of London.

Other varieties of salts were "coffins," called so probably from their shape; others were circular, with hollow stems and shallow containers; others with octagonal bases and circular bowls. From the seventeenth century onwards the pewterers copied the silversmiths.

Trencher salts in pewter were made as late as the time of J. Duncombe, or Duncumb.

Spoons of pewter are always being offered to collectors. Many of them are quite modern Dutch specimens, made of metal of very poor quality, and with circular bowls and frequently with circular or very slightly flattened stems. In nearly all early spoons, *i.e.*, from the fourteenth century to 1650, the bowls are irregularly ovate or fig-shaped, slightly curved upwards, with in many cases hexagonal stems; the reason for this, no doubt, being that as spoons had to be finished by hammering, so that they might thereby become hardened, the very fact of the hammering, *ipso facto*, changed the shape of the original section of the stem from round to oval, and by further hammering the result would easily be hexagonal. In the same way a square, or rather rhombic, sectioned stem would be caused by hammering.

Having arrived at a practical and beautiful bowl and an equally common-sense stem, the spoon-makers varied the knops or tops of the stem. In these knops the earliest type, according to the late Mr. Hilton Price, was that known as a "Ball knop." He ascribed it to the thirteenth or fourteenth century, and assigned to it the place of honour, as to age, in his collection. In his monograph on spoons he describes another similar spoon with a ball near the centre of the stem. This may have been produced at the time of making, or subsequently when some repair to the fragile stem was necessary, the ball in that case being a kind of "wiped joint."

English pewter spoons of the fig-shaped bowl type are divided by collectors into groups according to the type of finial or knop.

The knops are known as Acorns, Diamond-pointed, Maidenheads, Horned Head-dresses, Hexagons, Apostles, Writhen balls, Lions, Balusters, Seal-tops, Strawberries. They were, in nearly all cases, copies of the knops designed by contemporary silversmiths.

The list in tabular form on p. 101 will show the dates, by half-centuries, when, according to Mr. Price, the various spoons were being made.

The marks on pewter spoons are, as a rule, very small, but of far better workmanship than the bigger marks of the same period.

Snuff-boxes have been made of every conceivable shape, but of pewter snuff-boxes not much has been heard. The makers of them were never many in number, and at the present time there are scarcely any, and those not English.

As to the form of the boxes, none are perfectly square, for square boxes are not the most convenient for the pocket. None, too, are very large, as thin pewter, however good in

WHAT WAS MADE IN PEWTER

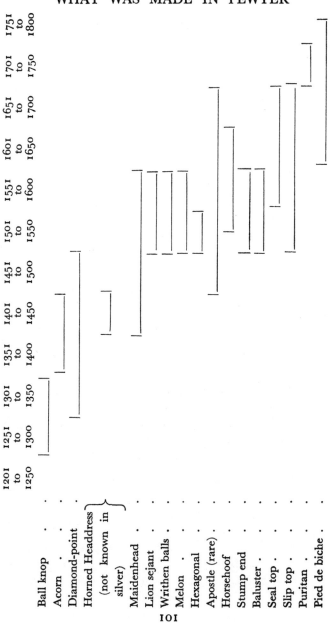

quality, would not be strong enough to withstand much wear and tear. Most of them are rectangular, with the corners either rounded off, or cut off so as to make the boxes octagonal. Circular boxes are not common, but are met with occasionally, as are also those of oval shape. Of the less practical fancy shapes there are the pistol pattern and the cockle-shell, one of each of which is shown in the illustrations between pp. 104 and 105. There are also several varieties of the lady's-slipper pattern.

None of those in pewter have been made to contain portraits or pictures of any description. In most cases the quality of the metal used is excellent. A cheap alloy consisting mainly of lead would have been useless for the making of boxes destined to be continually used, and worse than useless if designed to bear any raised ornament. The excellence of the hinges, especially in the specimens that have not been repaired, is worthy of notice, as they are fitted with the same amount of care that would be bestowed on a hinge made in a harder and more precious metal. It was of course essential that the boxes should not be too bulky nor too fragile—two points which also helped in establishing a high standard of quality for the metal employed in the manufacture.

The insides of many of the specimens show that gilding was often applied, and apparently covered with a transparent lacquer. In some more recent boxes the inside has been painted with gold paint to imitate the older method.

The standard of workmanship, whether the boxes were French, Dutch, German, or English, was like that of the material—a high one. Not one of the boxes illustrated in this volume bears any trace of careless, slipshod work. It is difficult to bring forward any evidence as to the place of origin. None of the boxes shown bears even the remotest trace of any maker's mark, either in the inside or on the outside. The reason for the absence of marks may be found in the thinness of the material, much of the sheet metal being less than $\frac{1}{32}$ of an inch in thickness.

The methods of construction used in the manufacture of the boxes are quite simple. Where it was possible from the shape of the box to cast it in two similar sections, this course was adopted, the lid being inserted later. A practised eye will very easily detect the line of junction by the slightly different colour of the solder employed. Some of the rectangular boxes have their sides formed by bending up the metal to the required angle, and by the application of solder. In some the sides of the boxes are formed of separate strips of metal which have been ornamented by being passed through rollers, and impressed in the process with some running ornament or embossed scroll-work.

Most of the lids are strengthened by being flanged or by being thickened at the edge. The ornamentation of the boxes is, as a rule, quite simple, as it should be in so soft a material, and is in most cases done by mechanical means—rolled strips for the sides, panels stamped in very slight relief, or in some cases floral scrolls, as designs for the centre, filled in with engine-turned work.

Occasionally some lightly engraved work of a simple kind is found, but it rarely looks effective on a box after a long period of use.

Turned borders, consisting of incised lines filled in with chased patterns, are frequently found. On some boxes a panel or ornament in another metal is added. Such a box is that shown at the foot of the illustration between the two shoes. This has an inset panel of pinchbeck or brass.

The bottoms of the boxes are generally plain, though in many the panel on the bottom is a replica of that on the

lid. The panels of ornament when added to a lid are often recessed below the rim, so as to save the design from undue wear and tear; and the same course is sometimes adopted in the case of small inserted panels in the sides.

In some of the ornamental panels which are so treated as to give the appearance of having been etched, the backgrounds show some faint traces of original colour, which was probably applied as a transparent lacquer to the box when first finished.

The subjects dealt with in the ornamentation are, as a rule, conventional scrolls and floral borders, with perhaps a basket of flowers or a hunting-scene as a centre-piece. One of those illustrated has a representation of the Last Supper, while another gives a peep.into a farmyard, with the tax collector making off with a pig. The box is titled "Take your tythe."

A group of Scottish mulls is shown facing p. 105. These are of ram's horn, deer's hoof or cow's horn and such like suitable materials, mounted with pewter. A maker of this type of mull is one Durie of Inverurie, about whom nothing further is known. His name, however, appears inside the lids of quite a number of such pieces.

Stone pots with pewter lids are a common feature in museum collections, where they naturally enough come in as pottery. The pewter collector will look at them from the point of view of the lids, and he will be disappointed. So many of the lids are missing or damaged, as was to be expected when the pots were so heavy and the lids so light and fragile. There are some excellent specimens in the British Museum with lids in good preservation, but they are in the main of foreign make.

One point of interest in the pot lids is that the method of fixing the pewter lids to-day is identical with that of five centuries ago. A small pit-like depression in the handle

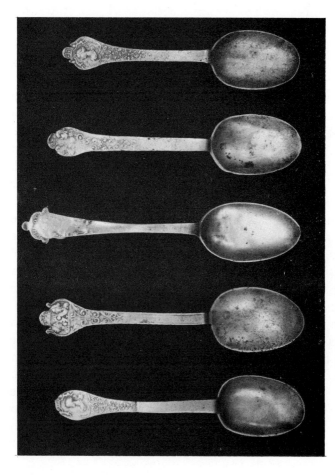

A GROUP OF SPOONS WITH CAST PORTRAITS OF ROYALTY
1 and 5, Queen Anne; 2 and 4, William and Mary; 3, George III.
(Michaelis Collection)

A GROUP OF PEWTER SNUFFBOXES
(*Michaelis Collection*)

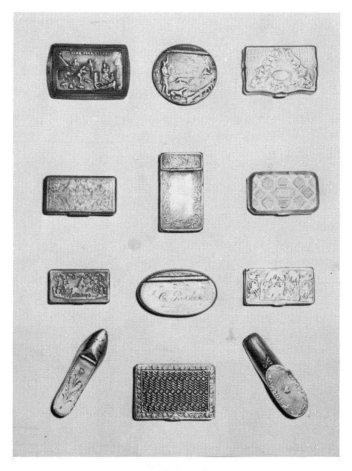

A GROUP OF PEWTER SNUFFBOXES

(*Michaelis Collection*)

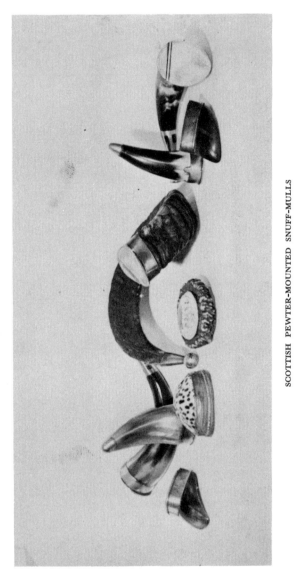

SCOTTISH PEWTER-MOUNTED SNUFF-MULLS

Late eighteenth and early nineteenth centuries

(*Michaelis Collection*)

receives, or is made to receive, a spur of the soft metal handle, and, when once the pewter is soldered in its place, the handle cannot shift.

As early as 1536 haberdashers, just as the drapers of to-day, seem to have outstepped the apparent limits of their trade, and to have sold stone-pot heads, small salts, and goblets.

Ladles of German origin, probably for domestic use as dippers, and for soup, are altogether larger than their English counterparts.

The Continental ladles also were shorter and thicker in the handle. Punch ladles were made in exact replica of those in silver, and are often found with twisted whalebone handles, tipped with pewter. Very few of those met with to-day are English.

Among the smaller objects made in pewter were pipe-stoppers, two of which are shown facing p. 145, together with a pewter dog-whistle. None of these objects, of early nineteenth-century manufacture, are easy to find to-day.

Perhaps the least interesting things ever made in a base metal were teapots and coffee-pots. There are one or two exceptions in the earlier pewter teapots by Richard Pitt, or Pitt and Dadley, but they are not generally popular with collectors. At least 99 per cent. of the so-called pewter teapots are not of pewter at all, but Britannia metal or "Ashberry" metal.

These follow the general lines of the silver and silver-plated articles produced in the mid nineteenth century and later, and in the dull grey metal are anything but elegant.

Tankards are of infinite variety, both as to size, shape, and ornament. Many so-called tankards are measures with lids, and the official stampings with dates of various years in succession as a rule should decide the matter.

Tourists occasionally bring home from abroad measures stamped with Government stamps, and engraved $\frac{1}{2}$ litre, imagining that they have secured a veritable treasure. Such measures are made by hundreds to-day, and are in common use wherever the metric system is the system of the country. If ever the litre is accepted over here, half-pint and pint pots will at once become rarities to be added to collectors' hoards.

German tankards are commonly slightly less in diameter at the top than they are at the foot. The lids are domed in most cases and the thumb-pieces are massive. Sometimes they are out of all proportion to the size and weight of the lid.

Tankards are often very dirty inside, and beneath the deposit in a German tankard there may be concealed a fine Tudor rose or a double-headed eagle, or some other device.

Some specimens have been spoilt by the addition of later feet.

Scandinavian tankards have perfectly cylindrical sides as a rule, and are left quite plain. Occasionally a little ornament in relief is found on the handles.

Occasionally flat-topped or slightly domed tankards have a coat of arms engraved, or else a coin, or a pewter cast of a coin, in the centre.

The Stuart, and William and Mary, type of English lidded tankards have a slightly tapering body and a flattened lid with serrated projections to the front of the lid. Later tankards of the time of Queen Anne and the Georges were made with domed (or double-domed) lids.

Some interesting types of *un*lidded tankards were produced during the years *c.*1690–1710, usually rather taller and more tapering than the lidded varieties.

As time progressed the shapes became more florid and

the handles, which hitherto had been a single sweep, became more complicated in design and can be described as of "double-ogee" pattern.

From this time onwards the styles generally deteriorated to what we now know as the Victorian tankards. These latter are of little interest to the serious collector unless he is forming a range of styles used throughout the ages, or is interested in making a collection of pieces bearing the names of inns or taverns.

In the course of his searches a collector may expect to come upon curious things even in a prosaic metal such as pewter. He need not be astonished by their unusual or strange forms.

A vessel in the form of a square-toed shoe (or was it a hot-water bottle?) was shown at Clifford's Inn in 1904, and was claimed by the owner to be a shoemaker's sign.

The same exhibitor lent a milk-jug in the form of a cow. It was a figure of some size, 16½ inches long and 9 inches in height, and of some capacity. The maker's name was Michel Pechel, a silversmith of Augsburg, and the cow was made as a wedding-present for Ignatz Muller and Xaver Alber.

The late Sir F. Dixon-Hartland had a ship in pewter, with all its sails and rigging. It was intended for use as a liqueur-bottle, to be passed round the table, the tap being contrived in the stern post. Pewter is hardly an ideal metal for keeping liqueur in for long, but perhaps the rule was that none should be allowed to remain.

Salts and pepper-pots in the form of pug-dogs are not uncommon in pewter. In later times salt-boats in the form of swans were made.

Maces in silver, corporation and otherwise, are sometimes found, but they, too, were made in pewter and of a very unusual form. The head of one such mace was a crescent moon, wedge-shaped in section, with a grotesque mask on the front where it was thickest. There were three of them in the set, but the original use of them was unknown to the then owner. The stems were too thin and weak, and had been strengthened by the addition of a collar soldered round the stem.

Pewter maces of some interest were carried by the mutes at the funeral of the Iron Duke in 1852. They were quite plain black wooden rods, with a knob at the lower end, a band of pewter half-way up the handle, and a head representing a phœnix rising from its ashes.

The late Mr. Buckmaster had a small three-faced figure, said to be a portrait of Queen Elizabeth, which was the top of the wand of a tipstaff. It had been converted into a seal when shown at the Clifford's Inn Exhibition.

As another variety of mace, the wand carried by the beadle of the Pewterers' Company may be cited as an instance.

A fine group of pewter maces or processional staves is shown facing p. 144. These were originally thought to have belonged to the Clothiers' Company of Bradford, but enquiries of the local Historical Society of that city failed to elicit any knowledge of such a company.

The group was divided among various pewter collectors many years ago and their present whereabouts are unknown.

Costrels, or pilgrim-bottles, were made of earthenware, and specimens may be seen in museums. There are several in the Guildhall Museum.

Another curious type of article sometimes found is that called in French *gut*. The body is bottle-shaped, of some considerable capacity, and the screw-top is fitted with a ring. By means of this ring the vessel was lowered down a well so as to cool the contents, usually wine. They are often found in a very battered condition, owing to their having come in contact with the sides of the well. Of three specimens known to the writer, two had been dredged up from wells, both, too, in the South of France. One of them had been repaired with a brass base, to replace the earlier one in pewter, and was fitted with brass rings.

The word *gut* is probably derived from the Latin *guttus*, a narrow-necked vessel, used by Pliny, Juvenal, and other writers. In the Saintonge patois the word is spelled "*got.*"

Among specimens of German pewter there will always be found some of the hexagonal vessels, with screw-tops, and rings to serve as handles. Some are found with spouts and others without, and herein is a possible clue to their exact use.

Those with spouts were used for containing *must*—the thick rich syrupy substance, highly intoxicating, left in a vat after the clear wine has been drawn.

The spouts are usually found fitted with lids, either screwed or hinged.

The spoutless kind are, by some, said to have been for carrying food, in the same way that enamelled or tin-plate vessels are carried by workmen of our time; but from the nature of the engravings found on them, in some cases, there is no doubt that they were wedding-presents— to a couple, not to a single member of the pair. They are, as a rule, more highly ornamented than the wine-flasks— sometimes all six faces of the hexagon being decorated, sometimes only the alternate faces being so treated. Sometimes four only of the six faces are enriched with ornament.

It is possible that they may have been intended for use as hot-water bottles, and were the gifts of some humorous members of the family, or circle of friends, who, thereby, implied that the nights might be chilly!

Some have maintained that these articles were intended to hold the personal effects, such as jewellery or cash, that a bride took with her when she left home to be married. In any case such vessels were in great request, for they are found with dates from 1660 down to 1840.

A prayer-slab (9 × 8) containing the following prayer—

> "Dass sey mein letzter Wille
> Gott drück das Siegel drauff
> Nun wart'ich in der Stille
> Bis dass ich meinen Lauff
> Durch Christi Tod Vollende
> So geh ich freudich hin
> Und weiss dass ich ohn Ende
> Des Himmels Erbe bin"—

was lent for exhibition at the Pewter Exhibition of 1904.

A clock-face in pewter will seem to many a strained use of the alloy, but there have been such things and they may be found again. The one known to the writer was of the usual "grandfather" shape. In the semicircular part over the dial proper was a relief representing the Holy Family. Immediately above the XII there was an eye, with a garnet or other red stone, set in the pewter. In the corners of the face the ornament was partly relief-work and partly pierced with gold and coloured background. The central part of the face contained the "Annunciation" in low relief, and the whole of it had probably been painted at one time. Its dimensions were 15 inches by 11 inches.

Sets of plates called motto plates are to be found. The set usually consists of six plates inscribed with a series of lettering. One such set bears the following wordings:—

WHAT WAS MADE IN PEWTER

"1. What is a merry man?
2. Let him do what he can
3. To entertain his guests,
4. With wine and merry jests.
5. But if his wife do frown
6. All merriment goes down."

Care should be taken in purchasing such a set, as they are known to have been faked, by inscriptions being added later to a perfectly genuine set of triple-reeded plates.

CHAPTER NINE

CHURCH PEWTER

IN the search for pewter the collector will be sure to be shown some that will be called Church pewter.

It is not only the possibility of fakes that need concern the novice, for he may be offered quite genuine *domestic* food basins described as baptismal bowls, ordinary plates labelled as patens, or Scottish lavers (ewers) as Church Communion flagons.

It has ever been the tendency for ignorant persons, or others who are not entirely honest, to give to their pieces what they suppose to be the added glamour of an ecclesiastical title. Far wiser to let the article be known by its commonplace name unless some undoubted proof is forthcoming to establish its religious connections.

The collector need not expect to be offered anything earlier than, say, the beginning of the seventeenth century. Church pewter earlier than this is known, but is mostly in safe-keeping in museums.

At the Council of Winchester in 1076 pewter was allowed to be used for chalices in poor parishes in place of the wooden ones then in use.

At a Council at Westminster in 1175 this ruling was reversed—the bishops being ordered not to consecrate pewter chalices.

The earliest pewter chalices known to exist are those which were buried with ecclesiastics in the thirteenth and fourteenth centuries. These were probably emblematical representations only, and it is doubtful if they had ever served any real use.

The bowls were wide spread, rather like a modern champagne-glass, and they stood upon a foot or stem rather like the trumpet-based candlesticks of the seventeenth century, see the specimen illustrated opposite p. 80.

Tall English Communion flagons in pewter dating from c.1610 onwards are occasionally met with, but will be of a prohibitive price.

Silver flagons for sacramental use were first made in 1602, and some of these, tall and with straight bodies, are to be found at New College, Oxford, 1602; Brasenose has some 1608, and there are some at Salisbury Cathedral of 1610. These silver standing pots, or stoups, as they were termed in the Canon of 1603–4, were almost at once copied by the pewterers, and the shape persisted with but slight variation for some considerable time. References may be found in most of the excellent accounts of county Church plate. But it may here be added by way of protest that the way in which sacramental plate, even though of pewter, has been sold out of the churches by unauthorised persons, and without the farce called a faculty, is nothing short of scandalous. If the plate has been Church plate, and used as such, so it should be allowed to remain. Almost every serious collector now has some specimens of flagons, chalices, and patens.

More than one collector has come upon Church plate that had thus been removed from its proper home, or resting-place, and after having had it most carefully restored returned it to the building from which it had been wrongfully removed.

English flagons at first had quite plain, tapering cylindrical drums standing on a slightly broadened base, with a similar structure round the neck.

The lid was domed, and the thumb-piece rather heavy and erect, not unlike that used on the later tappit-hens.

The handle was a single sweep, again somewhat similar to that on the tappit-hen, but with a small projection two inches or so above the terminal.

The handle was fixed to the drum of the flagon without the short connecting piece found on some later tankards and measures.

The next stage was the addition of a knob or finial to the lid, and a few mouldings to the base. The same general characteristics are followed in the third stage, with the exception of the lid, which now becomes a true "bun"-shape. This takes us up to about 1635, when additional types began to appear; these are too numerous to cover in detail, but it can be said that, generally speaking, from 1740 onwards it was a gradual decline in styles when the addition of florid mouldings at the base and centre of the drum, and the use of large spouts finally killed the grandeur and simplicity which had, hitherto, been the keynote of English flagons.

Scottish Communion pewter, which was used more recently than in our churches, and still is used, was on the whole more simple and restrained, and the specimens of the first few years of the nineteenth century have a dignity that is lacking in English contemporary work. They are entirely dissimilar to English flagons, with inverted saucer-shaped lids, and are plain with the exception of a band or fillet midway up the side, and some slight mouldings at the foot and round the rim.

Scottish chalices are larger in the bowl than those in use in English churches. They are frequently found in pairs, or sets of four.

Much Scottish ecclesiastical pewter seems to have left its native home at the time of the union of the Scottish

"York" Flagon

*c.*1735

Free Church and the United Presbyterian Church in 1900, and still more when the United Free Church joined with the Church of Scotland in 1929.

Font-basins are occasionally offered by dealers, but they are more likely to be domestic basins. There is one at the Church of Marston Morteyne, Bedfordshire (D. 13$\frac{3}{8}$), which by some has been ascribed to Puritan times, but from the marks on it, it would seem to be an eighteenth-century basin, probably ordered to replace a pewter predecessor. Such font-bowls were in use after the whole-sale damage to and destruction of fonts in the seventeenth century, and they are mentioned in churchwardens' accounts as late as the end of the eighteenth century. There is a good specimen at Lavenham, Suffolk. Many of these so-called fonts were merely basins, or *lavabos*, for the celebrant's ablution before Consecration.

Specimens survive in the West Country and have been secured by alert collectors.

The little cruets marked on the lids with A. for *Aqua* and V. for *Vinum* are frequently to be met with, and it is to be feared that, as they were in great request among a certain class of collectors, the demand has created a supply. It is probable that, as in the case of porringers and spoons, there are quite as many now, if not more, than there ever were in actual use.

Wafer-boxes are also met with sometimes, and still more rarely chrismatories. In both of these there is need for special vigilance on the part of the buyer.

Sepulchral plate—*i.e.*, plate used for interment with deceased ecclesiastics in place of the more precious— seems to have been of very poor metal, approximating lead, judging from the condition of the generality of specimens which have come down to us.

Patens are of two kinds—the small kind found as lids

to chalices, and the larger kind, some eight inches in diameter, often larger, especially in Scottish examples. They are often found with the name of the parish on the rim, a fact of interest which can generally be verified without much trouble.

Sometimes the patens were made with feet, and the genuine specimens are always interesting. Many of them are entirely without marks, especially those found in the West of England. One known to the writer is still in its own parish church. It is small, $7\frac{1}{8}$ inches in diameter and 3 inches high. Many of these patens have had feet added to them, some quite recently, to meet the demand for church plate, and many dishes on feet are called patens when in reality they are domestic in origin. They have been called—perhaps not seriously—Cromwellian cheese-dishes, and some are obviously French and look more like cake-dishes or cake-stands.

Apart from those which are known to be true patens there are many fine footed plates, quite genuine, which are more usually known as tazzas. These are quite popular with collectors, and date from the late seventeenth century to about 1775. Some of them may have had religious usage as wafer-plates or patens, but it is far more likely that the majority were purely household items.

It is a fact that in practically every case the weight of the flat plate (and possibly the contents) has caused the ring of the base to force its way upwards and to become visible from the top surface of the article. It is hardly likely that the small unleavened wafers would, in themselves, have been sufficiently weighty to have been a contributing cause.

Absolutely flat disks, with perhaps only a very slight moulding or thickening of the rim, have been described as patens or bread-trenchers; these have even been found mounted on a foot. They were, in all probability, originally scale plates before acquiring their glorified titles or their feet, which, incidentally, may have been perfectly good salts. One such "paten" is known where its owner went to the trouble of having the two pieces unsoldered, and he now has two *good* pieces of pewter to compensate for the effort. The salt thus reclaimed was of a type known to collectors as a "Capstan." (See illustration facing p. 97.)

The City Companies had large stores of pewter. At Pewterers' Hall in 1550 there was a good stock of pottle and of quart pots, of stope pints and some half-pints, salts with and without covers, and a garnish of dishes, platters, chargers, and saucers.

The Goldsmiths' Company ordered pewter plates and dishes at various times in their history. In 1601–2 the Merchant Taylors' Company in an inventory had nine great chargers, twelve 5 lb. platters, four dozen 4 lb. platters, two dozen and ten 3 lb. platters, three dozen 2 lb. platters, four dozen sallet dishes, five dozen plate trenchers, three dozen pie-plates, eight dozen and five saucers, and two dozen pottle pots; and eight years later they seem to have bought nearly as much again.

Of civic and other corporation pewter some is occasionally met with, and at one time must have existed in large quantities. Judging from the number of plates with the arms of the Corporation of Yarmouth, the inference to be drawn is that the Corporation had an enormous quantity of pewter plates, or else that someone has used the stamp with the arms of the borough in an enterprising but illegitimate manner.

Many of the colleges at Oxford, and some at Cambridge, have a few specimens left of their former stores. Worcester College has some marked "P.L.", *i.e.*, Provost's Lodging, the name still in use for the official lodging of the Head of the College. Queen's College has a fair amount, mainly hot-water dishes and plates. New College has some very interesting pewter which is not generally shown. It consists of some seventeenth-century pewter that belonged to the College, viz., a candlestick with a dodecagonal base (a somewhat unusual shape) bearing the arms of the College. With this was a much earlier plate, probably fifteenth-century, resembling a paten, with very deep circular depression, with the arms of the College in five places in all. This was in private hands and it is satisfactory to think that after an absence of many years this pewter is back again in its old home, and that it now is, and in future will be, carefully guarded.

Some years ago in some building alterations at All Souls College, Oxford, a disused drain was opened, and in it was found quite a small hoard of pewter from the seventeenth century onwards. A few of the pieces were stamped with the College arms, and some makers' marks were identified, which so far have not been found elsewhere. This may mean that the pewter was made locally, or brought from elsewhere. One or two of the pieces were of London manufacture.

The Fishmongers' Company, London, still use pewter plates at the banquets at which venison is served. The plates are dipped into boiling water to warm them just before they are required. Most of them date from about 1760, having been made by Thos. Swanson, the successor of Samuel Ellis, whose mark is on some of the plates. When a boy at school at Merchant Taylors'—then opposite Messrs. Truscott's printing works in Suffolk Lane—the writer used to go for dinner to the Bay Tree Tavern in St. Swithin's Lane. In the grill-room there the chops and steaks were served on pewter platters—quite flat with moulded rims. These were dipped by the cook into hot water when the meat was ready, and the water left on the platter constituted the gravy.

Pewter was used regularly by the various Inns of Court, and it was for a long time a kind of tradition that the Inns of Court, on giving up their silver plate to further the cause of Charles I, were graciously allowed to have pewter of the same shape and with the same hall-mark as evidence of the loan of the silver, and as a pledge of its eventual return. This tradition, however, is unlikely to be based on fact.

At the second Exhibition of Pewter held in Clifford's Inn Hall, in May 1908, there was a hot-water plate that belonged formerly to the Benchers of Gray's Inn. It was of very fine workmanship and in perfect condition, but of comparatively late date, with the touch of CARPENTER AND HAMBERGER (No. 1066 on the London touch-plates) superimposed with the name SWIFT. It is the only instance the writer has met with of marks being thus over-stamped. John Hamberger became a yeoman in 1794, and one W. Swift, perhaps his successor in the business, in 1809.

When Clifford's Inn was a legal society it was a rule that each member of it was to pay 13d. for vessels of pewter, and was obliged to have in the kitchen two plates and dishes for his own use.

There were similar regulations at the neighbouring Society of Staple Inn. Some of this pewter still survives— some in private hands and some in the Guildhall Museum. The late Mr. W. Churcher had some with the inscription Ex. I.K. dono. $\frac{Pr.}{}$ This was the gift of John Kock, president of the society in 1716, and bears the crest of the Inn, viz., a woolpack.

LATE TYPES OF COMMUNION PLATE

c. 1765. From Midhurst Church, Sussex

(Victoria and Albert Museum)

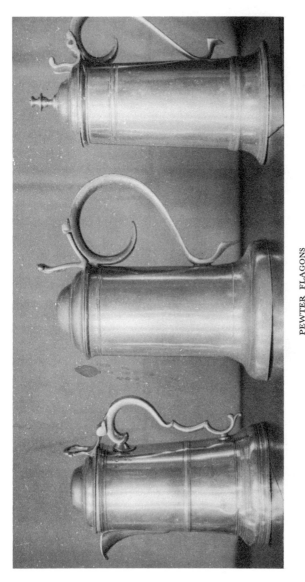

PEWTER FLAGONS

Irish, c. 1760
(*Ex-Shelley Collection*)

English, c. 1730

English, c. 1820

ALMS DISH DECORATED IN REPOUSSÉ WORK
By James Banckes of Wigan, *c.* 1750.
(*Formerly in Michaelis Collection*)

SERIES OF ENGLISH BALUSTER WINE MEASURES
From the gallon to the half-gill, all with "double-volute" thumb-
pieces, *c.* 1740–80
(*Collection of R. W. Cooper*)

THE "PIRLIE PIG"

A pewter fines box belonging to the Dundee Corporation

(*Photo by D. C. Thomson & Co., Ltd.*)

CHAPTER TEN

THE DECORATION OF PEWTER

PEWTER owes its chiefest charm to its soft grey colour and the patina that lapse of time alone can give to its surface. English pewter, as a rule, has been left quite plain and unadorned, and this is almost a characteristic of it in its best period. Scottish pewter was also left plain, and of the specimens now extant in museums and elsewhere in that country, at least two pieces survive which were originally decorated, viz., the "Pirlie Pig" (see opposite) and a basin or bowl in the Smith Institute at Stirling, figured in Mr. Ingleby Wood's book, *Scottish Pewterware and Pewterers*, Plate XX.

Foreign pewter was frequently decorated with ornaments of various kinds, and the mere presence of decoration on an article will generally indicate a foreign place of origin.

In arranging a scheme of ornament for his pewterware a workman had plenty of choice as to the means to be employed. He could make his moulds, if money and time were no object, as elaborate as he wished, and the moulds, when once completed, could be used again and again. In this way the pewter of François Briot and of Gaspar Enderlein was made and, after being put together, was finally worked over by competent chasers from the front, and all traces of joins and seams removed.

So, too, the delicately modelled plates known as Apostel-teller and Kaiser-teller were made in moulds and finished with great care afterwards. There is a mould in a German museum which would allow of a thick casting being made; and it would seem as though these plates were cast very thick, and that then, after the surface had been completed satisfactorily, they were turned down in a lathe to the required thinness. Sometimes the turner was too zealous, and left such a very thin shell, by way of a backing to his modelling, that the heavy centre has broken away from the rim.

Any speciments of these plates that show signs of coming to pieces can easily be reinforced by the addition of pewter to the back, but the metal added must be of a very low melting-point or the safety of the older plate will be endangered. It is expert pewterers' work.

It has sometimes been asserted that these decorative plates were never intended for use, but merely to be used as *pastiches* for ornament. They may have been, and it would account for the fact that they are occasionally found made of an alloy of so low a class that they seem to be lead rather than pewter. It may be that the lead ones are modern forgeries.

Many of the plates and trays figured in Demiani's monumental work on *Der Edelzinn*, especially those of Nicolaus Horchheimer, seem to have been cast with very shallow relief, so shallow that the relief looks as though the mould had been etched. In fact, in Ewrin Hintze's *Nurnberger Zinn* this is stated to be the case. A study of the edges of the scrolls and arabesques confirms this statement.

Some pewter has the appearance of having been cast from models in intaglio work and of having been subsequently worked up from the back. Roughly cast work with a tooled background looks extremely handsome.

Another means of adding ornament to a surface is by

stamping or by rolling. Most of the delicate work to be found on such small things as snuff-boxes is done in this way. The metal was rolled out between rollers and then cut up and joined up with great care. It is so thin in most cases that were it not for the octagonal form given to them they would never have survived the lifetime of the first owner and user. Much of the modern so-called pewter is apparently rolled and then soldered together.

Engraving with a burin was also done on pewter, and as a rule overdone. Plates with engraving all over the surface, such as hunting scenes and scenes after Hogarth's pictures, are examples of the engraver's skill, and a warning as to what not to attempt. The surface is so cut about with lines and shading that there is no chance for the beauty of the metal to appear, and the general effect obtained is that the dirt in the cuts seems the chief thing in the plate.

There is no possible objection to a well-engraved coat-of-arms on the edge of a plate, but the effect is distressing if badly done.

Incidentally, the beginner will need to ensure that the engraving is contemporary. Much ordinary, plain pewter has been "enhanced" by such additions in later years to make it readily saleable.

Etching, too, has been done on pewter, but specimens are rarely met with to-day. The effect is very pleasing, and the roughness of the dull background throws into pleasant relief the brighter portions of the design.

Chasing is also possible, but requires a hard alloy upon which the chaser may work. The chasing tools sink in far too deeply in a soft alloy and make high ridges on either side of the groove that is made, and the removal of the burred ridges has a tendency to make scratches. On a hard alloy the chaser may work quite easily and comfortably, either by outlining work, or by chasing the main lines of a scheme of ornament, the details of which are to be filled in by punches or stamps.

Pointille ornament is also effective and, though slight, stands wear and tear very well. It is usually bounded by plain lines, and these help to accentuate the prick marks of the tool.

Repoussé as applied to pewter requires care, and if overdone is bound to mar an otherwise good design or shape. Some cast work is cast very hollow—*e.g.*, some of the platters which are said to bear the device of François I— and is given the appearance of *repoussé*.

As a rule *repoussé* in the forms of bosses, etc., is a modern addition to older work—mainly to attract the eye of the buyer. An example of late *repoussé* work on an earlier dish may be seen between pp. 120 and 121. Much Tyrolese pewter, otherwise good, or at any rate inoffensive, has been mangled by the *repoussé* worker to make it appeal to the average tourist.

Pierced-work done deliberately is not common, and in the best specimens is kept quite simple. In porringer ears the pattern is obtained directly in the process of casting, while in pierced-work proper the pattern has been set out with compasses and then cut out or filed out, a laborious plan, but giving good results, especially when the metal was fairly thick.

In some cases the work, when pierced, is touched up a little with a graver, and in this way the *motif* of the design is accentuated.

What is known as wriggled work is perhaps the commonest and the most effective way of decorating pewter. It is quite easy to do, and it has the advantage that very little metal is removed from the object to be decorated, as compared with the amount removed by each separate cut made with a graver. The method is as follows. The workman takes a flat tool, say an ordinary carving chisel, $\frac{3}{16}$th of an inch wide, or a flat scorper, and holding it at an angle of 45 or 50 degrees, rocks it from side to side, and at the same time forces it away from him along the line he requires it to move. If the rocking be regular the pattern obtained will be the same, but will vary according to the width of the tool that is used, and also according to the acuteness of the angle at which it is held with reference to the work. If held quite vertically, no rocking motion or wriggling work is possible, and the motion, if continued, would result in a hole being bored in the plate. If, again, it is held too horizontally, it will slip on the surface and make scratches or gashes. Silver-plated teapots are adorned, or disfigured, by the same method. The tool used may be straight-edged like a chisel, or it may be round-nosed, or again it may be ground on the skew. Different results, too, may be obtained by reversing the tool, and, at the same time, modifying the angle, and also the rate of the rocking motion.

Some pieces of ceremonial pewter, such as rose-water dishes, have the central bosses richly enamelled. There were four such dishes at the Church of St. Katherine Cree, London, E.C.

Two of these remain at the church and the remaining pair, illustrated facing page 136, are in the keeping of the Guildhall Museum, London.

They all bear some emblem of King Charles I and are to be dated at about 1628—the date of the rebuilding of the church.

The rims are plain, with a single reeding, and the only other decorations, besides the centre bosses, are plain raised lines, beaten up from the back, and standing out clearly on the otherwise plain surface.

In one dish the enamelled centre bears the Royal Arms of England with C.R. at the top; in another are the insignia of the Coronation, viz., the Sceptre and the Sword of State, arranged in saltire, with palm leaves. In the four spaces thus contrived are:

1. C.R. and a regal crown.
2. A rose, crowned.
3. A thistle, crowned.
4. A harp, crowned.

On the third dish, the boss bears the Prince of Wales's feathers and the letters C.P. The fourth dish of the set has a double rose in the boss, but the dish has unfortunately been silver-plated. These bosses are apparently made of Dutch metal, and are affixed to the pewter. Another fine example, probably a little later, as it is said to have been one of a set of six supplied to Charles I in 1642 when at York, is ornamented with lenticular bosses. It has also a fine enamel boss in the centre (a similar one is illustrated between pp. 136 and 137).

Some articles made in pewter were enamelled, or rather lacquered, all over with a thin transparent lacquer, generally a blue, and then passed over to an engraver, who, by engraving his design with shallow and spoon-shaped cuts, displayed the grey metal underneath as though it were a decoration on the blue ground. Tea-caddies and snuff-boxes were decorated in this way, but the lacquer seems to kill the colour of the pewter. Those made to-day are usually sent out japanned. Paint pure and simple was applied to such things as tobacco-boxes. What the design on the paint was is likely to remain a mystery, for most of the specimens have been denuded of the paint so that their value as pewter may be enhanced. As pewter they are, as a rule, poor in quality, and are much more like lead. Gilding was often applied to any specimens of plates that were to be treated as merely decorative, such as the Kaiser-teller and Apostel-teller.

In France, gilding was confined to Church plate, but was later, in the reign of *le Grand Monarque*, permitted in the case of domestic pewter, after the silver plate of his subjects had been impounded.

In England, gilding was prohibited by decree of the Pewterers' Company, except in the case of small objects given away as presents, and not exposed publicly for sale.

Painting on pewter was allowed in certain cases, more especially the ornaments which were applied to furniture and affixed to beams and rafters.

Some of the signs of insurance offices affixed to house fronts were of pewter, painted in heraldic colours.

Pewter has been occasionally inlaid with other metals —more particularly brass. There was formerly in the Gurney Collection (later the property of Lord Swaythling) a very fine German flagon, quite Gothic in feeling and in some of its ornamental mouldings, most elaborately inlaid with brass, and the latter engraved with very fine and delicate line work. How the inlay was done at all is a matter for speculation, and for those interested a matter for practical experiment. The body was not thicker than stout brown paper in parts, and yet the inlay was as firmly embedded in the thin pewter as though it were part and parcel of it, and not an insertion.

In fact, this was probably the case. It is most likely that the thin brass was fitted to the mould before the molten pewter was poured in.

Appliqué work in pewter is found in the case of the Pechkrüge. The work is mainly scroll-work cut out with a saw, and either *appliqué* or slightly inlaid into the wooden body of the krug. They are not often to be met with in perfect condition, as the conditions of their manufacture are against their lasting intact for any length of time. If the waterproofing of pitch cracked, as it was bound to do sooner or later, the liquid in the krug would make the wooden side swell, and then the pewter would crack at the weakest point in the scroll-work and begin to work loose, the first stage in the rapid progress from dismemberment to utter decay.

Pewter has been inlaid with good effect in furniture, but the wood must be of a dark colour, otherwise the inlay loses its effect. It cannot tell unless there is a reasonable amount of contrast in the colour. Mahogany so treated looks well, so too does dark or darkened oak, but a light wood so inlaid, unless the metal is allowed to darken by being tarnished, is apt to suggest that the labour is misapplied. There was a fine mahogany cabinet in the Plantin Museum at Antwerp, richly inlaid with tin. It looked like silver and contrasted well with the warm tones of the cabinet-work. Whether or not this piece still remains, after two World Wars, has been impossible to ascertain. Other specimens of the same period may be found in private hands abroad or in museums.

Pewter in black wood and even in papier mâché has a good effect.

Specimens of Chinese pewter with brass or with copper inlay, mostly tea-caddies, are met with occasionally, but the work shows Russian influence in the character of its details.

In some specimens two or more of the methods here mentioned were combined with more or less skill. Cast-work required to be finished and surfaced, and was handed over to the chaser or the *repoussé* worker. Pierced-work was further defined by a few touches of the graver. Sometimes a brass figure was added to the top of a hanap

AN ENGRAVED DISH

Dated 1661, with inscription "Vivat Rex Carolus Secundus
Beati Pacifici"

(*British Museum*)

AN ENGRAVED DISH

With dated inscription "Vivat Rex Carolus Secundus
Beati Pacifici 1662"

(*Victoria and Albert Museum*)

or a small standing-cup; or hollow brass mouldings were fitted on to existing pewter ones. These additions do not show unless the metals are kept clean and bright. Their existence, however, can be detected by traces of verdigris, a sure sign of the added metal.

Lettering on pewter, as on copper-plate engravings, is dominated by the shape of the tool that is used and by the nature of the metal. If the lettering on a public-house tankard be studied, it will be found that the engraving is of a very simple type, so simple, in fact, that it gives rise to the idea that the engraver would not be able to engrave on any metal harder than pewter. There is no freedom of line anywhere. The letters, both capitals and small, are broken up into their simplest elements. What can be done with up-strokes of the graver is so done, and then, the piece being turned upside down, more up-strokes are made till all is finished. Where the two sets of strokes meet, but do not join as they should, little corrective touches are inserted afterwards. The cuts are generally shallow and V-shaped in section, and what with rough usage and still rougher cleaning soon show signs of wear and tear. Some of the lines are the reverse of steady. This must be put down partly to the workman's want of skill and partly to the custom of the artists, who seem to have required liquid refreshment administered at regular intervals in the particular vessels that they had just finished adorning.

Occasionally one finds a pot thoroughly well engraved in a good clerkly hand, with scrolls quite freely and prettily done. The assumption, probably justifiable, may be that the pot-engraver had been an engraver of card plates, who had fallen into evil ways, or perhaps on evil days.

On the German flagons and hanaps the script is smaller and quite characteristic, though the method, that of the up-strokes described above, is still the same. Initials of donors and long inscriptions are often done in large and small capitals, with remarkably good effect.

On the Seder-plätze, or Seder-schüsseln, used ceremonially by the Jews at Passover time, the Hebrew lettering, which might in itself be so grandly decorative, is often marred by the thick strokes the letters being broken in two and separated by a dot.

Mention must be made here of the pewter called by the German writers and collectors *Edelzinn*. It is really goldsmiths' work carried out in base metal, and it is so rare that it hardly comes within the ken of the everyday collector. Herr Demiani, of Leipzig, formed a unique collection, and his book has excellent reproductions of the best-known specimens.

Briot's original "Temperantia" salver and the ewer contain some very beautiful sculpture, but work more suited for a goldsmith than a pewterer. The salver seems to have been cast in one piece, then turned down in the lathe so as to remove all traces of any joins, and then very carefully worked up on the face and on the rim.[1] Not all the work ascribed to Briot seems to be really his. Most of the museums abroad have specimens of his work and show it side by side with the later and bolder work of Enderlein. Briot's salt in the museum at Dijon is a fine, bold piece of work, and much more suited for pewter than the salvers.

Other salvers of the Briot type are those with Pyramus and Thisbe, Hercules and the Lion, and on tankards and on ewers there are the well-known Ignis et Terra and the Susanna *motifs*. Enderlein did not slavishly copy all the subjects, but he produced the Mars salver, the Susanna—a mediæval favourite—the Adam and Eve, his Diana and

---

[1] The ewer, of necessity, had to be cast in a piece mould and then had to be soldered together.

Actæon, Lot and his Daughters, this latter in smaller size, the St. George and the Dragon, and smaller plates with Noah's sacrifice.

The theory that Briot copied his ideas from Enderlein is discredited by the fact that the latter died in 1633, many years subsequently to Briot.

The medallions in the salvers were used as decorative panels on smaller objects, and were sometimes cast in separate panels with an added border as wall decorations.

Under this same heading of *Edelzinn* must be classed the Apostel-teller, the Kurfurst-teller, the Sultan-teller, and the Arabesken-teller, which seem as a rule to have been made at Nuremberg. As their names imply, these plates have borders of the Apostles, with the Resurrection as a panel in the centre, the Emperor Ferdinand III and a border of six electors, or the Emperor Ferdinand II with a border of eleven Emperors of the House of Hapsburg.

These plates seem to have been produced from one mould, but by various makers, as the makers' marks vary in different specimens. They may have been the prototypes of the "Trifle from Lowestoft" or the "Present from Brighton"; for that they were intended for ornament and not for use is proved by the traces of gilding or painting that are found on them.

Eccentric articles may be found in pewter by those interested in grotesque forms. They are found chiefly in the deformation of cylindrical tankards, *e.g.*, when a simple tankard of the student type is converted into a semblance of a pine-apple, or has meaningless lines like those of emasculated gadroon curves worked in *repoussé*. In one collection a row of half a dozen tankards, all with added feet—some of the button type—as absurdly weak as they were flimsy, with lids overweighted with heraldic knobs, all distorted with pattern of sorts, some of it actually representing a lattice window or a brise-bise muslin, had a depressing effect. Fortunately they were in a kind of quarantine, being arranged by themselves on a lonely sideboard, in a dark and dismal corner.

CHAPTER ELEVEN

MARKS ON PEWTER—TOUCH-PLATES

IT would seem to be a common-sense proceeding for a maker—knowing the restrictions under which he lived as to the quality of his alloy, and the possibility of the unexpected searching of his premises, or the seizure of bad work subsequently to its sale—to put some kind of mark on his wares. The moulds, too, were often passed from one pewterer to another as they were required, for they were costly at the outset, and the searchers could not tell for certain whose pewter they condemned, without some more definite clue than that afforded by the place of seizure.

In the Règlement de la Pinterie of Limoges, dated 1394, one article distinctly states that every pewterer is to have his mark wherewith to mark his work, and that each man's mark is to be unlike those of his fellow-workmen.

At Rouen, in the Statuts des Etaimiers-Plombiers of 1554, about 150 years later, Article X provided that in a locked coffer a tablet of pewter was to be kept, on which the masters' marks were to be struck. In Article XX the regulation is made that each pewterer's mark is to be different from those of his fellows, and that a mark in the form of a little hammer, which is to be stamped as in Article X, is to be used on pure and fine tin, *i.e.*, pewter of the best quality. Article XXI ordains that no pewter of any quality is to be sold unmarked, under penalty of a fine of 12 sols for each piece.

The Paris pewterer was obliged to have two marks, one of them larger than the other. Of these the larger one was to have his initial and his name in full, while the smaller was to contain two letters, *i.e.*, the initials of the baptismal name and the surname.

The Nuremberg pewterers, according to Bapst, had to mark their pewter with the ordinary mark of the town, *i.e.*, an eagle. Each master, too, seems to have had his own eagle-mark, on the half of which he added his own private mark. He was also bound to hang up a piece of pewter with his mark impressed in it, so that his fellow-workmen and customers should know it as his. This was from the Regulations of 1576, which were probably nothing more than the codification of previous rules and customs of the trade.

A century and a half before this, 1419, the pewterers of York, perhaps the most important city in the north, and certainly a centre for pewterers at that early date, promulgated their regulations, or Ordinationes Peuderariorum, and it is interesting to find them stating as a preamble that they were the same as those of the pewterers of London.

In 1540 they added to their regulations a rule that "every of the said pewderers shall sett his marke of all such vessell as they shall cast hereafter, and to have a counterpane thereof to remain in the common chambre upon payne of every of them that lacks such a mark . . . to forfet therefor 3s. 4d. for every pece."

Sixty years or so later the mark was to be a "proper marke and two letters for his name," with the same penalty as above, together with a monthly penalty of 50s. per month till the mark was duly made and used.

It is an unfortunate fact that the touch-plates, which were obviously in being in York, have not come down to us, but nevertheless the names of many York Freemen are known.

Turning now to the London pewterers and their customs, we find that in 1475 the Company had a "ponchon of yrn with the brode arowe-hede for the forfet marke." This, no doubt, is the same iron that is referred to in an inventory which was made of the goods belonging to the Craft of Pewterers within the City of London in 1489. There are in it, among many items of interest, "a puncheon of iron with a brode arowe-hede gravyn therein." This was, as stated above, used for stamping all false wares when detected after official search.

But this "broad arrow-head" seems to have been used to mark the tin after being assayed, for in Welch, i. 249, mention is made of payment for a hammer and a chisel and mending the "brode arowhedd to saye the tynne."

In 1548–49 there is mention of a "markynge iron of the flowre de lyce" (or fleur de Lys) with which to mark stone pots, and four years later it was agreed "that all those that lyd stone potts should set their own marck on the insyde of the lyd, and to bring in all such stone potts into the hall whereby they may be vewed yf they be workmanly wrought and so be markyd with the marck of the hall on the owtside of the lyd." At the same meeting it was ordained that "every one that makyth such stone potts shall make a new marck such one as the Mr and Wardens shall be pleasid withall, whereby they maye be known from this day forward" (Welch, i. 175).

In 1555 there is an instance (quoted in Welch, i, 183) of one John Warying setting his mark (a Maltese cross with a pellet in each angle) as a witness of a promise to pay a debt partly in money and partly fine metal.

In 1564 William Curtis (Welch, i. 239) gave a book to the Craft, in which there were written the ordinances.

It distinctly states as follows (Welch, i. 241): "Also it is agreed that every one of the said fellowship that maketh any ware shall set his own mark thereon. And that no man shall give for his proper mark or touch the Rose and Crown with letters nor otherwise, but only to him to whom it is given by the fellowship. Nor that no man of the said Craft shall give one another's mark nother with letters nor otherwise, but every one to give a sundry mark, such one as shall be allowed by the master and the wardens for the time being, upon pain to forfeit and pay for every time (of) offending to the Craft box 13s. 4d."

Later, in 1574, it was made compulsory for founders of pewter to mark the strakes cast by them with their own mark, by making the penalty 1d. per pound.

Whatever the custom of the pewterers was, some pewter, at any rate, was marked. Two plates dug up at Kennington in 1909 were found to bear a crowned R. Mr. W. H. St. John Hope put down the earlier as Richard II and the later as Richard III. Of these two plates, both had been damaged by fire; one had no mark left, the other had a pewterer's hammer. The first plate may have had a mark on the missing portion. It certainly looks as though the marking of pewter was practised even in the fourteenth century.

By Act of Parliament 19 Hen. VII. c. 6 (*i.e.*, 1504) it was made compulsory for pewterers to register their marks. Welch (i. 94) gives it "Also that it may [by] the same auctorite be enacted and established, that no manner of person or persons of what degree or condicion soever he or they be of from henceforth make no hollowe wares of Pewter—that is to say Salts and Potts that is made of Pewter called Ley Metell but that it may be after the Assise of Pewter Ley Metell wrought within the City of

CHARLES I ALMS DISHES
From the Church of St. Katherine Cree, London
(By permission of the Guildhall Museum Authorities)

A ROSEWATER DISH
Charles I
(*In the possession of Mrs. Audrey Taylor*)

ALMS DISH

With arms of Charles I on enamel "boss," dated 1648

(*One of two from Mildenhall Church, Suffolk*)

THREE DOMED-LIDDED GEORGIAN TANKARDS

Of various sizes, all made by Richard Going, Bristol, *c.* 1720–40

(Michaelis Collection)

London; and that the makers of such wares shall marke the same wares with severall marks of their own to the intent that the [markers] of such wares shall avowe the same Wares by them as is aforesaid to be wrought, and that all and every of such wares not sufficiently made and wrought and not marked in the fourme abovesaid, founden in the possession of the same maker or seller to be forfeited, &c."

This consolidates into one Act the custom and makes compulsory what would seem to have been, up to that time, a voluntary practice. For in 1492 (Welch, i. 78) we find that the Company had caused to be made four *new* "marking irons for hollowe ware men." This entry shows that the old irons had become worn out.

We also find (Welch, i. 165) that in 1550 there was in existence "a table of pewter, with every man's marks therein." Unfortunately, this early touch-plate and its predecessors (if any) have not come down to our time, more is the pity, and we shall probably never know for certain what were the marks used by the sixteenth-century pewterers on their wares. It is only by a rare chance that one comes upon a good plate or other piece with a legible mark of that interesting period.

That some kind of compulsory touch-mark system was enforced prior to 1550 is evidenced by the fact that as early as 1526 a pewterer, one William Aprise, was fined 5s. for "delivering vessels unmarked with his touch according to the ordinances" (Cotterell, p. 58).

Again, within a few years of the first mention of the touch-plates, eighteen pewterers were fined for "naughty workmanship and not touching their ware."

In 1613 it was ordered by the Court in March that "every man's old touch shall be presently brought into the Hall, and new touches with difference there to be struck . . . all which to be done before the 13th day of this month."

This ordering of new touches was done on this occasion to prevent makers from selling ware less in weight than the standard which had been lately established. In the same year some makers of "lay" were found guilty of debasing their metal, and were ordered to bring their touches to the Hall and there to strike a new touch marked with "this year of 1614," that the offenders should be known.

By 14 Car. I (1638), every maker, worker, or manufacturer of tin, pewter, or lay metal was required to put his own "sign or note" to the said works, vessels, and manufactures.

This regulation was not obeyed any more than that of 1504, and there are many instances of fines on record.

Sometimes marks were exchanged privately, as witness many references in Mr. Welch's book.

Marks might be taken away if the pewterer did bad work. In these cases a badge of opprobrium was given him, containing a letter "f" (or a double "ff" for a repeated offence).

In two recorded cases defaulting pewterers were ordered to have new touches with their initials therein and "a knot about it" and the date 1656.

Besides the touch, and the rose and crown mark, and the crowned X as a quality mark for extraordinary ware, many makers were in the habit of stamping some of their wares, especially plates, with various devices, usually in small shields. These small marks, which occur in pewter as early as 1580, were, no doubt, put on the pewter with the intent to simulate the silver hall-marks. In many cases they were more than colourable imitations, for they were facsimiles in whole or in part. There was no reason why pewter should be stamped with the lion rampant, or the leopard's head, the Britannia seated, or a harp, unless it were that the makers wished to induce customers to think they were getting superior wares with marks like the silver-marks.

There do not seem to have been any complaints made by the buyers of pewter with simulated hall-marks—no doubt they were pleased to have them; but the Goldsmiths' Company in 1635 complained to the Privy Council of "a certain plate made of pewter having the stamps and marks upon it which only belongeth to the Companie of Goldsmiths of London, as if it had been of silver-plate of the assize of the said Companie."

In consequence the Pewterers' Company were directed to instruct the brethren that one stamp or mark was to be put on their wares, "as anciently hath been accustomed, and as the law in that case requireth." They were to search and examine not only what stamps are already engraven and made, but also what pewter is therewith marked and remaining amongst the pewterers, and take order that the same stamp be called in and delivered to the Warden of the Goldsmiths, to be defaced, and also that all pewter having more than one mark resembling the mark of the silver touch be forthwith melted down or the same mark defaced.

Little or nothing was done and the practice went on, with the one difference that some makers stamped one mark, such as a fleur-de-lis or a lion rampant, four times over on a plate, instead of using four different marks.

These small marks, however, were not considered by the Pewterers' Company to be enough, if they were the only marks on the pewter, and in 1682 a pewterer was fined for so doing.

Exactly the same kind of fancy marking is done by the

electroplate manufacturers of to-day. They stamp their wares with four small marks, sometimes containing the initials of the firm, a letter A or a B, to show the quality, and a shield perhaps with "E.P.N.S."—which means "electroplated on nickel silver." It is quite right they should be marked, but it is not right that they should in the least degree resemble the hall-marks that are by law put on silver.

It may be noted that these small marks may often be of great value in helping to decipher the name or date of a pewterer, by giving the initials of the maker whose name is, perhaps, indistinctly given in the larger touch.

Sometimes the initials in these small marks, or, as they are now generally called, hall-marks, are not the same as those of the name in the large touch. In these cases the actual touch is that of the maker, who made the pewter for another (possibly a middleman) and stamped thereon the silver marks adopted by the latter.

There are large numbers of plates with "S.E." in the small touch—for there were two pewterers by name Samuel Ellis—and they also made for Thomas Swanson, who later succeeded to S. Ellis's business, as is evidenced by a "label" used by Swanson in addition to his touch.

It must be understood that these hall-marks were put on by the pewterers themselves, and were no guarantee of quality, as were the hall-marks proper stamped by the Goldsmiths' Company at their Hall.

The nearest approach to a hall-mark on pewter was the X with (or occasionally without) a crown above it. This was supposed to be placed only on pewter of extra good quality. It was copied estensively by the pewterers of the Low Countries and is put on any inferior metal. It is also found on Scottish pewter.

There was another touch—the crowned rose—the use

of which is specified in 1580 (Welch, i. 288), which could not originally be used except by special permission of the Company.

If anything is entitled to be described as the "Hall Mark" it would be this.

In the year 1671 it had been determined that from that date no person should presume to strike the rose and crown with any additional letters of his own or another's name, whereby the mark, which was to be used only for exported goods, should in time become as other touches and not distinguished.

Towards the end of that same year it was ordered that "no member of the Mystery shall strike any other mark upon his ware than his touch or mark struck upon the plate at the Hall, and the Rose and Crown stamp, and also the Letter X upon extraordinary ware." At the same time it was left optional to any pewterer to add the word "London" to the rose and crown stamp, or in his touch. The stamping of the name in full upon all hard metal ware or extraordinary ware, which had been proposed, was expressly and plainly negatived.

In the autumn of 1692–93 it was decided that all such as have not their names within the compass of their touches should be allowed to put them at length within the same.

A contradictory regulation was made half a year later, and it was decided that "the practice of striking the name at length within or besides the touches registered or struck at the Hall is against the general good of the Company: and that all such persons as have set their names at length within their touches now in use shall alter their marks or touches by leaving out their names, and register and strike at the Hall their respective new or altered marks or touches without any person's name therein."

A later regulation (1697–98) prescribed that none should strike any other mark upon ware than his own proper touch and the rose and crown stamp; that any member may strike his name at length between his touch and the rose and crown, also the word "London," but that none may strike the letter X except upon extraordinary ware, commonly called "hard metal" ware.

From statements (in Welch) and rulings of the Court it would seem that there had at different times been unfair copying and counterfeiting of the marks and touches of the most successful pewterers. In 1702 a rule was made that each member was to deliver to the master "one peculiar and selected mark or touch solely and properly of itself and for yourself only, without adding thereunto any other man's mark in part or in whole, to be struck and impressed on the plate kept in the Hall . . . for that purpose; which said mark and none other he shall strike and set upon his ware of whatsoever sort that he shall make and sell, without diminution or addition."

The Company had always been averse to anything in the nature of an advertisement in the touches, and it seems that some pewterers had two touches—one which they had registered at the Hall, and another which they used on their wares. This had been complained of in 1688.

The last regulation as to touches was made as late as 1747, and runs as follows: "That all wares capable of a large touch shall be touched with a large touch with the Christian name and surname either of the maker or of the vendor at full length in plain Roman letters; and small wares shall be touched with the small touch"— under a penalty of 1d. per lb. for default.

With such contradictory amendments made at frequent intervals it was obvious that the pewterers were beginning to get out of hand, due, partly, to the fact that periodical searches were no longer possible, and from about the first quarter of the eighteenth century the decline of the Company's control can be seen. By the end of the eighteenth century its downfall was practically complete.

THE TOUCH-PLATES

The touch-plates preserved at Pewterers' Hall are five in number, and contain a large number, some 1,090 in all, of the touches or trade-stamps, or punches, with which pewterers used to be compelled to stamp, and in this way sign or vouch for, their wares. These, incomplete though they are, yet must be of the greatest interest to the serious collector.

They were photographed and reproduced in collotype many years ago and were originally issued in Mr. Welch's *History of the Pewterers' Company* in 1902.

They were also, by special permission of the Company, issued in the second edition, and that a limited one, of *Pewter Plate*, in 1910. In the latter volume they were described one by one (the description having been corrected where necessary by Mr. W. H. St. John Hope, F.S.A.), and the descriptions were numbered for more easy reference and carefully indexed. They were again reproduced in the late Howard H. Cotterell's *Old Pewter, its Makers and Marks*, in 1929.

Of the five existing London touch-plates, the earliest was purchased, after the Great Fire, in 1668. This was brought into use shortly afterwards and existing pewterers who had, undoubtedly, already struck their touches on one of the lost plates were invited to restrike them on the new plate.

Some of these restruck touches are dated, one being

as early as 1640, and some others, though undated, are even earlier. When restruck they were not placed in their original order, and this fact has caused early writers on the subject to have come to the conclusion that the marks were struck in a haphazard manner.

Much research into the touch-plate marks was undertaken by the late Howard Cotterell, and the results of his labours were published in his *Old Pewter, its Makers and Marks*. Many more of the marks on the plates, of which their owners were not known at that time, have now been allocated to their rightful owners, and will be found in their proper order in the list in this volume.

Disorderly as the touches on the plates may seem to the casual enquirer, the first few, at least, were struck in their particular order for a special reason. A reference to the list of owners of the touches will show that No. 1 is that of Robert Lucas, who was Master of the Company in 1667, and obviously the one who should head the new plate, having, undoubtedly, been responsible for many of the arrangements for rebuilding the Hall and instituting the system of restriking touches. No. 2 is of John Silk, who was made free in 1627; he was probably the oldest Past Master alive, and something of a doyen of the Company. This position on the plate would probably have been given to him as a mark of esteem. No. 3 is that of Anthony Mayor, a Warden of the Company in 1667. No. 4 of Nicholas Kelk, Master in 1665, the year preceding the fire. No. 5 of Thomas Haward, who was Master in the year 1666. No. 6 Theophilus Reading (this *is* out of place—and no logical explanation can be given). No. 7 is of Robert Martin, who was Kelk's Warden in 1666—and so on. Following these places of honour, so to speak, came the rank and file, who struck their touches as they were able to attend the Hall for the purpose. Inter-

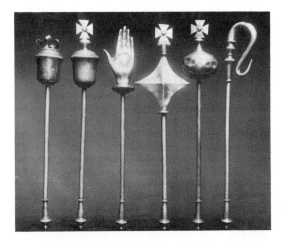

A FINE SERIES OF MACES, OR PROCESSIONAL STAVES
(*From a collection now dispersed*)

TWO ENGLISH PEWTER PORRINGERS
The standing item *c.* 1660–70; that with deep bowl *c.* 1675–80
(*Michaelis Collection*)

SMALL ITEMS IN PEWTER
Late eighteenth-century

A DOG-WHISTLE   TOBACCO STOPPER   TOBACCO STOPPER

spersed with them are those new Freemen who had leave to open shop at that time.

Most of the restruck touches come within the first 140 on the first plate, and after that the chronological sequence of striking by Freemen who were given leave to open shop is followed almost without a break. A few exceptions to this orderly sequence must be attributed to the fact that some later touches were struck in blank spaces on the plate which may have been left, originally, for Freemen who were eventually unable to make use of them.

In the present volume the figures quoted before the names give the number of the touch in the order in which it appears on the plates.

The early seventeenth-century touches were, as a rule, much smaller than those of later date, generally circular in form with a beaded edge, with some simple device as a distinctive badge. Most of those on the first and oldest touch-plate are circular or just slightly oval. Other types are the plain oval with two sprays of palm-leaves crossed and tied with a device in the plain space thus left between the palm-leaves. Before the end of the century, the Christian and the surnames of the maker appear in labels, top and bottom of the oval, and the palm-leaves have dwindled to such insignificant proportions that it is difficult to recognise them as palm-leaves. Sometimes the name is in the upper and the date in the lower label. In many the device is quite simple, flanked by initials on either side, and the last two figures of the year in the centre, below the device.

The same applies to the second touch-plate and part of the third, the only difference being that the size of the touches is somewhat larger, and they are better from the point of view of workmanship. Then about No. 670 begins a series of more or less square touches, or touches with straight sides, with a pillar at each side, and a slightly domed or a straight top. Many of them look like diminutive fire-backs.

Further on towards the end of the fourth touch-plate the oval with upper and lower labels is found in use, but the place once occupied by the remnants of the palm-leaves is cut out altogether, and the touch has a semi-circular recess on each side.

The touch-plates are made of thick sheets of pewter, weighing several pounds each, of varying shape and of varying size.

					Touches
1.	$19\frac{1}{2} \times 13\frac{3}{8}$ inches	.	.	.	1 to 351
2.	$17 \times 12\frac{7}{8}$,,	.	.	.	352 ,, 614
3.	$18 \times 13\frac{5}{8}$,,	.	.	.	615 ,, 849
4.	$21\frac{3}{8} \times 14$,,	.	.	.	850 ,, 1,069
5.	$21\frac{3}{4} \times 14\frac{1}{8}$,,	.	.	.	1,070 ,, 1,090

The earliest dated touch, as already stated, is 1640 (No. 47). Of the 351 touches there given, though many are 1655, the greater number are 1663, 1666, and 1668, and there are some of 1680 and even later.

In 1674, 6s. 6d. was spent on a new pewter plate to strike touches on. This may be the second plate now at Pewterers' Hall, but it must be an open question, for there are several touches on the first plate later than 1674. One certainly is dated 1680 and there are touches on it of men who did not take up their livery till 1699.

Touch-plate No. III begins with 1704 and is no doubt the one mentioned in Welch, ii. 174, under the year 1703–4, "Paid John ffrith for a plate to strike Touches on 8s. 9d."

Touch-plate No. IV has the touches of pewterers who flourished from 1731 onwards, including some who joined the Yeomanry in the last few years of the eighteenth century.

Judging from the number of touches that are met with belonging to pewterers who did not strike their touches at the Pewterers' Hall, the most probable inference to be drawn is that some of these may have used the early touch-plates which have been lost, and the pewterers themselves were either not able to restrike touches or had possibly even perished in the Plague. Many other touches will, of course, relate to provincial pewterers.

CHAPTER TWELVE

LISTS OF PEWTERERS AND THEIR DATES

THE following pages contain three lists of pewterers compiled as follows. All those pewterers who struck touches upon the five London plates and upon the two Edinburgh touch-plates.

The first two lists give, respectively, the order of the touches as they appear on the plates, and the third quotes owners of the touches, in alphabetical order, for easy reference.

It is not possible, for reasons of space, to include the names of all known pewterers, as these numbered over 5,000 at the time Cotterell's *Old Pewter, its Makers and Marks*, was published in 1929, and students who require to extend their studies to the limit will require to make frequent reference to that work. Nevertheless, the lists quoted in the present volume will be found of great value to the beginner in enabling him to decipher the marks which he is most likely to come across.

A list of London pewterers, in their order of striking touches, has not previously been published, and collectors who required such an arrangement for their own particular purposes have had to compile their own to the best of their ability from the various information available.

The editor of this book is able to give names of owners to many of the touches which have hitherto been in doubt, and for this reason the list will be of interest to all serious collectors.

Only the date of obtaining freedom (or joining the

Yeomanry) is shown against each pewterer, and it should be remembered that many of them worked on for a great number of years, so that a piece of pewter bearing a recorded mark may have been made many years later than the date shown against its maker.

A pewterer did not necessarily strike his touch immediately upon being made free, but only upon his "opening shop."

This meant that he had to acquire a certain amount of capital and attain a definite standard of skill before "leave to open and strike touch" was granted, and in many cases it was a matter of years before this state of affairs was reached.

It should be stated here that "joining the Yeomanry" and "obtaining Freedom" are correlative terms. A pewterers' apprentice, upon the termination of his period of servitude, applied to the Court of the Company to make him "free of the Company," and upon being accepted he was made, automatically, a member of the Yeomanry.

Livery (or Clothing) was awarded to a competent pewterer, usually only after some years' active working on his own account. Many pewterers never took Livery at all, but worked as journeymen to others and, hence, never struck touches for themselves.

In perusing the following lists it is interesting to note how certain families clung to the pewter trade, e.g. the Abernethys, the Fassons, the Inglises, the Quicks, and the Whites.

List 1 gives the touches on the London plates in numerical order.

List 2 gives the touches on the Edinburgh plates in numerical order.

List 3 gives a combination of the two lists in alphabetical order. Where L.T.P. or E.T.P. follows the touch number this indicates its position on the London or Edinburgh plates respectively.

An analytical index to the touches themselves is given in Chapter XIII.

Note.—Where initials only are quoted this means that the owner of this touch is not known for certain. In some cases a possible attribution has been given in brackets.

LIST I

LONDON TOUCH-PLATES

Plate 1	Name	Date of obtaining Freedom
1	Robert Lucas	1637
2a, b	John Silk	1627
3	Anthony Mayors	1648
4	Nicholas Kelk	1638
5	Thomas Haward, Sr.	1636
6	Theophilus Reading	1675
	(See also No. 263—out of place)	
7	Robert Marten	1638
8	W. G. (? Wm. Goddard, 1653; ? Wm. Gosnell 1659)	—
9	John French	1630
10	Alexander French	1657
11	S. I. (? Samuel Jackson, 1650)	—
12	Thomas Dickinson	1662
13	Nicholas Hunton	1661
14	I. B. or T. B.	—
15	John Leeson	1644–45
16	James Taudin	1657
17	Thomas Haward, Jr.	1663
18	Francis Lea	1651
19	Jonathan Ingles	1668
20	W. A.	—
21	(?) I. I.	—
22	C. S.	—
23	I. L. (? John Langdale, 1663)	—
24	William Cowley	1662

LISTS OF PEWTERERS AND THEIR DATES

Plate 1	Name	Date o obtaining Freedom
25	William Ayers	1663
26	W. I. (? Wm. Jones, 1668)	—
27	Robert Jones	1657
28	R. Horrod (dated 1664)	no trace
29	Henry Perris	1653
30	I. F. (dated 1663)	—
31	Thomas Cooper	1653
32	I. C.	—
33	George Abbott	1664
34	S. A.	—
35	Beza Boston	1661
36	Thomas Fountain	1626
37	Ralph Marsh, Sr.	1636
38	William Burton	1653
39⎫ 40⎭	Francis Lea (See No. 18—variations of touch)	—
41	Peter Duffield	1645
42	P. B. (? Peter Brocklesby, 1664)	—
43	W. A.	—
43a	Bennett Allett	1649
44	I. H.	—
45	T. B.	—
46	Ralph Hulls	1653
47	Nathaniel Mills	1639
48	T. S. (? Thos. Stone, 1664–65; Thos. Simpkins 1663)	—
49	John Coursey	1660
50	G. R. (dated 1663) (? Gabriel Redhead, 1662) (See also No. 109)	—
51	I. C.	—
52	Daniel Ingole	1656
53	William Withers	1654
54	Henry Brettell	1665
55	L. T.	—
56	E. A.	—
57	C. T. (? Charles Tough, 1654)	—
58	W. M. (dated 1666)	—
59	William Adams	1643
60	H. C.	—
61	E. H.	—
62	E. H. (? Edward Hodgkins, 1641)	—
63	Peter Brailsford	1659

Plate 1	Name	Date of obtaining Freedom
64	T. G.	—
65	F. G. (? Francis Gibbons, 1664)	—
66	W. B. (? Wm. Bowden, 1660)	—
67	James Bullevant	1660
68	William Jackson	1662
69	W. M. (? Wm. Mabbott, 1636)	—
70	T. S. (dated 1663)	—
71	Vincent Silk	1654
72	W. W. (? Wm. White, 1661)	—
73	W. P. (dated 1663)	—
74	W. P. (dated 1655)	—
75	W. E.	—
76	W. C.	—
77	W. (?)	—
78	W. W. (? William Wetter) (See also No. 402)	—
79	A. W. (Same as No. 154)	—
80	Thomas Vile	1641
81	W. D. (? Wm. Dyer, 1656)	—
82	T. B. (? Thos. Barford, 1665) (See also No. 145)	—
83	S. M. (? Samuel Mason, 1662; Samuel Martin, 1641)	—
84	R. A.	—
85	T. H. (? Thos. Hawford, c. 1658)	—
86	Thomas Batteson	1661
87	James Nicholls	1651
88	R. I.	—
89	(? N). H. (dated 1663)	—
90	I. I.	—
91	A. L. (? Adam Langley, 1656)	—
92	I. H. (? Joseph Hopkins, 1660; John Hickden, 1662) (See 99 and 136)	—
92a	W. F.	—
93	R. V. (? Richard Vernon, 1635)	—
94	Ralph Marsh, Jr.	1663
95	B. C.	—
96	Anthony Rolls	1645–46
97	John Bull	1660
98	Henry Hartwell	c.1665–66
99	I. H. (? Joseph Hopkins, John Hickden) (See No. 92 and 136)	—
100	I. P. (? John Prior, 1654)	—

Plate 1	Name	Date of obtaining Freedom
101	E. H. (dated 1670)	—
102	R. I. (dated 1670)	—
103	I. I. (dated 1668)	—
104	P. P. (dated 1668)	—
105	William Lewis	1667
106	Thomas Vile, Jr.	1664
107	W. D. (? Wm. Ditch, 1666)	—
108	B. B. (dated 1668)	—
109	? Gabriel Redhead (See also No. 50)	—
110	T. S. (? Thomas Stribblehill, 1668)	—
111	W. P. (? Wm. Pargiter, 1658)	—
112	I. H. (?Joseph Hewett, 1668)	—
113	W. A.	—
114	W. D. (dated 1663)	—
115	S. A.	—
116	I. I. (dated 1666)	—
117	I. R. (dated 1663)	—
118	W. (?)	—
119	T. S. (dated 1663)	—
120	I. A.	—
121	Robert Harding	1666
122	Thomas Templeman	1667
123	Stephen Lawrance	1661
124	Henry Freeman	1665
125	Thomas Elphick	1667
126	E. N. (? Edward Newboult, 1668)	—
127	R. T. (dated 1668) (? Richard Talver, 1666)	—
128	William Hall	1657
129	I. T. (? James Taylor, 1667)	—
130	I. H.	—
131	R. C. (? Richard Collier, 1664)	—
132	I. C. (? John Clarke, 1661)	—
133	L. D. (dated 1668)	—
134	R. M. (? Richard Masters, 1668; ? Richard Mastead, c.1666)	—
135	Lawrence Dyer	1648
136	I. H. (dated 1663) (? Joseph Hopkins) (See also Nos. 92 and 99)	—
137	T. O. (? Thomas Osborne, 1642)	—
138	F. P. (? Francis Parsons, 1666)	—
139	W. P. (? Wm. Pearse, 1669)	—

CHATS ON OLD PEWTER

Plate 1	Name	Date of obtaining Freedom
140 140a	Christopher Raper	1665
141	Charles Hallifax	1669
142	John Buxton	1667
143	Nicholas Hunton (See also No. 13)	1661
144	C. (?) H. (?)	—
145	(? Thos. Barford, 1665) (See also No. 82)	
146	T. D. (? Timothy Drinkwater, 1666)	—
147	Thomas Alder	1655
148	F. C. (? Francis Cook, 1655)	—
149	R. A.	—
150	C. R. (? Chas. Richardson, 1667)	—
151	I. M. (dated 1668)	—
152	George Rooke	1668
153	I. C.	—
154	A. W. (Same as No. 79)	—
155	I. G.	—
156	Jeremiah Loader	1667
157	Edward Goodman	1669
158	R. P. (dated 1671)	—
159	Henry Napton	1668
160	Ralph Brown	1660
161	William Hulls	1668
162	Richard Withebed	1669
163	David Budden	1668
164	Gilbert Cornhill	1669
165	Robert Seare	1667
166	Richard Jacobs	1668
167	William Smith	1668
168	William Paxton	1668
169	T. W. (dated 1670)	—
170	Jonathan Ingles	1668
171	John Wescott	1669
172	Joseph Collier	1669
173	Thomas Hicks	1669
174	E. H. (dated 1670)	—
175	Roger Reading	1668
176	John Skinn	1670
177	Richard Gardner	1669
178	Thomas Taylor	1670
179	Joseph Colson	1668

LISTS OF PEWTERERS AND THEIR DATES

Plate 1	Name	Date of obtaining Freedom
180	Joseph Parker	1663
181	Daniel Barton	1670
182	Bartholomew Vokins	1670
183	John Robinson	1659
184	Lewis James	1670
185	Benjamin Evans	1670
186	I. H. (? John Hamberlin, 1669)	—
187	John Greenwood	1669
188	Edward Dodd	1669
189	S. W. (? erased)	—
190	Jabez Boston	1663
191	John Widdowes	1670
192	Richard Heath	1666
193	William Richards	1664
194	Thomas Hunt	1666
195	John Rothwell	1669
196	Samuel Witter	1671
197	John Allen	1671
198	E . . . Lane	c.1670
199	Samuel Ingles	1666
200	Robert Wood	1671
201	Joseph Pratt	1670
202	Edward Relfe	1668
203	William Matthews	c.1669
204	William Howard	1671
205	William Atkinson	1672
206	Christopher Clark	1661
207	Lawrence Warren	1672
208	Ralph Hulls	1656
209	Stephen Mabberley	1661
210	Thomas Radcliff	1671
211	I. L. (dated 1672)	—
212	Richard Meddowes	1672
213	Samuel Quissenborough	1672
214	Daniel Mason	1669
215	Robert Gregg	1667
216	T. H.	—
217	Gabriel Hartwell	1667
218	Moses Winkworth	1671
219	John Redshaw (Obviously out of place)	1679
220	C. R. (dated 1674)	—

Plate 1	Name	Date of obtaining Freedom
221	Walter Sturt	1668
222	Benedictus Thompson	1669
223	Thomas Skinn	1672
224	John Waite	1670
225	Richard Belsher	1673
226	Thomas Middleton	c.1673
227	James Trew	1667
228	Egerton Bryan	1669
229	Richard Barford	1674
230	Hugh Quick	1674
231	John Slow	1672
232	Samuel Vernon	1674
233	Thomas Ridding	1674
234	Joseph Sandford	1674
235	John Milman	1673
236	Robert Jacombe (Jacob)	1660
237	John Leeson	1673
238	Henry Pratt	1674
239	John Saunders	1674
240	William Allen	1668
241	Humphrey Hyatt	1675
242	Henry Frith	1675
243	Samuel Facer	1675
244	John Emes	1673
245	George Hale	1675
246	Richard Walton	1675
247	Christopher Thorne	1675
248	William Only	1674
249	John Rawlinson	1675
250	John Kenton	1675
	(See also No. 490)	
251	John Snoxell	1675
252	John Smith	1675
253	Henry Jones	1675
254	(? John Horton, 1675)	—
255	John Teale	1675
256	John Hulls	1662
257	Edward Iles	1674
258 } 258a}	Thomas Smith	1675
259	Thomas King	1675
260	Obedience Robins	1671

LISTS OF PEWTERERS AND THEIR DATES

Plate 1	Name	Date of obtaining Freedom
261	James Knight	1675
262	John Cox	1676
263	Theophilus Reading	1675
	(See also No. 6)	
264	Anthony Redhead	1675
265	Henry Morse	1675
266	C. C.	—
267	T. G. (? Thomas Gowland, 1675)	—
268	Henry Bradley	1675
269	David Heyrick	1676
270	James Glazebrook	1676
271	Paul Hayton	1676
272	Thomas Deacon	1675
273	George Vibart	1668
274	Ralph Benton	1676
275	John Russell	1676
276	Thomas Cutlove	1670
277	Thomas Hodgson	1676
278	William Hurst	1676
279	Humphrey Penn	1676
280	William Adams	1675
281	Thomas Hickling	1676
282	John Jackson	1674
283	Robert Morse	1676
284	Joseph Higdon	1676
285	Moses West	1677
286	Robert Tillott	1676
287	Thomas Shakle	1675
288	Samuel Mabbs	1676
289	William Waters	1670
290	John Paynell	1677
291	William Kenrick	1670
292	Richard Donne	1677
293	John Castle	1675
294	Edward Groves	1677
295	John Dove	1676
296	Thomas Tidmarsh	1677
297	John Laughton (see also No. 480)	1668
298	Daniel Barton	1670
	(See also No. 181)	
299	John Williams	1675
300	John Stribblehill	1676

Plate 1	Name	Date of obtaining Freedom
301	Richard Smith	1677
302	Henry Hatch	1675
303	Robert Lock	1677
304	Thomas Leach	1677
305	John Cropp	1677
306	Francis Paradice	1675
307	Jonathan Bonkin, Sr.	c.1677
308	William Mors	1676
309	F. L. (? Francis Larkin, 1677)	—
310	Willaim Vinmont	1678
311	I. N. (dated 1676)	—
312	Richard Fletcher	1677
313	William Green	1676
314	Edward Pusey	1676
315	C. B. (? Chris. Bentley, 1678)	—
316	Jeremiah Cole	1676
317	John Pepper	1678
318	R. B. (dated 1678) (? Rice Brooks, Jr., 1678)	—
319	Thomas Kelk	1663
320	Benjamin Blackwell	1676
321	Thomas Faulkner	1678
322	William Pettiver	1676
323	John Blunt	1676
324	John Grimsted	1676
325	Thomas Waite (Waight ?)	1677
326	Thomas Cooper, Jr.	1678
327	Luke Porter	1679
328	William Fly	1676
329	John Hamlin	1678
330	Andrew Rudsby	1677
331	Nathaniel Rider	1675
332	Nicholas Johnson	1667
333	Edward Randall	1677
334	William Tibbing	1662
335	William Heaton (?) (See also No. 342)	c.1677
336	Edward Traherne	1679
337	Thomas Simms	1675
338	William Hall	1680
339	Benjamin Cooper	1677
340	Francis Perkins	1674
341	Thomas Betts	1676

Plate 1	Name	Date of obtaining Freedom
342	William Heaton (See above, No. 335)	—
343	H. T. (dated 1680)	—
344	Jaques Taudin, Jr.	1673
345	Francis Knight	1678
346	Richard Shurmur	1678
347	Thomas Clark	1676
348	George Scott	1675
349	John Pettiver	1677
350	Thomas Pickfat	1677
350a	Thomas Powell	1676
350b	William Sandys	1680
	(See also No. 491)	
351	William Crooke	1679
Plate 2		
352	Robert Parr	1703
	(This touch should have been struck at end of this plate, or at the beginning of plate 3.)	
353	George Smith	1651
	(This apparently should have been re-struck earlier)	
354	William Burton (a variant of his touch No. 38)	
355	Charles Rack	1681
356	William Braine	1681
357	Stephen Lawrance	1661
	(See also No. 123)	
358	M. C. (dated 1676)	—
359	W. H.	—
360	H. D.	—
361	William Johnson	1676
362	Thomas Smith	1682
363	John Marsh	1658
364	Thomas Gardiner	1679
365	Edward Burchall	1681
366	John Bonvile	1677
367	Joseph Brooker	1679
368	T. P.	—
369	John Savidge	1678
370	Thomas Watterer	1674
371	Giles Madgwick	1681
372	Henry Sibley	1682

Plate 2	Name	Date of obtaining Freedom
373	Henry Wiggin	1670
374	John Goble	1680
375	Samuel Hancock	1677
376	William Hunton	1682
377	William Attwood	1683
378	John Cooper	1681
379	Joseph King	1682
380	Edward Walker	1682
381	Robert Hands	1673
382	Benjamin Cotton (or Cotterell)	1679
383	Joseph Cable	1680
384	John Parkinson	c.1680
385	Edward Kent	1677
386	William Foster	1675
387	Samuel Seaton	1679
388	T. S.	—
389	Robert Sturrop	1677
390	I. S. (dated 1683)	—
391	Anthony James	1675
392	James Carter	1683
393	John Joyce	1683
394	Thomas Porter	1683
395	Henry Harford	1677
396	Richard Gray	1682
397	Richard Smalpiece	1682
398	Peter Moulesworth	1662
399	Thomas Wright	1683
400	William Long	1677
401	Gabriel Grunwin	1681
402	? William Wetter (See also No. 78)	c.1684
403	Daniel White	1676
404	Thomas Saunders	1684
405	Joshua Fairhall	1684
406	Thomas Marshall	1684
407	Joseph Piddel	1684
408	Richard Brafield	1684
409	Edward Willett (See also No. 412)	1681
410	John Cormell	1683
411	Thomas Lock	1684
412	Edward Willet. (Same as No. 409)	—

Plate 2	Name	Date of obtaining Freedom
413	Charles Osborne	1681
414	Philemon Angel	1684
415 415a }	John Pettitt	1683
416	John Shakle	1672
417	William Nicholl	1685
418	E. A.	—
419	Samuel Sheppard	1683
420	John Smith	1685
421	Joseph Mountford	1680
422	John Donne	1683
423	Charles Royce	1684
424	James Nicholls	1684
425	Edward Roberts	1679
426	John Lawrance	1684
427	I. S. (dated 1685)	—
428	Thomas Smith. (A variation of 258 and 258a)	
429	Thomas Cary	1685
430	John Coursey	1685
431	Henry Adams	1665
432	John Dyer	1680
433	Thomas Paddon	1683
434	William Buttery	1686
435	Nicholas Marriott	1686
436	Thomas Smith	1686
437	?	—
438	William Withers	1684
439	John Wyatt	1685
440	D. S. (? Danl. Sherwin, 1686; ? Danl. Stephens, 1685)	—
441	Daniel Parker	1678
442	Charles Tough	1687
443	Thomas Roberts	1688
444	W. B.	—
445	Edward Walmesley	1685
446	T. B.	—
447	William Hall	1687
448	Richard White	1686
449	James Tisoe	1688
450	H. I.	—
451	Edward Quick	1687
452	Nathaniel Shortgrave	1687

Plate 2	Name	Date of obtaining Freedom
453	John Stile	1688
454	Edward Holman	1688
455	I. W.	—
456	John French	1686
457 457a }	Alexander Cleeve	1688
458	Richard Webb	1685
459	Thomas Palmer	1672
460	John Cambridge	1687
461	John Holley	1689
462	Robert Nicholson	1687
463	Thomas Castle	1685
464	John Trout	1689
465	John Cooper	1688
466	Charles Hulse	1690
467 468 }	Edward Smith	1680
469	Samuel Smalley	1683
470	William Eden	1689
471	T. A. O. B. (?)	—
472	Edward Matthews	1691
473	Thomas Cowderoy	1689
474	John Baskerville	1681
475	Elizabeth Witter	c.1691
476	Francis Cliffe	1687
477	James Brettell	1688
478	John Oliver	1687
479	Samuel Jackson	1667
480	John Laughton (2nd touch. See also No. 297)	1668
481	Daniel Wilson	1690
482	Robert Williams	1689
483	William Bravell	1684
484	William Clark	1687
485	Benjamin Whitaker	1691
486	I. G. (dated 1692)	—
487	Isaac Cooke	1692
488	John Donne. (May be 2nd touch. See No. 422)	—
489	I. S. (dated 1692) (? John Sharp, 1692)	—
490	John Kenton (See also 250)	1675

Plate 2	Name	Date of obtaining Freedom
491	William Sandys (Possibly a 2nd touch. See No. 350*b*)	—
492	Thomas Leapidge	1691
493	James Hughes	1691
494	John Page	1692
495	Philip Ruddock	1690
496	Thomas Buttery	1692
497	William Smith	1691
498	(Sir) John Fryers	1692
499	I. S.	—
500	? Joseph Pickard	1691
501	Robert Atterson	1693
502	William Colman	1683
503	E (?). M. (dated 1693)	—
504	William Buckley	1689
505	F. B. (? Francis Beesley, 1693)	—
506	H. M.	—
507	John Elderton	1693
508	Charles Cranley	1692
509	Thomas Winchcombe	1691
510	Harry Goodman	1693
511	Benjamin Boyden	1693
512	John Coke	1694
513	? John Reynolds (If so, this is out of place)	1696
514	Josiah Clark	1690
515	George Hammond	1693
516	Samuel Newell	1689
517	Martin Brown	1686
518	George Canby	1694
519	John Heath	1694
520	Robert Iles	1691
521	D. I. (dated 1694)	—
522	Joseph Smith	1695
523	Thomas Spring	1676
524	Charles Middleton	1690
525	John Hankinson	1693
526	Lawrence Child	1693
527	Stephen Bridges	1692
528	Henry Feild	1693
529	William Clarke	1695
530	Joseph Rayne	1693

Plate 2	Name	Date of obtaining Freedom
531	William Dymoke	1696
532	George Everard	1696
533	William Atlee	1696
534	Henry Brasted	1692
535	Richard Clerk	1696
536	John Gisburne	1696
537	John Carr	1695
538	Jabez Harris	1694
539	George North	1693
540	William Ellwood	1693
541	Solomon Jempson (Tompson)	1696
542	Joseph Bowden	1687
543	John Summers	1696–7
544	Anthony Waters	1685
545	John Thomas	1698
546	Richard Warkman	1697
547	Edward Stone	1695
548	William Plivey	1697
549	Thomas Tillyard	1698
550	William Gillam	1698
551	William Matthews	1698
552	William Stevens	1697
553	John Jones, Sr.	1700
554	John Barlow	1698
555	Robert Daken	1698
556	William Heyford	1698
557	Jonas Durand	1692
558	Richard Dyer	1699
559	William Raves	1682
560	Basil Graham	1699
561	Nicholas Sweatman	1698
562	John Blake	1690
563	John Compere	1696
564	Thomas Bosworth	1699
565	Thomas Cooke	1690
566	John Warren	1697
567	Peter Carter	1699
568	Edward Leapidge	1699
569	William Digges	1699
570	Charles Render	1699
571	Francis Litchfield	1697
572	Charles Randall	1699

Plate 2	Name	Date of obtaining Freedom
573	Daniel Barton, Jr.	1700
574	William Hux	1700
575	Anthony Smith	1698
576	Thomas Parker	1695
	(See also No. 579)	
577	Bernard Babb	1700
578	John Emes	1700
579	Thomas Parker	—
	(See also No. 576, a variation)	
580	Thomas Bennett	1700
581	John Newham	1699
582	Robert Deane	1692
583	John Prince	1697
584	Thomas Hopkins	1700
585	John Ewen (Yewen)	1700
586	John Child	1700
587	John Carpenter	1701
588	Fulk Humphrey Wormlayton	1691
589	Samuel Boss	1695
590	John Calcott	1699
591	John Quick	1699
592	Thomas Buckby (? Buckley)	1701
593	James Hitchman	1701
594	Robert Bordman	1700
595	Thomas Burges	1700
596	Nicholas Okeford	1699
597	John Kirton	1699
598	George Hume	1700
599	Anthony Sturton	1686
600	Thomas Spencer	1702
601	Thomas Frith	1693
602	Thomas Greener	1700
603	Nathaniel Bessant	1702
604	David Brock	1702
605	David Budden, Jr.	1701
606	William Ellis	1702
607	Tristram Pierce	1702
608	George Winter	1701
609	Williams Waylett	1701
610	Thomas Scattergood	1700
611	Thomas Beckett	1702
612	Nicholas Jackman	1699

Plate 2	Name	Date of obtaining Freedom
613	John Smith	1702
614	Joseph Slow	1702

Plate 3		
615	James Tidmarsh	1701
616	Samuel Pettiver	1695
617	Benjamin Casimer	1704
618	Robert Reynolds	1704
619	Abraham Roberts	1687
620	John Savage	1699
621	Robert Jupe	1697
622	Thomas Horrod	1693
623	Howell Gwilt	1697
624	Jonathan Cotton, Sr.	1704
625	Robert Pilkington	1704
626	Daubeny Turbeville	1703
627	William Turner	1702
628	Edward Hanns (Hands)	1704
629	William Brown	1705
630	Thomas Wigley	1699
631	John Spicer	1699
632	Thomas Smith	1705
633	Thomas Arnott	1702
634	William Seare	1705
635	Thomas Peisley (See also No. 670)	1693
636	James Paxton	1698
637	Everard Gillam	1702
638	Joseph Pixley	1706
639	Benjamin Foster	1706
640	James Gisburne	1691
641	Richard Heslopp	1700
642	Henry Hammerton	1706
643	Robert Morse	1702
644	William Townsend	1699
645	William Fenwick	c.1706
646	Robert Crossfield	1701
647	Timothy Richards	1699
648	Richard King	1698
649	Richard Collier	1706
650	Thomas Boyden	1706

Plate 3	Name	Date of obtaining Freedom
651	Abraham Wiggin	1707
652	John Blewett	1707
653	Philip Rogers	1708
654	Thomas Sheppard	1705
655	Richard Wilkes	1708
656	William King	1706
657	Edward Quick	1708
658	Henry Sewdley	1706
659	John Peacock	1706
660	John Harris	1709
661	Hellier Perchard	1709
662	Spackman & Grant	c.1709
663	William Hitchens	1705
664	Philip Stevens	1709
665	Robert Oudley	1708
666	Richard James	1709
667	Richard Dale	1709
668	William Cox	1708
669	Humphrey Sankey	1710
670	Thomas Peisley (See also No. 635, a variation)	—
671	Thomas Goodwin	1707
672	Arthur Engley (Ingles)	1710
673	Henry Feildar	1704
674	Greenhill Lindsay	1708
675	Timothy Fly	1710
676	George Smith	1712
677	Richard Grunwin	1713
678	Peter Redknap	1713
679	John Walmsley	1702
680	Theodore Jennings	1713
681	Thomas Giffin	1709
682	Richard Drinkwater	1712
683	William Beamont (Beaumont)	1706
684	John Laffar	1706
685	William Newham	1708
686	George Underwood	1712
687	John Osborn	1701
688a	John Waite	1706
688b	John Lawson	1713
689	Samuel Knight	1703
690	John Woodeson	1708

Plate 3	Name	Date of obtaining Freedom
691	Lawrence Dyer	1704
	(Had leave to *alter* his touch in 1712)	
692	Thomas Wheeler	1692
693	John Palmer	1702
694	James Everett	1711
695	John Walker	1713
696	Edward Randall	1715
697	John Tidmarsh	1713
698	Thomas Cartwright	1712
699	John Neaton	1714
700	Richard Partridge	1715
701	Thomas Webb	1714
702	Thomas Matthews	1711
703	John Strickland	1703
704	William Meadows	1714
705	Abraham Cross	1695
706	William Miles	1715
707	Thomas Claridge	1716
708	John Ansell	1714
709	George Peisley	1718
710	John Rolt	1716
711	Gray & King	c.1718
712	William Hulls	1717
713	John Langford	1719
714	Seth Jones	1719
715	Francis Whittle	1715
716	Thomas Lincolne	1718
717	Abraham Ford	1719
718	John Carpenter	1711
719	William Warkman	1713
720	John Merriweather	1718
721	John Osborne, Jr.	1713
722	Jonathan Bonkin, Jr.	1699
723	Richard King	1714
724	Pendelbury Spring	1717
725	Thomas Leach	c.1720
726	Arthur Smalman	1713
727	John Langley	1716
728	William Nicholson	1720
729	Benjamin Withers	1719
730	Peter Collier	1720
731	John Trapp	1695

Plate 3	Name	Date of obtaining Freedom
732	Joseph Watson	1713
733	William Clark	1721
734	Thomas Rhodes	1721
735	Jonathan Brodhurst	1719
736	John Kent	1718
737	Richard Wright	1712
738	Robert Pole	1717
739	John Wyatt	1718
740	Thomas Hickling	1717
741	Edward Lawrence	1713
742	John Edwards	1718
743	White & Bernard	c.1721
744	John Heath	1711
745	George Taylor (See also No. 758)	1722
746	Samuel Ellis	1721
747	John Randall	1723
748	Robert Wass	1712
749	Luke Johnson	1713
750	Alexander Lancaster	1711
751	James Excell	1718
752	John Carr	1722
753	Joseph Pratt, Jr.	1709
754	Thomas Hux	1723
755	Edward Nash	1717
756	Catesby Chapman	1721
757	Thomas Stevens	1716
758	George Taylor (duplicate of No. 745)	
759	Edward Ubly	1716
760	Henry Jackson	1723
761	Thomas Wyatt	1723
762	John Norgrove	1722
763	Richard Cox	1713
764	Richard Spooner	1719
765	John Cole	c.1722
766	Paul Mitchell	1721
767	Simon Pattinson	1715
768	Thomas Bacon	1719
769	John Paxton	1717
770	Edward Merifield	1716
771	Richard Leggatt	1722
772	Thomas Stribblehill	1704

Plate 3	Name	Date of obtaining Freedom
773	Thomas Kirke	1728
774	Joseph Wingod	1721
775 } 775a	Henry Elwick	1707
776	Samuel Miles	1726
777	Thomas James	1726
778	William Ellis	1726
779	John Shaw	1726
780	James Matthews	1722
781	James Bishop	1724
782	Rowland Poole	1717
783	Robert Matthews	1721
784	Thomas Phillips	1727
785	Edward Bradstreet	1720
786	Mark Cripps	1727
787	Henry Smith	1724
788	John Smith	1724
789	John Payne	1725
790	John Hathaway	1725
791	Alexander Cleeve	1715
792	John Cater	1725
793	John Rogers	1717
794	Thomas Gosling	1720
795	John Davis	1715
796	Samuel Smith	1727
797	John Blenman	1726
798	Joseph Carter	c.1726
799	William Martin	1726
800	Thomas Piggott	1698
801	John Watts	1725
802	Thomas Swindell	1705
803	Ann Tidmarsh	1728
804	Joseph Donne (Same as No. 807)	1727
805	Richard Bowcher	1727
806	Thomas Kirby	1722
807	Joseph Donne	1727
808	Smith & Leapidge	c.1728
809	Joseph Sherwin	1726
810	Joseph Claridge	1724
811	Daniel Pickering	1723
812	William Horton	1725
813	Samuel Cooke	1727

LISTS OF PEWTERERS AND THEIR DATES

Plate 3	Name	Date of obtaining Freedom
814	Benjamin Brown	1726
815	William Norwood	1727
816	William Rowell	1726
817	William Stevens	1729
818	Richard Bradstreet	1727
819	John Williams	1724
820	George Stafford	1730
821	Joseph Pedder	1727
822	John Jones, Jr.	1727
823	Andrew Rudsby	1712
824	Cooke & Freeman	c.1731
825	Samuel Spateman	1719
826	John Fasson	1725
827	William Sandys Green	1725
828	John Jordan	1727
829	William Smith	1732
830	Simon Halford	1726
831	Richard Wildman	1728
832	Giles Cleeve	1706
833	John de St. Croix	1729
834	Richard Hands	1727
835	Thomas Barnes	1726
836	Edward Drew	1728
837	Richard Brown	1729
838	John Cowley	1724
839	Alexander Hamilton	1721
840	James Smith	1732
841	William Phillips	1719
842	William Charlesley	1729
843	Darling & Meakin	c.1732
844	William Cooch	1731
845	Samuel Grey	1729
846	William Foxon	1723
847	Benjamin Foster, Jr.	1730
848	Edward Yorke	1732
849	William Shayler	1734
Plate 4		
850	Samuel Taylor	1731
851	Samuel Righton	1732
852	James Tidmarsh	1734
853	Johnson & Chamberlain	1732

Plate 4	Name	Date of obtaining Freedom
854	James Tisoe	1733
855	John Jackson	1728
856	Samuel Jefferys	1734
857	William Murray	1734
858	Robert Peircey	1722
859	John Scattergood	1732
860	Richard Smith	1733
861	Henry Maxted	1731
862	Thomas Collett	1735
863 864	William Deane	1731
865	John Langton	1731
866	Jonathan Cotton, Jr.	1735
867	Robert Massam	1735
868	John Piggott	1736
869	Philip (or Philemon) Matthews	1736
870	John Wright	1717
871	Daniel Grendon	1735
872	Alexander Stout	1733
873	Thomas Scattergood	1736
874	Fly & Thompson	c.1737
875	Henry Little	1734
876	Thomas Groce	1737
877	Robert Hitchman	1737
878	John Jupe	1735
879	Samuel Grigg	1734
880	Patrick Garioch	1735
881	Edmund Sharrock	1737
882	Roger Pye	1737
883	Robert Patience	1734
884	William Handy	1728
885	John Kenrick	1737
886	Francis Piggott	1736
887	George Alderson	1728
888	Philip Roberts	1738
889	Robert Skinner	1738
890	John Belson	1734
891	Bartholomew Elliott	1738
892	William Cowling	1737
893	Wood & Mitchell	c.1742
894	William Highmore	1741
895	W. S.	—

172

Plate 4	Name	Date of obtaining Freedom
896	Thomas Ubly	1741
897	John Foster	1735
898	Thomas Matthew	1736
899	Thomas Boardman	1728
900	Edward Quick	1735
901	Samuel Sweatman	1728
902	Richard Norfolk	1736
903	John Williams	1729
904	John Benson	1740
905	Lawrence Yates	1738
906	Henry Joseph	1736
907	Robert Crooke	1738
908	George Holmes	1742
909	John Perry	1743
910	John Boteler	1743
911	William Palmer	1743
912	Edward Toms	1744
913	Acquila Dackombe	1742
914	William Farmer (?)	(?) 1743
915	Jonathan Stevens	1744
916	William Taylor	1728
917	James Gibbs	1741
918	John Hayton	1743
919	John Bromfield	1745
920	William Howard	1745
921	George Bacon	1746
922	Jonathan Leach	1742
923	John Wynn	1746
924	Richard Pitt	1747
925	John Hartwell	1736
926	Richard Newman	1747
927	Joseph White	1747
928	John Townsend	1748
929	Burford & Green	c.1748
930	Richard Poole	1747
931	William Harrison	1748
932	James Lethard	1745
933	William Glover Annison (See also No. 947)	1742
934	John Wingod	1748
935	John Sellon	1740
936	John Cornelius Merriweather	1747

Plate 4	Name	Date of obtaining Freedom
937	William Bampton	1742
938	Daniel Lawson	1749
	(See also No. 942)	
939	George Beeston	1743
940	Isaac Read	1743
941	Mathew Tonkin	1749
942	Daniel Lawson. (Same as No. 938)	
943	Henry Appleton	1749
944	John Ubly	1748
945	William Phipps	1743
946	James Bullock	1750
947	Wm. Glover Annison. (Same as No. 933)	
948	Rowland Smith	1734
949	William Phillips	1744
950	Charles P. Maxey	1750
951	Bouchier Cleeve, Jr.	c.1750
952	Henry Irving	1750
953	Richard Peake	1750
954	William White	1751
955	Robert Randall	1748
956	James Boost	1744
957	John Walker	1748
958	Matthew Underwood	1752
959	Richard Alderwick	1748
960	William Healey	1752
961	James Fontain	1752
962	Richard Pawson	1752
963	John Edwards	1739
964	John Fasson, Jr.	1753
965	John Home	1749
966	William Harris	1746
967	Benjamin Townsend	1744
968	James Steevens	1753
969	Thomas Langford	1751
970	William de Jersey	c.1738
971	John White	1755
972	Isaac Reeve	1754
973	Thomas Buttery	1756
974	Henry Bowler	1757
975	Thomas Hawkins	1756
976	George Grenfell	1757
977	William Fasson	1758

Plate 4	Name	Date of obtaining Freedom
978	Thomas Munday	1754
979	Benjamin Bacon	1749
980	Robert Scatchard	1756
981	Charles Claridge	1756
982	Joseph Spackman	1749
983	James Puleston	1752
984	William Hitchens	1759
985	John Vaughan	1753
986	Joseph Jefferys	1757
987	William Frome	1760
988	Mary Willey	1760
989	Thomas Smith	1739
990	Thomas Jones	1755
991	Brown & Swanson	c.1760
991b	Thomas Swanson	1753
992	Munden & Grove	c.1760
993	William Wightman	1758
994	Bennett & Chapman	c.1761
995	John King	1757
996	Ralph Wharram	1756
997	Thomas Greenwood	1759
998	William Bennett	1758
999	Robert (1760), and Thomas, Porteous	1762
1000	Nathaniel Meakin, Jr.	1761
1001	Richard Bowler	1755
1002	John & Joseph Brown and J. Lewis	1757
1003	James Fiddes	1754
1004	Thomas Thompson	1755
1005	Thomas Smith	1755
1006	Thomas Giffin	1759
1007	Clark & Greening	c.1765
1008	Thomas Swanson	1753
1009	John Perry	1765
1010	John Alderson	1764
1011	Charles Smith	1765
1012	Townsend & Reynolds	c.1766
1013	William Snape	1764
1014	William Farmer	1765
1015	Anthony Jenner	1754
1016	Thomas Smith	1761
1017 (2)	Stephen Kent Hagger	1754
1018	Pitt & Floyd	c.1769

Plate 4	Name	Date of obtaining Freedom
1019	Henry Wood	1768
1020a 1020b	Samuel Law	1768
1021	John Hudson	1770
1022	Joseph Monk	1757
	(See also No. 1030)	
1023	John Gurnell	1768
1024	John Hinde	1767
1025	Robert Hodges	1772
1026	Thomas Dodson	1769
1027	Edward Sidey	1772
1028	William Phillips	1750
1029 (3)	William Cooch	1775
1030	Joseph Monk. (Same as No. 1022)	
1031	Richard Yates	1772
1032	John Appleton	1768
1033 (2)	Samuel Higley	1775
1034 (2)	William Barnes	1770
1035	Richard Alderwick	1776
1036 (2)	Cornelius Swift	1770
1937 (2)	Nathaniel Barber	1777
1038	Samuel Salter Bowler	1779
1039	Samuel Priddle	1773
1040	Robert Jupe	1776
1041 (2)	William Wright	1764
1042 (2)	Robert Lupton	1775
1043 (2)	Pitt & Dadley	c.1781
1044	William Millin	1776
1045	Joseph and James Spackman	1785
1046 (2)	Robert Walker	1779
1047	Joseph Foster	1757
1048 (2)	Thomas Fasson	1783
1049	Richard Bache	1779
1050	Charles Wm. Loader	1784
1051	Robert Jackson	1780
1052	Joseph Spackman & Co.	c.1785
1053	Robert Knight	1770
1054 (2)	Henry & Richard Joseph	c.1787
1055	Edward Lockwood	1768
1056	Philip White	1778
1057	William Harrison King	1786
1058	Richard Bagshaw	1772

Plate 4	Name	Date of obtaining Freedom
1059 (2)	Robert Barnett	1783
1060	William Wadsworth	1780
1061 (2)	Peter Le Keux	1779
1062 (2)	Charles Jones	1786
1063 (2)	Coney John Brown	1786
1064	Edward Seawell	1779
1065 (2)	Randall Moring	1780
1066	Carpenter & Hamberger	c.1794
1067 (2)	Wood & Hill	c.1794
1068 (2)	John Gray Green	1793
1069 (2)	Josiah Maynard	1772
Plate 5		
1070 (2)	William Bathus	1797
1071 (2)	Paul Fisher	1798
1072 (2)	William Nettlefold	1785
1073 (2)	Thomas Phillips	1795
1074	I. F.	—
1075 (2)	Samuel Turner	1790
1076 (2)	William Groome	1798
1077 (2)	William Gibbs	1804
1078 (2)	Roger Moser	1806
1079 (2)	William Walker	1787
1080 (2)	Samuel Cocks	1819
1081 (2)	Joseph Godfrey	1807
1082 (2)	Robert Stanton	1810
1083 (2)	James Ashley	1820
1084 (2)	Sir George Alderson	1817
1085 (2)	Richard Mister	1802
1086 (2)	W. M.	—
1087 (2)	John Hornby Maw	1822
1088 (2)	William Cornelius Swift	1809
1089 (2)	James Stanton	1815
1090 (2)	Thomas Ashley	1821
1091	William J. Englefield	1875

EDINBURGH TOUCH-PLATES

Touches	Name	Date of obtaining Freedom
1 and 2	I. R. (? John Rebate, 1588)	—
3 and 4	John Weir	c.1580
5 and 6	James Sibbet	1600
7 and 8	L. M.	struck c.1600
9 and 10	Q. V. (or W.)	struck c.1600
11 and 12	I. R. (? John Reddeth, 1603)	—
13	Thomas Weir	1596
14 and 15	Richard Weir	1597
16 and 17	A. H. (dated 1600)	struck c.1600
18 and 19	Cornelious Tayleur	1610
20 and 21	George Gledstone	1610
22 and 23	Alexander Sibbald	1605
24	Patrick Walker	1607
25	Andro Bothwick	1620
26	William Garmentin	1613
27	Thomas Inglis	1616
	(See also Nos. 29 and 30)	
28	William Hamiltone	1613
29 and 30	Thomas Inglis	1616
	(See No. 27)	
31	R. H.	struck c. 1620
32	G. B.	struck c. 1620
33	James Sibbald	1631
34	A. S. (dated 1631)	—
35	V. T. (dated 1631)	—
36 and 37	Robert Thompson	struck c.1631
38	William Scott	1634
39	Robert Simpsone	1631
40	Joseph Goldie	1633
41	James Monteith	1634
42	James Abernethie	1640
43	James Buclennand	1643
44	James Monteith	1643
45	John Harvie	1643
46	Robert Weir	1646
47 and 48	Thomas Inglis	1648
49	William Abernethie	1649
50	James Hernie	1651

Touches	Name	Date of obtaining Freedom
51	This touch is a castle without initials and probably belongs to either No. 50 or No. 52	
52	William Christie	1652
53	. . . (?). B. (? William Borthwick) (dated 1653)	—
54	Thomas Edgar	1654
55	A. F. (dated 1654) (? Alexander Ferguson, 1660)	—
56	D. B. (dated 1654) (? David Bryce, 1660)	—
57	James Harvie	1654
58	William Anderson	1654
59	I. S. (dated 1655) (? John Syde, 1660)	—
60	Alexander Grahame (dated 1655)	1654
61	I. L. (dated 1655) (? John Law, 1660)	—
62	Andrew M'Clean	1660
63	John Ramsay	1659
64	Samuel Walker	1660
65	Robert Inglis	1663
66	James Abernethie (dated 1663)	1660
67	George Crichtoune	1664
68	Archibald Napier	1666
69	James Herring	c.1667
70	James Abernethie	1669
71	John Watson	1671
72	William Harvie	1672
73	. . . (?) C. (dated 1675)	—
74	Alexander Walker	1676
75	T. C. (dated 1675)	—
76	A. M. (dated 1672) (? Alexander Moir, 1675)	—
77	A. F. (dated 1676) (? Alexander Ferguson, 1678)	—
78	R. W. (dated 1676) (? Robert Walker)	—
79	George Whyte	1676
80	Alexander Munroe	1677
81	John Guld	1677
82	John Ferguson	1678
83	John Syde	1680
84	Alexander Hunter	1682
85	Robert Edgar	1684
86	T (or I). W. (dated 1685)	—
87	Thomas Inglis	1686
88	Touch of a castle, probably belongs to No. 89	—
89	John Herring	1688
90	William Davidsone	1693
91	James Herring	1692

Touches	Name	Date of obtaining Freedom
92	David Symmer	1692
93	William Herring	1693
94	John Andersone	1693
95	David Penman	1693
96	Robert Burns	1694
97	James Symontoun	1696
98	Robert Andersone	1697
99	John Napier	1700
100	John Tait	1700
101	John Weir	1701
102	John Grier	1701
103	Alexander Browne	1717
104	R. F. (dated 1703) (? Robert Findlay, 1717)	—
105	A. B. (dated 1704) (? Alexander Bryden, 1717)	—
106	James Cowper	1704
107	Thomas Mitchell	1704
108	George Tennent	1706
109	William Harvie	1706
110	Alexander Coulthard	1708
111	James Edgar	1709
112	Mungo Burton	1709
113	Walter Patasone	1710
114	Thomas Cockburn	1711
115	John Cuthbertson	1712
116	Alexander Waddel	1714
117	John Jolly	1714
118	Robert Kellowe	1715
119	Robert Reid	1718
120	John Letham	1718
121	James Rait	1718
122	Edward Gibson	1719
123	Thomas Inglis	1719
124	James Clark	1722
125	Robert Veitch	1725
126	Thomas Simpson	1728
127	Edward Bunkell	c.1728
128	W. B. (dated 1729) (? William Browne)	—
129	John Wilson	1732
130	Archibald Inglis	1732
131	Alexander Wright	1732
132	R. B. (dated 1733) (? Robert Brown)	—
133	A. N. (dated 1733)	—

Touches	Name	Date of obtaining Freedom
134	A. A. (dated 1734) (? Adam Anderson, c.1734)	—
135	W. S. (dated 1735) (? William Scott)	—
136	I. G. (dated 1737) (? John Glover)	—
137	William Ballantyne	1742
138	Adam Tait	1747
139	William Ballantyne	1749
140	William Hunter	1749
141	Andrew Kinnear	1750
142	John Brown	1761
143	John Gardiner	1764

LIST III

ALPHABETICAL LIST OF PEWTERERS

Abernethie, James, Edinburgh	.	1640 F.	42 E.T.P.	
Abernethie, James, ,,	.	1660 F.	66 E.T.P.	
Abernethie, James, ,,	.	1669 F.	?70 E.T.P.	
Abernethie, William, ,,	.	1649 F.	49 E.T.P.	
Adams, Henry, London	.	1685 Y.	431 L.T.P.	
Adams, William, ,,	.	1643 Y.	59 L.T.P.	
Adams, William, ,,	.	1675 Y.	280 L.T.P.	
Alderson, George, ,,		1728 Y.	887 L.T.P.	
Alderson, Sir George, ,,	.	1817 Y.	1084 L.T.P.	
Alderson, John, ,,	.	1764 Y.	1010 L.T.P.	
Alderwick, Richard, ,,	.	1748 Y.	959 L.T.P.	
Alderwick, Richard, ,,	.	1776 Y.	1035 L.T.P.	
Allen, John, ,,	.	1671 Y.	197 L.T.P.	
Allen, William, ,,	.	1668 Y.	240 L.T.P.	
Anderson, Adam, Edinburgh	.	1734 F.	?134 E.T.P.	
Anderson, William, ,,	.	1654 F.	?58 E.T.P.	
Andersone, John, ,,	.	1693 F.	94 E.T.P.	
Andersone, Robert, ,,	.	1697 F.	98 E.T.P.	
Angel, Philemon, London	.	1684 Y.	414 L.T.P.	
Annison, Wm. Glover, ,,	.	1742 Y.	933 and 947 L.T.P.	
Ansell, John, ,,	.	1714 Y.	708 L.T.P.	
Appleton, Henry, ,,	.	1749 Y.	943 L.T.P.	
Appleton, John, ,,	.	1768 Y.	1032 L.T.P.	
Arnott, Thomas, ,,	.	1702 Y.	633 L.T.P.	
Ashley, James, ,,	.	1820 Y.	1083 L.T.P.	
Ashley, Thomas J. T. ,,	.	1821 Y.	1090 L.T.P.	

Atkinson, William,	London	.	1672 Y.	205 L.T.P.
Atlee, William,	,,	.	1696 Y.	533 L.T.P.
Atterton, Robert,	,,	.	1693 Y.	501 L.T.P.
Attwood, William,	,,	.	1683 Y.	377 L.T.P.
Ayers, William,	,,	.	1663 Y.	25 L.T.P.
Babb, Bernard,	,,	.	1700 Y.	577 L.T.P.
Bache, Richard,	,,	.	1779 Y.	1049 L.T.P.
Bacon, Benjamin,	,,	.	1749 Y.	979 L.T.P.
Bacon, George,	,,	.	1746 Y.	921 L.T.P.
Bacon, Thomas,	,,	.	1719 Y.	768 L.T.P.
Bagshaw, Richard,	,,	.	1772 Y.	1058 L.T.P.
Ballantyne, William, Edinburgh		.	1742 F.	137 E.T.P.
Ballantyne, William, Edinburgh		.	1749 F.	139 E.T.P.
Bampton, William, London .		.	1742 Y.	937 L.T.P.
Barber, Nathaniel,	,,	.	1777 Y.	1037 L.T.P.
Barford, Richard,	,,	.	1674 Y.	229 L.T.P.
Barlow, John,	,,	.	1698 Y.	554 L.T.P.
Barnes, Thomas,	,,	.	1726 Y.	835 L.T.P.
Barnes, William,	,,	.	1770 Y.	1034 L.T.P.
Barnett, Robert,	,,	.	1783 Y.	1059 L.T.P.
Barton, Daniel,	,,	.	1670 Y.	181 and 298 L.T.P.
Barton, Daniel, Jr.	,,	.	1700 Y.	573 L.T.P.
Baskerville, John,	,,	.	1681 Y.	474 L.T.P.
Bathus, William,	,,	.	1797 Y.	1070 L.T.P.
Batteson, Thomas,	,,	.	1661 Y.	86 L.T.P.
Beamont, William,	,,	.	1706 Y.	683 L.T.P.
Beckett, Thomas,	,,	.	1702 Y.	611 L.T.P.
Beeston, George,	,,	.	1743 Y.	939 L.T.P.
Belsher, Richard,	,,	.	1673 Y.	225 L.T.P.
Belson, John,	,,	.	1734 Y.	890 L.T.P.
Bennett & Chapman,	,,	.	c. 1761.	994 L.T.P.
Bennett, Thomas,	,,	.	1700 Y.	580 L.T.P.
Bennett, William,	,,	.	1758 Y.	998 L.T.P.
Benson, John,	,,	.	1740 Y.	904 L.T.P.
Benton, Ralph,	,,	.	1676 Y.	274 L.T.P.
Bessant, Nathaniel,	,,	.	1702 Y.	603 L.T.P.
Betts, Thomas,	,,	.	1676 Y.	341 L.T.P.
Bishop, James,	,,	.	1724 Y.	781 L.T.P.
Blackwell, Benjamin,	,,	.	1676 Y.	320 L.T.P.
Blenman, John,	,,	.	1726 Y.	797 L.T.P.
Blewett, John,	,,	.	1707 Y.	652 L.T.P.
Blunt, John,	,,	.	1676 Y.	323 L.T.P.
Boardman, Thomas,	,,	.	1728 Y.	899 L.T.P.
Bonkin, Jonathan, Sr.	,,	.	c. 1678 Y.	307 L.T.P.

Bonkin, Jonathan, Jr., London	. 1699 Y.	722 L.T.P.
Bonvile, John, ,,	. 1677 Y.	366 L.T.P.
Boost, James, ,,	. 1744 Y.	956 L.T.P.
Bordman, Robert, ,,	. 1700 Y.	594 L.T.P.
Borthwick, Andro, Edinburgh	. 1620 F.	25 E.T.P.
Borthwick, William, ,, .	. c. 1653	?53 E.T.P.
Boss, Samuel, London .	. 1695 Y.	589 L.T.P.
Boston, Beza, ,,	. 1661 Y.	35 L.T.P.
Boston, Jabez, ,, .	. 1663 Y.	190 L.T.P.
Bosworth, Thomas, ,, .	. 1699 Y.	564 L.T.P.
Boteler, John, ,, .	. 1743 Y.	910 L.T.P.
Bowcher, Richard, ,, .	. 1727 Y.	805 L.T.P.
Bowden, Joseph, ,, .	. 1687 Y.	542 L.T.P.
Bowler, Henry, ,, .	. 1757 Y.	974 L.T.P.
Bowler, Richard, ,, .	. 1755 Y.	1001 L.T.P.
Bowler, Samuel, ,, .	. 1779 Y.	1038 L.T.P.
Boyden, Benjamin, ,, .	. 1693 Y.	511 L.T.P.
Boyden, Thomas, ,, .	. 1706 Y.	650 L.T.P.
Bradley, Henry, ,, .	. 1675 Y.	268 L.T.P.
Bradstreet, Edward, ,, .	. 1720 Y.	785 L.T.P.
Bradstreet, Richard, ,, .	. 1727 Y.	818 L.T.P.
Brafield, Richard, ,, .	. 1684 Y.	408 L.T.P.
Brailsford, Peter, ,, .	. 1659 Y.	63 L.T.P.
Braine, William, ,, .	. 1681 Y.	356 L.T.P.
Brasted, Henry, ,, .	. 1692 Y.	534 L.T.P.
Bravell, William, ,, .	. 1684 Y.	483 L.T.P.
Brettell, James, ,, .	. 1688 Y.	477 L.T.P.
Bridges, Stephen, ,, .	. 1692 Y.	527 L.T.P.
Brocks, David, ,, .	. 1702 Y.	604 L.T.P.
Brodhurst, Jonathan, ,, .	. 1719 Y.	735 L.T.P.
Bromfield, John, ,, .	. 1745 Y.	919 L.T.P.
Brooker, Joseph, ,, .	. 1679 Y.	367 L.T.P.
Brown, Alexander, Edinburgh	. 1717 F.	103 E.T.P.
Brown, Benjamin, London .	. 1726 Y.	814 L.T.P.
Brown, Coney John, ,, .	. 1786 Y.	1063 L.T.P.
Brown, John, Edinburgh .	. 1761 F.	142 E.T.P.
Brown, John and Joseph, and John Lewis (partnership), London	. c. 1757.	1002 L.T.P.
Brown Martin, London .	. 1686 Y.	517 L.T.P.
Brown, Ralph, ,, .	. 1660 Y.	160 L.T.P.
Brown, Richard, ,, .	. 1729 Y.	837 L.T.P.
Brown, Robert, Edinburgh .	. c. 1733.	132 E.T.P.
Brown, William, ,, .	. c. 1729.	?128 E.T.P.
Brown, William, London .	. 1705 Y.	629 L.T.P.

Browne & Swanson, London .	. *c.* 1760.	991	L.T.P.
Bryan, Egerton, ,, .	. 1669 Y.	228	L.T.P.
Bryce, David, Edinburgh .	. 1660 F.	56	E.T.P.
Bryden, Alexander, ,, .	. 1717 F.	?105	E.T.P.
Buckby, Thomas, London .	. *c.* 1700 Y.	592	L.T.P.
Buckley, William, ,, .	. 1689 Y.	504	L.T.P.
Buclennand, James, Edinburgh	. 1643 F.	43	E.T.P.
Budden, David, London .	. 1668 Y.	163	L.T.P.
Budden, David, ,, .	. 1701 Y.	605	L.T.P.
Bull, John, ,, .	. 1660 Y.	97	L.T.P.
Bullevant, James, ,, .	. 1660 Y.	?67	L.T.P.
Bullock, James, ,, .	. 1750 Y.	946	L.T.P.
Bunkell, Edward, Edinburgh	. *c.* 1720.	?127	E.T.P.
Burchall, Edward, London .	. 1681 Y.	365	L.T.P.
Burford & Green, ,, .	. *c.* 1748.	929	L.T.P.
Burges, Thomas, ,, .	. 1701 Y.	595	L.T.P.
Burns, Robert, Edinburgh .	. 1694 F.	96	E.T.P.
Burton, Mungo, ,, .	. 1709 F.	112	E.T.P.
Burton, William, London .	. 1653 Y.	38 and 354	L.T.P.
Buttery, Thomas, ,, .	. 1692 Y.	496	L.T.P.
Buttery, Thomas, ,, .	. 1756 Y.	973	L.T.P.
Buttery, William, ,, .	. 1686 Y.	434	L.T.P.
Buxton, John, ,, .	. 1667 Y.	142	E.T.P.
Cable, Joseph, London .	. 1680 Y.	383	L.T.P.
Calcott, John, ,, .	. 1699 Y.	590	L.T.P.
Cambridge, John, ,, .	. 1687 Y.	460	L.T.P.
Canby, George, ,, .	. 1694 Y.	518	L.T.P.
Carpenter, John, ,, .	. 1701 Y.	587	L.T.P.
Carpenter, John, ,, .	. 1711 Y.	718	L.T.P.
Carpenter & Hamberger, ,, .	. *c.* 1794.	1066	L.T.P.
Carr, John, ,, .	. 1696 Y.	537	L.T.P.
Carr, John, ,, .	. 1722 Y.	752	L.T.P.
Carter, James, ,, .	. 1683 Y.	392	L.T.P.
Carter, Joseph, ,, .	. *c.* 1726.	798	L.T.P.
Carter, Peter, ,, .	. 1699 Y.	567	L.T.P.
Cartwright, Thomas, ,, .	. 1712 Y.	698	L.T.P.
Cary, Thomas, ,, .	. 1685 Y.	429	L.T.P.
Casimer, Benjamin, ,, .	. 1704 Y.	617	L.T.P.
Castle, John, ,, .	. 1675 Y.	293	L.T.P.
Castle, Thomas, ,, .	. 1685 Y.	463	L.T.P.
Cater, John, ,, .	. 1725 Y.	792	L.T.P.
Chamberlain & Johnson, ,, .	. *c.* 1734.	853	L.T.P.
Chapman, Catesby, ,, .	. 1721 Y.	756	L.T.P.
Charsley, William, ,, .	. 1729 Y.	842	L.T.P.

Child, John, London	.	. 1700 Y.	586 L.T.P.
Child, Lawrence, ,,		. 1693 Y.	526 L.T.P.
Chrichtoune, George, Edinburgh	.	1664 F.	67 E.T.P.
Christie, William, ,,		. 1652 F.	52 E.T.P.
Claridge, Charles, London		. 1756 Y.	981 L.T.P.
Claridge, Joseph, ,,	.	. 1724 Y.	810 L.T.P.
Claridge, Thomas, ,,	.	. 1716 Y.	707 L.T.P.
Clark, Christopher, ,,	.	. 1661 Y.	206 L.T.P.
Clark, James, Edinburgh	.	. 1722 F.	124 E.T.P.
Clark, John, London	.	. 1661 Y.(?)132 L.T.P.	
Clark, Josiah, ,,		. 1690 Y.	514 L.T.P.
Clark, Richard, ,,	.	. 1696 Y.	535 L.T.P.
Clark, Thomas, ,,	.	. 1671 Y.	347 L.T.P.
Clark, William, ,,	.	. 1695 Y.	529 L.T.P.
Clark(e), William, ,,	.	. 1687 Y.	484 L.T.P.
Clark, William, ,,	.	. 1721 Y.	733 L.T.P.
Clark & Greening, ,,	.	. c. 1765.	1007 L.T.P.
Cleeve, Alexander, ,,	.	. 1688 Y.	457 L.T.P.
Cleeve, Alexander, ,,	.	. 1715 Y.	791 L.T.P.
Cleeve, Bourchier, ,,	.	. 1736 Y.	951 L.T.P.
Cleeve, Giles, ,,	.	. 1706 Y.	832 L.T.P.
Cliffe, Francis, ,,	.	. 1687 Y.	476 L.T.P.
Cockburn, Thomas, Edinburgh	.	1711 F.	114 E.T.P.
Cocks, Samuel, London	.	1819 Y.	1080 L.T.P.
Coke, John, ,,		. 1694 Y.	512 L.T.P.
Cole, Jeremiah, ,,	.	. 1676 Y.	316 L.T.P.
Cole, John, ,,	.	. c. 1722.	765 L.T.P.
Collet, Thomas, ,,	.	. 1735 Y.	862 L.T.P.
Collier, Joseph, ,,	.	. 1669 Y.	172 L.T.P.
Collier, Peter, ,,	.	. 1720 Y.	730 L.T.P.
Collier, Richard, ,,	.	. 1664 Y.	131 L.T.P.
Collier, Richard, ,,	.	. 1706 Y.	649 L.T.P.
Colman, William, ,,	.	. 1683 Y.	502 L.T.P.
Colson, Joseph, ,,	.	. 1668 Y.	179 L.T.P.
Compere, John, ,,	.	. 1696 Y.	563 L.T.P.
Cooch, William, ,,	.	. 1731 Y.	844 L.T.P.
Cooch, William, ,,	.	. 1775 Y.	1029 L.T.P.
Cooke, Isaac, ,,	.	. 1692 Y.	487 L.T.P.
Cooke, Samuel, ,,	.	. 1727 Y.	813 L.T.P.
Cooke, Thomas, ,,	.	. 1690 Y.	565 L.T.P.
Cooke & Freeman, ,,	.	. c. 1731.	824 L.T.P.
Cooper, Benjamin, ,,	.	. 1677 Y.	339 L.T.P.
Cooper, John, ,,	.	. 1681 Y.	378 L.T.P.
Cooper, John, ,,	.	. 1688 Y.	465 L.T.P.
Cooper, Thomas, ,,	.	. 1653 Y.	31 L.T.P.

Cooper, Thomas,	London .	. 1678 Y.	326 L.T.P.
Cormell, John,	,,	. 1683 Y.	410 L.T.P.
Cornhill, Gilbert,	,,	. 1669 Y.	164 L.T.P.
Cotton, Benjamin,	,,	. 1679 Y.	382 L.T.P.
Cotton, Jonathan,	,,	. 1704 Y.	624 L.T.P.
Cotton, Jonathan, Jr.	,,	. 1735 Y.	866 L.T.P.
Coulthard, Alexander, Edinburgh		1708 F.	110 E.T.P.
Coursey, John, London	.	. 1660 Y.	49 L.T.P.
Coursey, John,	,,	. 1685 Y.	430 L.T.P.
Cowderoy, Thomas, London		. 1689 Y.	473 L.T.P.
Cowling, William,	,,	. 1737 Y.	892 L.T.P.
Cowper, James, Edinburgh .		. 1704 F.	106 E.T.P.
Cox, John,	London .	. 1676 Y.	262 L.T.P.
Cox, Richard,	,,	. 1713 Y.	763 L.T.P.
Cox, William,	,,	. 1708 Y.	668 L.T.P.
Cranley, Charles,	,,	. 1692 Y.	508 L.T.P.
Cripps, Mark,	,,	. 1727 Y.	786 L.T.P.
Crooke, Robert,	,,	. 1738 Y.	907 L.T.P.
Crooke, William,	,,	. 1679 Y.	351 L.T.P.
Cropp, John,	,,	. 1677 Y.	305 L.T.P.
Cross, Abraham,	,,	. 1695 Y.	705 L.T.P.
Crosfeild, Robert,	,,	. 1701 Y.	646 L.T.P.
Cuthbertson, John, Edinburgh		. 1712 F.	115 E.T.P.
Cutlove, Thomas, London	.	. 1670 Y.	276 L.T.P.
Dackombe, Aquila, London		. 1742 Y.	913 L.T.P.
Daken, Robert,	,,	. 1698 Y.	555 L.T.P.
Dale, Richard,	,,	. 1709 Y.	667 L.T.P.
Darling & Meakin,	,,	. c. 1732.	843 L.T.P.
Davidsone, William, Edinburgh		. 1693 F.	90 E.T.P.
Davis, John,	London .	. 1715 Y.	795 L.T.P.
Deacon, Thomas,	,,	. 1675 Y.	272 L.T.P.
Deane, Robert,	,,	. 1692 Y.	582 L.T.P.
Deane, William,	,,	. 1731 Y.	864 L.T.P.
de Jersey, William,	,,	. c. 1738.	970 L.T.P.
de St. Croix, John,	,,	. 1729 Y.	833 L.T.P.
Digges, William,	,,	. 1699 Y.	569 L.T.P.
Ditch, William,	,,	. 1666 Y.(?)	107 L.T.P.
Dodd, Edward,	,,	. 1669 Y.	188 L.T.P.
Dodson, Thomas,	,,	. 1769 Y.	1026 L.T.P.
Donne, John,	,,	. 1683 Y.	422 L.T.P.
Donne, John,	,, (Probably same as above)		488 L.T.P.
Donne, Joseph,	,,	. 1727 Y.	804 & 807 L.T.P.
Donne, Richard,	,,	. 1677 Y.	292 L.T.P.
Dove, John,	,,	. 1676 Y.	295 L.T.P.

Drew, Edward,	London	.	.	1728 Y.	836 L.T.P.
Drinkwater, Richard,	,,	.	.	1712 Y.	682 L.T.P.
Drinkwater, Timothy,	,,	.	.	1666 Y.(?)	146 L.T.P.
Duffield, Peter,	,,	.	.	1645 Y.	41 L.T.P.
Durand, Jonas,	,,	.	.	1692 Y.	557 L.T.P.
Dyer, John,	,,	.	.	1680 Y.	432 L.T.P.
Dyer, Lawrence,	,,	.	.	1648 Y.	135 L.T.P.
Dyer, Lawrence,	,,	.	.	1704 Y.	691 L.T.P.
Dyer, Richard,	,,	.	.	1699 Y.	558 L.T.P.
Dymoke, William,	,,	.	.	1696 Y.	531 L.T.P.
Eden (Eddon), William,	London	.	.	1689 Y.	470 L.T.P.
Edgar, James,	Edinburgh	.	.	1709 F.	111 E.T.P.
Edgar, Robert,	,,	.	.	1684 F.	85 E.T.P.
Edgar, Thomas,	,,	.	.	1654 F.	54 E.T.P.
Edwards, John,	London	.	.	1718 Y.	742 L.T.P.
Edwards, John,	,,	.	.	1739 Y.	963 L.T.P.
Elderton, John,	,,	.	.	1693 Y.	507 L.T.P.
Elliott, Bartholomew,	,,	.	.	1738 Y.	891 L.T.P.
Ellis, Samuel,	,,	.	.	1721 Y.	746 L.T.P.
Ellis, William,	,,	.	.	1702 Y.	606 L.T.P.
Ellis, William,	,,	.	.	1726 Y.	778 L.T.P.
Ellwood, William,	,,	.	.	1693 Y.	540 L.T.P.
Elwick, Henry,	,,	.	.	1707 Y.	775 L.T.P.
Emes, John,	,,	.	.	1673 Y.	244 L.T.P.
Emes, John	,,	.	.	1700 Y.	578 L.T.P.
Englefield, Wm. J.	,,	.	.	1875 Y.	1091 L.T.P.
Engley, Arthur,	,,	.	.	1710 Y.	672 L.T.P.
Everard, George,	,,	.	.	1696 Y.	532 L.T.P.
Everett, James,	,,	.	.	1711 Y.	694 L.T.P.
Ewen (or Yewen), John,	,,	.	.	1700 Y.	585 L.T.P.
Excell, James,	,,	.	.	1718 Y.	751 L.T.P.
Facer, Samuel,	London	.	.	1675 Y.	243 L.T.P.
Fairhall, Joshua,	,,	.	.	1684 Y.	405 L.T.P.
Farmer, William,	,,	.	. c.	1744.	914 L.T.P.
Farmer, William,	,,	.	.	1765 Y.	1014 L.T.P.
Fasson, John,	,,	.	.	1725 Y.	826 L.T.P.
Fasson, John,	,,	.	.	1753 Y.	964 L.T.P.
Fasson, Thomas,	,,	.	.	1783 Y.	1048 L.T.P.
Fasson, William,	,,	.	.	1758 Y.	977 L.T.P.
Faulkner, Thomas,	,,	.	.	1678 Y.	321 L.T.P.
Feild, Henry,	,,	.	.	1693 Y.	528 L.T.P.
Feildar, Henry,	,,	.	.	1704 Y.	673 L.T.P.
Ferguson, Alexander,	Edinburgh	.	.	1660 F.	?55 E.T.P.

Ferguson, Alexander, Edinburgh	.	1678 F.	?77 E.T.P.
Ferguson, John,	,,	1678 F.	82 E.T.P.
Fiddes, James, London	.	1754 Y.	1003 L.T.P.
Findlay, Robert, Edinburgh	.	1717 F.	?104 E.T.P.
Fisher, Paul, London	.	1798 Y.	1071 L.T.P.
Fletcher, Richard, ,,	.	1677 Y.	312 L.T.P.
Fly & Thompson, ,,	. c. 1737.		874 L.T.P.
Fly, Timothy, ,,	.	1710 Y.	675 L.T.P.
Fly, William, ,,	.	1676 Y.	328 L.T.P.
Fontain, James, ,,	.	1752 Y.	961 L.T.P.
Ford, Abraham, ,,	.	1719 Y.	717 L.T.P.
Foster, Benjamin, ,,	.	1706 Y.	639 L.T.P.
Foster, Benjamin, ,,	.	1730 Y.	847 L.T.P.
Foster, John, ,,	.	1735 Y.	897 L.T.P.
Foster, Joseph, ,,	.	1757 Y.	1047 L.T.P.
Foster, William, ,,	.	1675 Y.	386 L.T.P.
Fountain, Thomas, ,,	.	1626 Y.	36 L.T.P.
Foxon, William, ,,	.	1723 Y.	846 L.T.P.
Freeman, Henry, ,,	.	1665 Y.	124 L.T.P.
French, Alexander, ,,	.	1657 Y.	10 L.T.P.
French, John, Sr. ,,	.	1630 Y.	9 L.T.P.
French, John, Jr. ,,	.	1686 Y.	456 L.T.P.
Frith, Henry, ,,	.	1675 Y.	242 L.T.P.
Frith, Thomas, ,,	.	1693 Y.	601 L.T.P.
Froome, William, ,,	.	1760 Y.	987 L.T.P.
Fryers, Sir John, Bart. ,,	.	1692 Y.	498 L.T.P.
Gardiner, John, Edinburgh .	.	1764 F.	143 E.T.P.
Gardiner, Richard, London .	.	1669 Y.	177 L.T.P.
Gardiner, Thomas, ,, .	.	1679 Y.	364 L.T.P.
Garioch, Patrick, ,, .	.	1735 Y.	880 L.T.P.
Garmentin, William, Edinburgh	.	1613 F.	26 E.T.P.
Gibbs, James, London .	.	1741 Y.	917 L.T.P.
Gibbs, William, ,, .	.	1804 Y.	1077 L.T.P.
Gibson, Edward, Edinburgh	.	1719 F.	122 E.T.P.
Giffin, Thomas, London .	.	1709 Y.	681 L.T.P.
Giffin, Thomas, ,, .	.	1759 Y.	1006 L.T.P.
Gillam, Everard, ,, .	.	1702 Y.	637 L.T.P.
Gillam, William, ,, .	.	1698 Y.	550 L.T.P.
Gisburne, James, ,, .	.	1691 Y.	640 L.T.P.
Gisburne, John, ,, .	.	1696 Y.	536 L.T.P.
Glazebrook, James, ,, .	.	1676 Y.	270 L.T.P.
Gledstane, George, Edinburgh	.	1610 F.	20 & 21 E.T.P.
Glover, John, ,,	. c. 1737.		?136 E.T.P.
Goble, Nicholas, London .	.	1680 Y.	374 L.T.P.

Godfrey, Joseph Henry, London .	1807 Y.	1081	L.T.P.
Goldie, Joseph, Edinburgh . .	1633 F.	40	E.T.P.
Goodman Edward, London . .	1669 Y.	157	L.T.P.
Goodman, Harry, ,, . .	1693 Y.	510	L.T.P.
Goodwin, Thomas, ,, . .	1707 Y.	671	L.T.P.
Gosling, Thomas, ,, . .	1720 Y.	794	L.T.P.
Graham, Basill, ,, . .	1699 Y.	560	L.T.P.
Grahame, Alexander, Edinburgh .	1654 F.	60	E.T.P.
Gray, Richard, London . .	1682 Y.	396	L.T.P.
Gray & King, ,, . .	c.1718.	711	L.T.P.
Green, John Gray, ,, . .	1793 Y.	1068	L.T.P.
Green, William, ,, . .	1676 Y.	313	L.T.P.
Green, Wm. S. ,, . .	1725 Y.	827	L.T.P.
Greener, Thomas, ,, . .	1700 Y.	602	L.T.P.
Greenwood, John, ,, . .	1669 Y.	187	L.T.P.
Greenwood, Thomas, ,, . .	1759 Y.	997	L.T.P.
Gregge, Robert, ,, . .	1667 Y.	215	L.T.P.
Grendon, Daniel, ,, . .	1735 Y.	871	L.T.P.
Grenfell, George, ,, . .	1757 Y.	976	L.T.P.
Grier, John, Edinburgh . .	1701 F.	102	E.T.P.
Grigg, Samuel, London . .	1734 Y.	879	L.T.P.
Grimsted, John, ,, . .	1676 Y.	324	L.T.P.
Groce, Thomas, ,, . .	1737 Y.	876	L.T.P.
Groome, William, ,, . .	1798 Y.	1076	L.T.P.
Grove, Edward, ,, . .	1677 Y.	294	L.T.P.
Grunwin, Gabriel, ,, . .	1681 Y.	401	L.T.P.
Grunwin, Richard, ,, . .	1713 Y.	677	L.T.P.
Guld, John, Edinburgh . .	1677 F.	81	E.T.P.
Gurnell, John, London . .	1768 Y.	1023	L.T.P.
Guy, Samuel, ,, . .	1729 Y.	845	L.T.P.
Gwilt, Howell, ,, . .	1697 Y.	623	L.T.P.
Hagger, Stephen Kent, London .	1754 Y.	1017	L.T.P.
Hale (?Hare), George, ,, .	1675 Y.	245	L.T.P.
Halford, Simon, ,, .	1726 Y.	830	L.T.P.
Hall, William, ,, .	1657 Y.	128	L.T.P.
Hall, William, ,, .	1680 Y.	338	L.T.P.
Hall, William, ,, .	1687 Y.	447	L.T.P.
Hallifax, Charles, ,, .	1669 Y.	141	L.T.P.
Hamilton, Alexander, ,, .	1721 Y.	839	L.T.P.
Hamiltone, William, Edinburgh .	1613 F.	28	E.T.P.
Hamlin, John, London .	1678 Y.	329	L.T.P.
Hammerton, Henry ,, .	1706 Y.	642	L.T.P.
Hammond, George, ,, .	1693 Y.	515	L.T.P.
Hancock, Samuel, ,, .	1677 Y.	375	L.T.P.

Hinde, John,	London	. 1767 Y.	1024 L.T.P.
Hitchins, William,	,,	. 1705 Y.	663 L.T.P.
Hitchins, William,	,,	. 1759 Y.	984 L.T.P.
Hitchman, James,	,,	. 1701 Y.	593 L.T.P.
Hitchman, Robert,	,,	. 1737 Y.	877 L.T.P.
Hodge, Robert Peircy,	,,	. 1772 Y.	1025 L.T.P.
Hodgkins, Edward,	,,	. 1641 Y.	(?)62 L.T.P.
Hodgson, Thomas,	,,	. 1676 Y.	277 L.T.P.
Holley, John,	,,	. 1689 Y.	461 L.T.P.
Holman, Edward,	,,	. 1688 Y.	454 L.T.P.
Holmes, George,	,,	. 1742 Y.	908 L.T.P.
Home, John,	,,	. 1749 Y.	965 L.T.P.
Hopkins, Joseph,	,,	. 1660 Y.	(?) 92 or 99 L.T.P.
Hopkins, Thomas,	,,	. 1700 Y.	584 L.T.P.
Horrod, R.,	,,	. c.1664.	28 L.T.P.
Horrod, Thomas,	,,	. 1693 Y.	622 L.T.P.
Horton, William,	,,	. 1725 Y.	812 L.T.P.
Howard, William,	,,	. 1671 Y.	204 L.T.P.
Howard, William,	,,	. 1745 Y.	920 L.T.P.
Hudson, John,	,,	. 1770 Y.	1021 L.T.P.
Hughes, James,	,,	. 1691 Y.	493 L.T.P.
Hulls, John,	,,	. 1662 Y.	256 L.T.P.
Hulls, Ralph,	,,	. 1653 Y.	46 & 208 L.T.P.
Hulls, William,	,,	. 1717 Y.	712 L.T.P.
Hulse, Charles,	,,	. 1690 Y.	466 L.T.P.
Hume, George,	,,	. 1700 Y.	598 L.T.P.
Hunt, Thomas,	,,	. 1666 Y.	194 L.T.P.
Hunter, Alexander,	Edinburgh	. 1682 F.	84 E.T.P.
Hunter, William,	,,	. 1749 F.	140 E.T.P.
Hunton, Nicholas,	London .	. 1661 Y.	(?) 13 & 143 L.T.P.
Hunton, William,	,, .	. 1682 Y.	376 L.T.P.
Hurst, William,	,, .	. 1676 Y.	278 L.T.P.
Hux, Thomas,	,, .	. 1723 Y.	754 L.T.P.
Hux, William	,, .	. 1700 Y.	574 L.T.P.
Hyatt, Humphrey	,, .	. 1675 Y.	241 L.T.P.
Iempson, Solomon,	London .	. 1696 Y.	541 L.T.P.
Iles, Edward,	,, .	. 1674 Y.	257 L.T.P.
Iles, Robert,	,, .	. 1691 Y.	520 L.T.P.
Ingles, Jonathan,	,, .	. 1668 Y.	19 & 170 L.T.P.
Ingles, Samuel,	,, .	. 1666 Y.	199 L.T.P.
Ingley, Arthur (see Engley)			
Inglis, Archibald,	Edinburgh	. 1732 F.	130 E.T.P.
Inglis, Robert,	,, .	. 1663 F.	65 E.T.P.
Inglis, Thomas,	,, .	. 1616 F.	27, 29 & 30 E.T.P.

Inglis, Thomas, Edinburgh .	.	1647 F.	47 & 48 E.T.P.
Inglis, Thomas, ,,	.	1686 F.	87 E.T.P.
Inglis, Thomas, ,,	.	1719 F.	123 E.T.P.
Ingole, Daniel, London	.	1656 Y.	52 L.T.P.
Irving, Henry, ,,	.	1750 Y.	952 L.T.P.
Jackman, Nicholas, London	.	1699 Y.	612 L.T.P.
Jackson, Henry, ,,	.	1723 Y.	760 L.T.P.
Jackson, John, ,,	.	1674 Y.	282 L.T.P.
Jackson, John, ,,	.	1728 Y.	855 L.T.P.
Jackson, Robert, ,,	.	1780 Y.	1051 L.T.P.
Jackson, Samuel, ,,	.	1667 Y.	479 L.T.P.
Jackson, Samuel, ,,	.	1659 Y. (?)	11 L.T.P.
Jackson, William, ,,	.	1662 Y.	68 L.T.P.
Jacob, Richard, ,,	.	1668 Y.	166 L.T.P.
Jacomb (?Jacob), Robert, London		1660 Y.	236 L.T.P.
James, Anthony, London	.	1675 Y.	391 L.T.P.
James, Lewis, ,,	.	1670 Y.	184 L.T.P.
James, Thomas, ,,	.	1726 Y.	777 L.T.P.
Jefferys, Joseph, ,,	.	1757 Y.	986 L.T.P.
Jefferys, Samuel, ,,	.	1734 Y.	856 L.T.P.
Jenner, Anthony, ,,	.	1754 Y.	1015 L.T.P.
Jennings, Theodore, ,,	.	1713 Y.	680 L.T.P.
Johnson, Luke, ,,	.	1713 Y.	749 L.T.P.
Johnson, Nicholas, ,,	.	1667 Y.	332 L.T.P.
Johnson, William, ,,	.	1676 Y.	361 L.T.P.
Jolly, John, Edinburgh	.	1714 F.	117 E.T.P.
Jones, Charles, London	.	1786 Y.	1062 L.T.P.
Jones, Henry, ,,	.	1675 Y.	253 L.T.P.
Jones, John, ,,	.	1700 Y.	553 L.T.P.
Jones, John, Jr. ,,	.	1727 Y.	822 L.T.P.
Jones, Seth, ,,	.	1719 Y.	714 L.T.P.
Jones, Thomas, ,,	.	1755 Y.	990 L.T.P.
Jordan, John, ,,	.	1727 Y.	828 L.T.P.
Joseph, Henry, ,,	.	1736 Y.	906 L.T.P.
Joseph, Henry and Richard, London c.1787.			1054 L.T.P.
Joyce, John, London .	.	1683 Y.	393 L.T.P.
Jupe, John, ,,	.	1735 Y.	878 L.T.P.
Jupe, Robert, ,,	.	1697 Y.	621 L.T.P.
Jupe, Robert, ,,	.	1776 Y.	1040 L.T.P.
Kelk, Nicholas, London	.	1638 Y.	4 L.T.P.
Kelk, Thomas, ,,	.	1663 Y.	319 L.T.P.
Kellowe, Robert, Edinburgh	.	1715 F.	118 E.T.P.
Kendrick, John, London	.	1737 Y.	885 L.T.P.

Kendrick, William, London .	.	1670 Y.	291 L.T.P.
Kent, Edward, ,,	.	. 1677 Y.	385 L.T.P.
Kent, John, ,,	.	. 1718 Y.	736 L.T.P.
Kenton, John, ,,	.	. 1675 Y.	250 & 490 L.T.P.
King, James (Gray & King), London		1716 Y.	711 L.T.P.
King, John, London	.	. 1757 Y.	995 L.T.P.
King, Joseph, ,,	.	. 1682 Y.	379 L.T.P.
King, Richard, ,,	.	. 1714 Y.	723 L.T.P.
King, Robert, ,,	.	. 1698 Y.	648 L.T.P.
King, Thomas, ,,	.	. 1675 Y.	259 L.T.P.
King, William, ,,	.	. 1786 Y.	1057 L.T.P.
Kinnear, Andrew, Edinburgh	.	1750 F.	141 E.T.P.
Kirby, Thomas, London .	.	1722 Y.	806 L.T.P.
Kirke, Thomas, ,,	.	. 1728 Y.	773 L.T.P.
Kirton, John, ,,	.	. 1699 Y.	597 L.T.P.
Knight, Francis, ,,	.	. 1678 Y.	345 L.T.P.
Knight, James ,,	.	. 1675 Y.	261 L.T.P.
Knight, Robert, ,,	.	. 1770 Y.	1053 L.T.P.
Knight, Samuel, ,,	.	. 1703 Y.	689 L.T.P.
Laffar, John, London	.	1706 Y.	684 L.T.P.
Lancaster, Alexander, ,,	.	1711 Y.	750 L.T.P.
Lane, E., ,,	.	c.1671.	198 L.T.P.
Langford, John, ,,	.	1719 Y.	713 L.T.P.
Langford, Thomas, ,,	.	1751 Y.	969 L.T.P.
Langley, Adam, ,,	.	1656 Y.	(?) 91 L.T.P.
Langley, John, ,,	.	1716 Y.	727 L.T.P.
Langton, John, ,,	.	1731 Y.	865 L.T.P.
Laughton, John, ,,	.	1668 Y.	297 & 480 L.T.P.
Law, John, Edinburgh	.	1660 F.	? 61 E.T.P.
Law, Samuel, London .	.	1768 Y.	1020 L.T.P.
Lawrance, Edward, ,,	.	1713 Y.	741 L.T.P.
Lawrance, John, ,,	.	1684 Y.	426 L.T.P.
Lawrance, Stephen, ,,	.	1661 Y.	123 & 357 L.T.P.
Lawson, Daniel, ,,	.	1749 Y.	938 & 942 L.T.P.
Lawson, John, ,,	.	1713 Y.	688 L.T.P.
Lea, Francis, ,,	.	1651 Y.	18, 39 & 40 L.T.P.
Leach, Jonathan, ,,	.	1742 Y.	922 L.T.P.
Leach, Thomas, ,,	.	1677 Y.	304 L.T.P.
Leach, Thomas, ,,	.	c.1721.	725 L.T.P.
Leapidge, Edward, ,,	.	1699 Y.	568 L.T.P.
Leapidge, Thomas, ,,	.	1691 Y.	492 L.T.P.
Leeson, John, ,,	.	1644 Y.	15 L.T.P.
Leeson, John, ,,	.	1673 Y.	237 L.T.P.
Leggatt, Richard, ,,	.	1722 Y.	771 L.T.P.

Meriefield, Edward,	London	. 1716 Y.	770 L.T.P.
Merriweather, John,	,,	. 1718 Y.	720 L.T.P.
Merriweather, John,	,,	. 1747 Y.	936 L.T.P.
Middleton, Charles,	,,	. 1690 Y.	524 L.T.P.
Middleton, Thomas,	,,	. c.1673.	226 L.T.P.
Miles, Samuel,	,,	. 1726 Y.	776 L.T.P.
Miles, William,	,,	. 1715 Y.	706 L.T.P.
Millin, William,	,,	. 1776 Y.	1044 L.T.P.
Millman, John,	,,	. 1673 Y.	235 L.T.P.
Mills, Nathaniel,	,,	. 1639 Y.	47 L.T.P.
Mister, Richard,	,,	. 1802 Y.	1085 L.T.P.
Mitchell, Paul,	,,	. 1721 Y.	766 L.T.P.
Mitchell, Thomas, Edinburgh		. 1704 F.	107 E.T.P.
Moir, Alexander,	,,	. 1675 F.	(?)76 E.T.P.
Monk, Joseph, London	.	. 1757 Y.	1030 L.T.P.
Monteith, James, Edinburgh		. 1634 F.	41 E.T.P.
Monteith, James,	,,	. 1643 F.	44 E.T.P.
Morse, Henry,	London .	. 1675 Y.	265 L.T.P.
Morse, Robert,	,, .	. 1676 Y.	283 L.T.P.
Morse, Robert,	,, .	. 1702 Y.	643 L.T.P.
Morse, William,	,, .	. 1676 Y.	308 L.T.P.
Moser, Roger,	,, .	. 1806 Y.	1078 L.T.P.
Moulesworth, Peter,	,, .	. 1662 Y.	398 L.T.P.
Mountford, Joseph,	,, .	. 1680 Y.	421 L.T.P.
Munday, Thomas,	,, .	. 1754 Y.	978 L.T.P.
Munden (Wm.) & Grove (Edmund),			
London	.	. c.1760.	992 L.T.P.
Munroe, Andrew, Edinburgh		. 1677 F.	80 E.T.P.
Murray, William, London	.	. 1734 Y.	857 L.T.P.
Napier, Archibald, Edinburgh		. 1666 F.	68 E.T.P.
Napier, John,	,,	. 1700 F.	99 E.T.P.
Napton, Henry,	London .	. 1668 Y.	159 L.T.P.
Nash, Edward,	,, .	. 1717 Y.	755 L.T.P.
Neaton, John,	,, .	. 1714 Y.	699 L.T.P.
Nettlefold, William,	,, .	. 1785 Y.	1072 L.T.P.
Newell, Samuel,	,, .	. 1689 Y.	516 L.T.P.
Newham, John,	,, .	. 1699 Y.	581 L.T.P.
Newham, William,	,, .	. 1708 Y.	685 L.T.P.
Newman, Richard,	,, .	. 1747 Y.	926 L.T.P.
Nicholls, James,	,, .	. 1651 Y.	87 L.T.P.
Nicholls, James, Jr.,	,, .	. 1684 Y.	424 L.T.P.
Nicholls, William,	,, .	. 1685 Y.	417 L.T.P.
Nicholson, Robert,	,, .	. 1690 Y.	462 L.T.P.
Nicholson, William,	,, .	. 1720 Y.	728 L.T.P.

Norfolk, Richard, London . . 1736 Y. 902 L.T.P.
Norgrove, John,   ,, . . 1722 Y. 762 L.T.P.
North, George,   ,, . . 1693 Y. 539 L.T.P.
Norwood, William,   ,, . . 1727 Y. 815 L.T.P.

Okeford, Nicholas, London . . 1699 Y. 596 L.T.P.
Oliver, John,   ,, . . 1687 Y. 478 L.T.P.
Only, William,   ,, . . 1674 Y. 248 L.T.P.
Osborne, Charles,   ,, . . 1681 Y. 413 L.T.P.
Osborne, John,   ,, . . 1701 Y. 687 L.T.P.
Osborne, John,   ,, . . 1713 Y. 721 L.T.P.
Oudley, Robert,   ,, . . 1708 Y. 665 L.T.P.

Paddon, Thomas, London . . 1683 Y. 433 L.T.P.
Page, John,   ,, . . 1692 Y. 494 L.T.P.
Palmer, John,   ,, . . 1702 Y. 693 L.T.P.
Palmer, Thomas,   ,, . . 1672 Y. 459 L.T.P.
Palmer, William,   ,, . . 1743 Y. 911 L.T.P.
Paradice, Francis   ,, . . 1675 Y. 306 L.T.P.
Pargiter, William,   ,, . . 1658 Y. (?) 111 L.T.P.
Parker, Daniel,   ,, . . 1678 Y. 441 L.T.P.
Parker, Joseph,   ,, . . 1663 Y. 180 L.T.P.
Parker, Thomas,   ,, . . 1694 Y. 576 L.T.P.
Parker, Thomas,   ,, . . 1695 Y. 579 L.T.P.
Parkinson, John,   ,, . c.1680. 384 L.T.P.
Parr, Robert,   ,, . . 1703 Y. 352 L.T.P.
Partridge, Richard, ,, . . 1715 Y. 700 L.T.P.
Patasone, Walter, Edinburgh 1710 F. 113 E.T.P.
Patience, Robert, London . . 1734 Y. 883 L.T.P.
Pattinson, Simon,   ,, . . 1715 Y. 767 L.T.P.
Pawson, Richard,   ,, . . 1752 Y. 962 L.T.P.
Paxton, James,   ,, . . 1698 Y. 636 L.T.P.
Paxton, John,   ,, . . 1717 Y. 769 L.T.P.
Paxton, William,   ,, . . 1668 Y. 168 L.T.P.
Payne, John,   ,, . . 1725 Y. 789 L.T.P.
Paynell, John,   ,, . . 1677 Y. 290 L.T.P.
Peake, Richard,   ,, . . 1750 Y. 953 L.T.P.
Pedder, Joseph,   ,, . . 1727 Y. 821 L.T.P.
Peircey, Robert,   ,, . . 1722 Y. 858 L.T.P.
Peisley, George,   ,, . . 1718 Y. 709 L.T.P.
Peisley, Thomas,   ,, . . 1693 Y. 635 & 670 L.T.P.
Penman, David, Edinburgh . . 1693 F. 95 E.T.P.
Penn, Humphrey, London . . 1676 Y. 279 L.T.P.
Pepper, John,   ,, . . 1678 Y. 317 L.T.P.

Perchard, Hellary, London (or Hellier)	.	.	1709 Y.	661	L.T.P.
Perkins, Francis,	,,	.	. 1674 Y.	340	L.T.P.
Perris, Henry,	,,	.	. 1653 Y. (?)	29	L.T.P.
Perry, John,	,,	.	. 1743 Y.	909	L.T.P.
Perry, John,	,,	.	. 1765 Y.	1009	L.T.P.
Pettit, John,	,,	.	. 1683 Y.	415	L.T.P.
Pettiver, John,	,,	.	. 1677 Y.	349	L.T.P.
Pettiver, Samuel,	,,	.	. 1695 Y.	616	L.T.P.
Pettiver, William. Sr.	,,	.	. 1655 Y. (?)	74	L.T.P.
Pettiver, William, Jr.	,,	.	. 1676 Y.	322	L.T.P.
Phillips, Thomas,	,,	.	. 1727 Y.	784	L.T.P.
Phillips, Thomas,	,,	.	. 1795 Y.	1073	L.T.P.
Phillips, William,	,,	.	. 1719 Y.	841	L.T.P.
Phillips, William,	,,	.	. 1744 Y.	949	L.T.P.
Phillips, William,	,,	.	. 1750 Y.	1028	L.T.P.
Phipps, William,	,,	.	. 1743 Y.	945	L.T.P.
Pickard, Joseph,	,,	.	. 1691 Y. ?	500	L.T.P.
Pickering, Daniel,	,,	.	. 1723 Y.	811	L.T.P.
Pickfat, Thomas,	,,	.	. 1677 Y.	350	L.T.P.
Piddel, Joseph,	,,	.	. 1684 Y.	407	L.T.P.
Pierce, Tristram,	,,	.	. 1702 Y.	607	L.T.P.
Piggott, Francis,	,,	.	. 1736 Y.	886	L.T.P.
Piggott, John,	,,	.	. 1736 Y.	868	L.T.P.
Piggott, Thomas,	,,	.	. 1698 Y.	800	L.T.P.
Pilkington, Robert,	,,	.	. 1704 Y.	625	L.T.P.
Pitt & Dadley,	,,	.	. c.1781.	1043	L.T.P.
Pitt & Floyd,	,,	.	. c.1769.	1018	L.T.P.
Pitt, Richard,	,,	.	. 1747 Y.	924	L.T.P.
Plivey, William,	,,	.	. 1697 Y.	548	L.T.P.
Pole, Robert,	,,	.	. 1717 Y.	738	L.T.P.
Poole, Richard,	,,	.	. 1747 Y.	930	L.T.P.
Poole, Rowland,	,,	.	. 1717 Y.	782	L.T.P.
Porter, Luke,	,,	.	. 1679 Y.	327	L.T.P.
Porter, Thomas,	,,	.	. 1683 Y.	394	L.T.P.
Porteus, Robert & Thomas, London		c.1762.		999	L.T.P.
Powell, Thomas, London	.	.	1676 Y.	350A	L.T.P.
Pratt, Henry,	,,	.	. 1674 Y.	238	L.T.P.
Pratt, Joseph,	,,	.	. 1670 Y.	201	L.T.P.
Pratt, Joseph,	,,	.	. 1709 Y.	753	L.T.P.
Priddle, Samuel,	,,	.	. 1773 Y.	1039	L.T.P.
Prince, John,	,,	.	. 1697 Y.	583	L.T.P.
Puleston, James,	,,	.	. 1752 Y.	983	L.T.P.
Pusey, Edward,	,,	.	. 1676 Y.	314	L.T.P.
Pye, Roger,	,,	.	. 1737 Y.	882	L.T.P.

Quick, Edward, London	.	.	1687 Y.	451 L.T.P.
Quick, Edward, ,,	.	.	1708 Y.	657 L.T.P.
Quick, Edward, ,,	.	.	1735 Y.	900 L.T.P.
Quick, Hugh, ,,	.	.	1674 Y.	230 L.T.P.
Quick, John, ,,	.	.	1699 Y.	591 L.T.P.
Quissenborough, Samuel, London			1672 Y.	213 L.T.P.
Rack, Charles, London	.	.	1681 Y.	355 L.T.P.
Radcliff, Thomas, ,,	.	.	1671 Y.	210 L.T.P.
Rait, James, Edinburgh	.	.	1718 F.	121 E.T.P.
Ramsay, John, ,,	.	.	1659 F.	63 E.T.P.
Randall, Charles, London		.	1699 Y.	572 L.T.P.
Randall ,Edward, ,,		.	1677 Y.	333 L.T.P.
Randall, Edward, ,,		.	1715 Y.	696 L.T.P.
Randall, John, ,,		.	1723 Y.	747 L.T.P.
Randall, Robert, ,,		.	1748 Y.	955 L.T.P.
Raper, Christopher, ,,		.	1665 Y.	140 L.T.P.
Raves, William, ,,		.	1682 Y.	559 L.T.P.
Rawlinson, John, ,,		.	1675 Y.	249 L.T.P.
Rayne, Joseph, ,,		.	1693 Y.	530 L.T.P.
Read, Isaac, ,,		.	1743 Y.	940 L.T.P.
Reading, Roger, ,,		.	1668 Y.	175 L.T.P.
Reading, Theophilus, ,,		.	1675 Y.	6 & 263 L.T.P.
Rebate, John, Edinburgh		.	1588 F.	? 1 & 2 E.T.P.
Redhead, Anthony, London		.	1675 Y.	264 L.T.P.
Redhead, Gabriel, ,,		.	1662 Y.	? 50 L.T.P.
Redknap, Peter, ,,		.	1713 Y.	678 L.T.P.
Redshaw, John, ,,		.	1679 Y.	219 L.T.P.
Reeve, Isaac, ,,		.	1754 Y.	972 L.T.P.
Reid, Robert, Edinburgh		.	1718 F.	119 E.T.P.
Relfe, Edward, London		.	1668 Y.	202 L.T.P.
Render, Charles, ,,		.	1699 Y.	570 L.T.P.
Reynolds, John, ,,		.	1693 Y.	(?) 513 L.T.P.
Reynolds, Robert, ,,		.	1704 Y.	618 L.T.P.
Rhodes, Thomas, ,,		.	1721 Y.	734 L.T.P.
Richards, Timothy, ,,		.	1699 Y.	647 L.T.P.
Richards, William, ,,		.	1664 Y.	193 L.T.P.
Richardson, Charles, ,,		.	1667 Y.(?)	150 L.T.P.
Ridding, Thomas, ,,		.	1674 Y.	233 L.T.P.
Rider, Nathaniel, ,,		.	1675 Y.	331 L.T.P.
Righton, Samuel, ,,		.	1732 Y.	851 L.T.P.
Roberts, Abraham, ,,		.	1687 Y.	619 L.T.P.
Roberts, Edward, ,,		.	1679 Y.	425 L.T.P.
Roberts, Philip, ,,		.	1738 Y.	888 L.T.P.
Roberts, Thomas, ,,		.	1688 Y.	443 L.T.P.

Robins, Obedience, London .	.	1671 Y.	260	L.T.P.
Robinson, John,	,, .	. 1659 Y.	183	L.T.P.
Rogers, John,	,, .	. 1717 Y.	793	L.T.P.
Rogers, Philip,	,, .	. 1708 Y.	653	L.T.P.
Rolls, Anthony,	,, .	. 1645 Y.	96	L.T.P.
Rolt, John,	,, .	. 1716 Y.	710	L.T.P.
Rooke, George,	,, .	. 1668 Y.	152	L.T.P.
Rothwell, John,	,, .	. 1669 Y.	195	L.T.P.
Rowell, William,	,, .	. 1726 Y.	816	L.T.P.
Royce, Charles,	,, .	. 1684 Y.	423	L.T.P.
Rudduck, Philip,	,, .	. 1690 Y.	495	L.T.P.
Rudsby, Andrew,	,, .	. 1677 Y.	330	L.T.P.
Rudsby, Andrew,	,, .	. 1712 Y.	823	L.T.P.
Russell, John,	,, .	. 1677 Y.	275	L.T.P.
Sandford, Joseph, London .	.	1674 Y.	234	L.T.P.
Sandys, William,	,, .	. 1680 Y.	491	L.T.P.
Sandys, William,	,, .	. 1681 Y.	350B	L.T.P.
Saunders, John,	,, .	. 1674 Y.	239	L.T.P.
Saunders, Thomas,	,, .	. 1684 Y.	404	L.T.P.
Savage, John,	,, .	. 1699 Y.	620	L.T.P.
Savidge, John,	,, .	. 1678 Y.	369	L.T.P.
Scatchard, Robert,	,, .	. 1756 Y.	980	L.T.P.
Scattergood, John,	,, .	. 1732 Y.	859	L.T.P.
Scattergood, Thomas, ,,	.	. 1700 Y.	610	L.T.P.
Scattergood, Thomas, ,,	.	. 1736 Y.	873	L.T.P.
Scott, George,	,, .	. 1675 Y.	348	L.T.P.
Scott, William, Edinburgh .	.	c. 1735. (?)	135	E.T.P.
Scott, William,	,, .	. 1734 F.	38	L.T.P.
Seare (Sayers), Robert, London	.	1667 Y.	165	L.T.P.
Seaton, Samuel,	,,	. 1679 Y.	387	L.T.P.
Seawell, Edward,	,,	. 1779 Y.	1064	L.T.P.
Sellon, John,	,,	. 1740 Y.	935	L.T.P.
Sewdley, Henry,	,,	. 1706 Y.	658	L.T.P.
Shakle, John,	,,	. 1672 Y.	416	L.T.P.
Shakle, Thomas,	,,	. 1675 Y.	287	L.T.P.
Sharp, John,	,,	. 1692 Y.(?)	489	L.T.P.
Sharrock, Edmund,	,,	. 1737 Y.	881	L.T.P.
Shaw, John,	,,	. 1726 Y.	779	L.T.P.
Shayler, William,	,,	. 1734 Y.	849	L.T.P.
Sheppard, Samuel,	,,	. 1683 Y.	419	L.T.P.
Sheppard, Thomas,	,,	. 1705 Y.	654	L.T.P.
Sherwin, Joseph,	,,	. 1726 Y.	809	L.T.P.
Shorey, John,	,,	. 1683 Y.	390	L.T.P.
Shortgrave, Nathaniel,	,,	. 1687 Y.	452	L.T.P.

Shurmur, Richard, London	.	1678 Y.	346 L.T.P.
Sibbald, Alexander, Edinburgh	.	1605 F.	22 & 23 E.T.P.
Sibbald, James, "	.	1631 F.	33 E.T.P.
Sibbett, James, "	.	1600 F.	5 & 6 E.T.P.
Sibley, Henry, London	.	1682 Y.	372 L.T.P.
Sidey, Edward, "	.	1772 Y.	1027 L.T.P.
Silk, John, "	.	1627 Y.	2 L.T.P.
Silk, John, "	.	1693 Y.	499 L.T.P.
Silk, Vincent, "	.	1654 Y.	71 L.T.P.
Simms, Thomas, "	.	1675 Y.	337 L.T.P.
Simpson, Robert, Edinburgh	.	1631 F.	39 E.T.P.
Simpson, Thomas, "	.	1728 F.	126 E.T.P.
Skinn, John, London	.	1670 Y.	176 L.T.P.
Skinn, Thomas, "	.	1672 Y.	223 L.T.P.
Skinner, Robert, "	.	1738 Y.	889 L.T.P.
Slow, John, "	.	1672 Y.	231 L.T.P.
Slow, Joseph, "	.	1702 Y.	614 L.T.P.
Smalley, Samuel, "	.	1683 Y.	469 L.T.P.
Smalman, Arthur, "	.	1713 Y.	726 L.T.P.
Smalpiece, Richard, "	.	1682 Y.	397 L.T.P.
Smith, Anthony, "	.	1698 Y.	575 L.T.P.
Smith, Charles, "	.	1765 Y.	1011 L.T.P.
Smith, Edward, "	.	1680 Y.	467 & 468 L.T.P.
Smith, George, "	.	1651 Y.	353 L.T.P.
Smith, George, "	.	1712 Y.	676 L.T.P.
Smith, Henry, "	.	1724 Y.	787 L.T.P.
Smith, James, "	.	1732 Y.	840 L.T.P.
Smith, John, "	.	1675 Y.	252 L.T.P.
Smith, John, "	.	1685 Y.	420 L.T.P.
Smith, John, "	.	1702 Y.	613 L.T.P.
Smith, John, "	.	1724 Y.	788 L.T.P.
Smith, Joseph, "	.	1695 Y.	522 L.T.P.
Smith, Richard, "	.	1677 Y.	301 L.T.P.
Smith, Richard, "	.	1733 Y.	860 L.T.P.
Smith, Rowland, "	.	1734 Y.	948 L.T.P.
Smith, Samuel, "	.	1727 Y.	796 L.T.P.
Smith, Thomas, "	.	1675 Y.	258 L.T.P.
Smith, Thomas, "	.	1682 Y.	362 L.T.P.
Smith, Thomas, "	.	1686 Y.	436 L.T.P.
Smith, Thomas, (?) "	.	(?)	388 L.T.P.
Smith, Thomas, "	.	1705 Y.	632 L.T.P.
Smith, Thomas, "	.	1739 Y.	989 L.T.P.
Smith, Thomas, "	.	1755 Y.	1005 L.T.P.
Smith, Thomas, "	.	1761 Y.	1016 L.T.P.
Smith, William, "	.	1668 Y.	167 L.T.P.

Smith, William, London	.	1691 Y.	497 L.T.P.
Smith, William, ,,	.	1732 Y.	829 L.T.P.
Smith (Saml.) & Leapidge (Anne), London	.	. c.1728.	808 L.T.P.
Snape, William, London	.	1764 Y.	1013 L.T.P.
Snoxell, John, ,,	.	1675 Y.	251 L.T.P.
Spackman & Grant, ,,	.	c.1709.	662 L.T.P.
Spackman, Joseph, ,,	.	1749 Y.	982 L.T.P.
Spackman, Joseph & James, London	c.1782.		1045 L.T.P.
Spackman, Joseph & Co., ,,	c.1785.		1052 L.T.P.
Spateman, Samuel, London	.	1719 Y.	825 L.T.P.
Spencer, Thomas, ,,	.	1702 Y.	600 L.T.P.
Spicer, John, ,,	.	1699 Y.	631 L.T.P.
Spooner, Richard, ,,	.	1719 Y.	764 L.T.P.
Spring, Pendlebury, ,,	.	1717 Y.	724 L.T.P.
Spring, Thomas, ,,	.	1676 Y.	523 L.T.P.
Stafford, George, ,,	.	1730 Y.	820 L.T.P.
Stanton, James, ,,	.	1815 Y.	1089 L.T.P.
Stanton, Robert, ,,	.	1810 Y.	1082 L.T.P.
Steevens, James, ,,	.	1753 Y.	968 L.T.P.
Stevens, Jonathan, ,,	.	1744 Y.	915 L.T.P.
Stevens, Philip, ,,	.	1709 Y.	664 L.T.P.
Stevens, Thomas, ,,	.	1716 Y.	757 L.T.P.
Stevens, William, ,,	.	1697 Y.	552 L.T.P.
Stevens, William, ,,	.	1729 Y.	817 L.T.P.
Stile, John, ,,	.	1688 Y.	453 L.T.P.
Stone, Edward, ,,	.	1695 Y.	547 L.T.P.
Stout, Alexander, ,,	.	1733 Y.	872 L.T.P.
Stribblehill, John, ,,	.	1676 Y.	300 L.T.P.
Stribblehill, Thomas, ,,	.	1704 Y.	772 L.T.P.
Strickland, John, ,,	.	1703 Y.	703 L.T.P.
Sturrop, Robert, ,,	.	1677 Y.	389 L.T.P.
Sturt, Walter, ,,	.	1668 Y.	221 L.T.P.
Sturton, Anthony, ,,	.	1686 Y.	599 L.T.P.
Summers, John, ,,	.	1696–7 Y.	543 L.T.P.
Swanson, Thomas, ,,	.	1753 Y.	991B & 1108 L.T.P.
Sweatman, Nicholas, ,,	.	1698 Y.	561 L.T.P.
Sweatman, Samuel, ,,	.	1728 Y.	901 L.T.P.
Swift, Cornelius, ,,	.	1770 Y.	1036 L.T.P.
Swift, William Cornelius, London		1809 Y.	1088 L.T.P.
Swindell, Thomas, London	.	1705 Y.	802 L.T.P.
Syde, John, Edinburgh	.	1660 F.	(?) 59 E.T.P.
Syde, John, ,,	.	1680 F.	83 E.T.P.
Symmer, David, ,,	.	1692 F.	92 E.T.P.
Symontoun, James, ,,	.	1696 F.	97 E.T.P.

Tait, Adam, Edinburgh	. .	1747 F.	138 E.T.P.
Tait, John, ,,	. .	1700 F.	100 E.T.P.
Taudin, James (Jaques), Sr., London		1657 Y.	16 L.T.P.
Taudin, James (Jaques), Jr., London		1673 Y.	344 L.T.P.
Tayleour, Cornelius, Edinburgh	.	1610 F.	18 & 19 E.T.P.
Taylor, George, London	. .	1722 Y.	745 & 758 L.T.P.
Taylor, James, ,,	. .	1667 Y.	(?) 129 L.T.P.
Taylor, Samuel, ,,	. .	1731 Y.	850 L.T.P.
Taylor, Thomas, ,,	. .	1670 Y.	178 L.T.P.
Taylor, William, ,,	. .	1728 Y.	916 L.T.P.
Teale, John, ,,	. .	1675 Y.	255 L.T.P.
Templeman, Thomas, London	.	1667 Y.	122 L.T.P.
Tennent, George, Edinburgh	.	1706 F.	108 E.T.P.
Thomas, John, London	.	1698 Y.	545 L.T.P.
Thompson, Benedictus, London	.	1669 Y.	222 L.T.P.
Thompson, Robert, Edinburgh	. c.1631.		36 & 37 E.T.P.
Thompson, Thomas, London	.	1755 Y.	1004 L.T.P.
Thorne, Christopher, ,,	.	1675 Y.	247 L.T.P.
Tibbing, William, ,,	.	1662 Y.	334 L.T.P.
Tidmarsh, Ann, ,,	.	1728 Y.	803 L.T.P.
Tidmarsh, James, ,,	.	1701 Y.	615 L.T.P.
Tidmarsh, James, ,,	.	1734 Y.	852 L.T.P.
Tidmarsh, John, ,,	.	1713 Y.	697 L.T.P.
Tidmarsh, Thomas, ,,	.	1677 Y.	296 L.T.P.
Tillott, Robert, ,,	.	1676 Y.	286 L.T.P.
Tillyard, Thomas, ,,	.	1698 Y.	549 L.T.P.
Tisoe, James, ,,	.	1688 Y.	449 L.T.P.
Tisoe, James, ,,	.	1733 Y.	854 L.T.P.
Toms, Edward, ,,	.	1744 Y.	912 L.T.P.
Tonkin, Matthew, ,,	.	1749 Y.	941 L.T.P.
Tough, Charles, ,,	.	1654 Y.	(?) 57 L.T.P.
Tough, Charles, ,,	.	1687 Y.	442 L.T.P.
Townsend, Benjamin, ,,	.	1744 Y.	967 L.T.P.
Townsend, John, ,,	.	1748 Y.	928 L.T.P.
Townsend, J., & Reynolds, R., London	. c.1766.		1012 L.T.P.
Townsend, William, London	.	1699 Y.	644 L.T.P.
Traherne, Edward, ,,	.	1679 Y.	336 L.T.P.
Trapp, John, ,,	.	1695 Y.	731 L.T.P.
Trew, James, ,,	.	1667 Y.	227 L.T.P.
Trout, John, ,,	.	1689 Y.	464 L.T.P.
Turberville, Daubeny, ,,	.	1703 Y.	626 L.T.B.
Turner, William, ,,	.	1702 Y.	627 L.T.P.
Ubly, Edward, London	.	1716 Y.	759 L.T.P.

Ubly, John,	London	.	1748 Y.	944	L.T.P.
Ubly, Thomas,	,,	.	1741 Y.	896	L.T.P.
Underwood, George,	,,	.	1712 Y.	686	L.T.P.
Underwood, Matthew,	,,	.	1752 Y.	958	L.T.P.
Vaughan, John, London	.	.	1753 Y.	985	L.T.P.
Veitch, Richard, Edinburgh	.	.	1635 F. (?)	93	E.T.P.
Vernon, Richard, London	.	.	1635 Y. (?)	93	L.T.P.
Vernon, Samuel,	,,	.	1674 Y.	232	L.T.P.
Vibart, George,	,,	.	1668 Y.	273	L.T.P.
Vile, Thomas,	,,	.	1641 Y.	80	L.T.P.
Vile, Thomas,	,,	.	1664 Y.	106	L.T.P.
Vinmont, William,	,,	.	1678 Y.	310	L.T.P.
Vokins, Bartholomew, London	.	.	1670 Y.	182	L.T.P.
Waddel, Alexander, Edinburgh	.	.	1714 F.	116	E.T.P.
Wadsworth, William, London	.	.	1780 Y.	1060	L.T.P.
Waite, John,	,,	.	1670 Y.	224	L.T.P.
Waite, John,	,,	.	1706 Y.	688	L.T.P.
Waite, Thomas,	,,	.	1677 Y.	325	L.T.P.
Walker, Alexander, Edinburgh	.	.	1676 F.	74	E.T.P.
Walker, Edward, London	.	.	1682 Y.	380	L.T.P.
Walker, John,	,,	.	1713 Y.	695	L.T.P.
Walker, John,	,,	.	1748 Y.	957	L.T.P.
Walker, Patrick, Edinburgh	.	.	1607 F.	24	E.T.P.
Walker, Robert,	,,	.	c.1676. (?)	78	E.T.P.
Walker, Samuel,	,,	.	1660 F.	64	E.T.P.
Walker, William, London	.	.	1787 Y.	1079	L.T.P.
Waller, Robert,	,,	.	1779 Y.	1046	L.T.P.
Walmsley, Edward,	,,	.	1685 Y.	445	L.T.P.
Walmsley, John,	,,	.	1702 Y.	679	L.T.P.
Walton, Richard,	,,	.	1675 Y.	246	L.T.P.
Warkman, Richard,	,,	.	1697 Y.	546	L.T.P.
Warkman, William,	,,	.	1713 Y.	719	L.T.P.
Warren, John,	,,	.	1697 Y.	566	L.T.P.
Warren, Lawrence,	,,	.	1669 Y.	207	L.T.P.
Wass, Robert,	,,	.	1712 Y.	748	L.T.P.
Waters, Anthony,	,,	.	1685 Y.	544	L.T.P.
Waters, William,	,,	.	1670 Y.	289	L.T.P.
Watson, John, Edinburgh	.	.	1671 F.	71	E.T.P.
Watson, Joseph, London	.	.	1713 Y.	732	L.T.P.
Watterer, Thomas,	,,	.	1674 Y.	370	L.T.P.
Watts, John,	,,	.	1725 Y.	801	L.T.P.
Waylett, William,	,,	.	1701 Y.	609	L.T.P.
Webb, Richard,	,,	.	1685 Y.	458	L.T.P.

Webb, Thomas, London	.	. 1714 Y.	701 L.T.P.
Weir, John, Edinburgh	.	. c.1584.	3 & 4 E.T.P.
Weir, John, ,,	.	. 1701 F.	101 E.T.P.
Weir, Richard, ,,	.	. 1597 F.	14 & 15 E.T.P.
Weir, Robert, ,,	.	. 1646 F.	46 E.T.P.
Weir, Thomas, ,,	.	. 1596 F.	13 E.T.P.
Wescott, John, London	.	. 1669 Y.	171 L.T.P.
West, Moses, ,,	.	. 1677 Y.	285 L.T.P.
Wetter (?), William, ,,	.	. c.1666.	78 L.T.P.
Wharram, Ralph, ,,	.	. 1756 Y.	996 L.T.P.
Wheeler, Thomas, ,,	.	. 1692 Y.	692 L.T.P.
Whitaker, Benjamin, ,,	.	. 1691 Y.	485 L.T.P.
White, Daniel, ,,	.	. 1676 Y.	403 L.T.P.
White, John, ,,	.	. 1755 Y.	971 L.T.P.
White, Joseph, ,,	.	. 1747 Y.	927 L.T.P.
White, Philip, ,,	.	. 1778 Y.	1056 L.T.P.
White, Richard, ,,	.	. 1686 Y.	448 L.T.P.
White, William, ,,	.	. 1661 Y. (?)	72 L.T.P.
White, William, ,,	.	. 1751 Y.	954 L.T.P.
White & Bernard, ,,	.	. c.1721.	743 L.T.P.
Whittle, Francis, ,,	.	. 1715 Y.	715 L.T.P.
Whyte, George, Edinburgh	.	. 1676 F.	79 E.T.P.
Widdowes, John, London	.	. 1670 Y.	191 L.T.P.
Wiggin, Abraham, ,,	.	. 1707 Y.	651 L.T.P.
Wiggin, Henry, ,,	.	. 1679 Y.	373 L.T.P.
Wightman, William, ,,	.	. 1758 Y.	993 L.T.P.
Wigley, Thomas, ,,	.	. 1699 Y.	630 L.T.P.
Wildman, Richard, ,,	.	. 1728 Y.	831 L.T.P.
Wilkes, Richard, ,,	.	. 1708 Y.	655 L.T.P.
Willet, Edward, ,,	.	. 1681 Y.	409 & 412 L.T.P.
Willey, Mary, ,,	.	. 1760 Y.	988 L.T.P.
Williams, John, ,,	.	. 1675 Y.	299 L.T.P.
Williams, John, ,,	.	. 1724 Y.	819 L.T.P.
Williams, John, ,,	.	. 1729 Y.	903 L.T.P.
Williams, Robert, ,,	.	. 1689 Y.	482 L.T.P.
Wilson, Daniel, ,,	.	. 1690 Y.	481 L.T.P.
Wilson, John, Edinburgh	.	. 1732 F.	129 E.T.P.
Winchcombe, Thomas, London	.	1691 Y.	509 L.T.P.
Wingod, John, ,,	.	. 1748 Y.	934 L.T.P.
Wingod, Joseph, ,,	.	. 1721 Y.	774 L.T.P.
Winkworth, Moses, ,,	.	. 1671 Y.	218 L.T.P.
Winter, George, ,,	.	. 1701 Y.	608 L.T.P.
Withebed, Richard, ,,	.	. 1669 Y.	162 L.T.P.
Withers, Benjamin, ,,	.	. 1719 Y.	729 L.T.P.
Withers, William, ,,	.	. 1654 Y.	53 L.T.P.

Withers, William, London	.	.	1684 Y.	438 L.T.P.
Witter, Elizabeth, ,,	.	.	1691 Y.	475 L.T.P.
Witter, Samuel, ,,	.	.	1671 Y.	196 L.T.P.
Wood, Henry, ,,	.	.	1768 Y.	1019 L.T.P.
Wood, Robert, ,,	.	.	1671 Y.	200 L.T.P.
Wood & Hill, ,,	.	. c.1798.		1067 L.T.P.
Wood & Mitchell, ,,	.	. c.1742.		893 L.T.P.
Woodeson, John, ,,	.	.	1708 Y.	690 L.T.P.
Wormlayton, Fulk Humphrey, London	. . .	.	1701 Y.	588 L.T.P.
Wright, Alexander, Edinburgh	.		1732 F.	131 E.T.P.
Wright, John, London	.	.	1717 Y.	870 L.T.P.
Wright, Richard, ,,	.		1712 Y.	737 L.T.P.
Wright, Thomas, ,,	.		1683 Y.	399 L.T.P.
Wright, William, ,,	.		1764 Y.	1041 L.T.P.
Wyatt, John, ,,	.		1685 Y.	439 L.T.P.
Wyatt, John, ,,	.		1718 Y.	739 L.T.P.
Wyatt, Thomas, ,,	.		1723 Y.	761 L.T.P.
Wynne, John, ,,	.		1746 Y.	923 L.T.P.
Yates, Lawrence, London	.	.	1738 Y.	905 L.T.P.
Yates, Richard, ,,	.	.	1772 Y.	1031 L.T.P.
Yorke, Edward, ,,	.	.	1732 Y.	848 L.T.P.

CHAPTER THIRTEEN

ANALYTICAL INDEX TO THE DEVICES CONTAINED IN THE TOUCHES ON THE FIVE TOUCH-PLATES NOW IN EXISTENCE

IN indexing the touches from the point of view of the devices contained therein, the chief object has been to take the most important feature in the device as a whole, and under that feature the number of the touch as given in the numerical list in the previous chapter will be found. By the numbers of the touches their position on the touch-plates can easily be found. This can be seen from the table:

Touch-plate.	Touches.
1	1 to 351
2	352 to 614
3	615 to 849
4	850 to 1069
5	1070 to 1090

It will be found that some touches, more particularly those which are purely heraldic, are indexed under "Arms." It is no easy task to draw a hard-and-fast line, but as a rule those on a shield are to be found under "Arms."

The saving of time in using this list will be evident to any collector keen on identifying marks. Take, for instance, a touch which occurs once only on the touch-

plates as *an artichoke and a mullet*. From the index it is
No. 733, and the table just given shows it to be on the
3rd touch-plate, and about half-way down. To hunt
through 1,090 touches with no clue at all is a very slow
process. Some touches, such as the *fleur-de-lis* and a *lion
rampant*, occur frequently—the former twenty-six times,
the latter twenty-one times. In each case there is some
little differentiating mark which should make rapid
identification possible.

For abbreviations used in this list see page 244.

CHATS ON OLD PEWTER

			No.
Arm and hand with dagger . .	p.c.	GEO. HAMMOND	515
Arm (mailed) and sphere . .	—	HENRY FEILD	528
Arm (mailed) issuing from a coronet, holding 3 ladles	—	JOHN PRINCE	583
Arm, on a torse, holding a heart .	b.c.	T. H. (? THOS. HAWFORD)	85
Arm with bundle of rods, 1646 .	b.o.	ANTHONY ROLLS	96
Arms of London, with 2 swords .	—	THOMAS LEACH	725
Arms, a chevron (vair), and 3 griffins' heads erased	—	EDWARD QUICK	900
Arms, a chevron cotised indented and 3 lions, with 3 crosses paty on the chevron; and crest, a demi-lion holding a cross paty	—	WILLIAM HEALEY	960
Arms, a cross engrailed and a crescent on the cross. Also crescent in the quarter for difference. Crest, a two-headed eagle	—	SAMUEL HIGLEY	1033
Arms, a cross with 2 crosslets fitchy in chief, impaling 3 stags tripping	—	BURFORD & GREEN	929
Arms, a double-headed eagle with a crown in chief	—	JOHN BENSON	904
Arms, a fess between a goat's head couped and 3 scallop-shells in base	—	RALPH WHARRAM	996
Arms, a fess engrailed and 3 apples slipped in the stalks	—	HENRY APPLETON	943
Arms, a lion passant and 3 stars, impaling a chief ermine with a demi-lion on the chief	b.p.	THOMAS BOARDMAN	899
Arms, a lion passant and 3 fleurs-de-lis	—	RD. NORFOLK	902
Arms, a lion rampant . . .	b.p.	JOHN WYNN	923
Arms, a lion rampant, and in chief 3 mullets. Crest, a demi-lion	—	ROBERT SCATCHARD	980
Arms, a lion rampant, impaling party per bend sinister 6 martlets	—	JOHN HOME	965
Arms, a lion rampant, impaling party per bend sinister 6 martlets	—	NATHANIEL BARBER	1037
Arms, a rose and 4 fleurs-de-lis .	—	GEORGE HOLMES	908
Arms, a stag's head couped with a crown between the antlers	—	JOHN WILLIAMS	903
Arms, a trefoil and an orb of 8 mullets	—	WILLIAM PHIPPS	945
Arms, barry ermine and a lion rampant	—	JAMES GISBURNE	640

208

ANALYTICAL INDEX

ANALYTICAL INDEX

No.

Coronet, ducal, between fleurs-de-lis and 2 crosses paty; a cross paty and 2 crossed palm-branches below	—	JOSEPH & JAMES SPACKMAN	1045
Coronet (earl's) with, above, a mullet in a crescent	—	WM. SHAYLER	849
Coronet (earl's), with shield . .	p.l.c.	HENRY HATCH	302
Cranes, 3	b.o.	EDWD. TRAHERNE	336
Crescent	b.c.	E. G. (? ERASMUS GIBBONS)	65
Crescent	p.c.	THOS. BOYDEN	650
Crescent	b.o.	WM. TAYLOR	916
Crescent and a bird . . .	s.s.	S. W.	189
Crescent, and signs of Zodiac in border	b.o.	JOHN WILLIAMS	819
Crescent and rainbow . . .	b.c.	JOSEPH RAYNE	530
Crescent and star . . .	c.	W. M. (? WM. MABBOTT)	69
Crescent and 2 mullets . .	b.c.	JOHN NEATON	699
Crescent and 2 stars, with 87 .	—	W. HEATON	335
Crescent and 2 stars . . .	b.c.	JOSEPH KING	379
Crescent, crowned . . .	p.l.	ANT. SMITH	575
Crescent (or moon) and 7 stars .	b.p.	JOHN PAYNE	789
Crescent with 6 stars . . .	b.c.	WM. PALMER	911
Crescent with 6 stars . . .	—	JAMES BOOST	956
Crescents, 2, with ducal coronet above	—	ARTHUR ENGLEY	672
Crook, crowned, 1657 . . .	c.	ROBERT JONES	27
Cross, crosslet, and 3 crescents .	p.l.	BERNARD BABB	577
Cross, crosslet between 2 roses and 2 stags' heads	—	WILLIAM WIGHTMAN	993
Cross, flory, with 78 . . .	d.	R.B. (? RICE BROOKS, Jr.)	318
Cross, paty, 1674 . . .	s.b.c.	HUGH QUICK	230
Cross, with 5 lions rampant . .	—	EDW. YORKE	848
Crosses, paty, 3 . . .	bordered c.	ANDREW RUDSBY	330
Crown	s.b.c.	JOHN SKINN	176
Crown	b.c.	RICHARD GARDNER	177
Crown	b.o.	RICHARD DYER	558
Crown, with 77	s.p.s.	T. O. (?)	137
Crown, also angel and palm, with 73	pl.	THO. SKINN	223
Crown and a pear (?) . . .	—	JOHN EDWARDS	742
Crown and a tun, 1707 . .	b.c.	HENRY HAMMERTON	642
Crown and dolphin, with 96 . .	—	RICHARD CLARKE	535
Crown and horseshoe, 1676 . .	p.l.c.t.	C. C.	266
Crown and mitre . . .	l.b.c.	J. WIDDOWES	191

ANALYTICAL INDEX

215

ANALYTICAL INDEX

ANALYTICAL INDEX

			No.
Goat and wheatsheaf . . .	p.l.	THOMAS LEAPIDGE	492
Goat and wheatsheaf . . .	—	EDW. LEAPIDGE	568
Goat's head couped, transfixed with a spear, crown, and tent behind	—	WILLIAM COX	668
Goat's head erased and coronet .	s.b.c.	W. H.	359
Gog and Magog and bell . .	—	I. SAVIDGE	369
Golden Fleece	—	SAMUEL ELLIS	746
Golden Fleece between four rings and a fleur-de-lis	—	THOMAS SWANSON	1008
Grasshopper	$\dfrac{\text{p.o.}}{\text{p.l.c.}}$	RALPH HULLS	208
Grasshopper and crown . .	—	EDWARD RANDALL	365
Grasshopper, and o5 . . .	—	WILLIAM TURNER	627
Grasshopper, with 2 keys crossed and a roundel	—	PHILIP STEVENS	664
Greyhound	$\dfrac{\text{l.b.c.}}{\text{p.l.c.t.}}$	THO. HUNT	194
Greyhound coursing . . .	—	JOHN REDSHAW	219
Greyhound running, star above .	—	SAM. SALTER BOWLER	1038
Greyhound's head erased, on a torse, with a crown and LONDON	s.	— (? BARFORD)	145
Griffin	—	SIMON HALFORD	830
Griffin	—	JOSEPH MONK	1024
Griffin on a ragged staff . .	—	GEORGE GRENFELL	976
Griffin passant	b.c.	CHAS. ROYCE	423
Griffin sejant	—	W. SANDYS	827
Griffin sejant on a torse . .	—	WILLIAM SANDYS	491
Griffin, winged	p.l.c.t.	HENRY MORSE	265
Griffin's head couped with crown over	b.o.	LAWRENCE YATES	905
Griffin's head couped with snake in its mouth	p.o.	WILLIAM HULLS	712
Griffin's head ducally gorged on a torse	—	GEORGE NORTH	539
Griffin's head erased . . .	—	I. C.	32
Griffin's head erased and 2 frets .	—	THOMAS CLARIDGE	707
Griffin's head erased with 2 frets and a crown	—	RICHARD BARFORD	229
Griffin's head erased on a torse .	—	ROBT. LUPTON	1042
Griffin's head erased with a marquis's coronet above, and 2 stars	—	RICHARD YATES	1031
Griffin's head erased, with crown and 2 stars above	b.c.	ISAAC REEVE	972

ANALYTICAL INDEX

			No.
Griffin's head erased with a star, and 66	b.c.	S.A.	34
Griffin's head issuant from a crown	—	WILLIAM WRIGHT	1041
Griffins' heads (3) erased . .	b.p.	GILES CLEEVE	832
Gull	s.b.c.	JOHN BLAKE	562
Gun and carriage with 5 mullets .	o.	THO. JONES	990
Gunner and cannon . . .	p.l.	THO. BURGES	595
Guy, Earle of Warwick, with dragon's head	—	THOMAS WIGLEY	630
Hammer crowned, 1666 . .	b.c.	I. I.	116
Hammer crowned between 2 fleurs-de-lis	—	WILLIAM NORWOOD	815
Hammer with shears and 80 .	b.c.	H. T.	343
Hammer and 93	b.c.	I. P. (? JOSEPH PICKARD)	500
Handbell	—	THOS. WRIGHT	399
Handbell, 1679	b.c.	THOS. WAIGHT	325
Handcart and 99 . . .	b.c.	PETER CARTER	567
Hand and anchor . . .	b.c.	E. A.	56
Hand and crook, with 73 . .	p.s.	MOSES WINKWORTH	218
Hand and crowned anchor . .	p.l.	T. WATTERER	370
Hand and dagger . . .	s.b.c.	W. A.	43
Hand and key, crowned . .	p.l.c.	THO. CARY	429
Hand and thistle . . .	b.c.	GEO. SCOTT	348
Hand and thistle, crowned . .	—	IOHN YEWEN	585
Hand (left) crowned . . .	b.c.	JOSEPH COLLIER	172
Hand grasping a dove with olive branch	—	JOSEPH CLARIDGE	810
Hand holding a heart, 1714 . .	b.c.	JAMES EVERETT	694
Hand outstretched, with a knife on the palm, 1758	—	CHARLES CLARIDGE	981
Hand, sleeved, holding a marigold or daisy	—	EDWARD MERIEFIELD	770
Hand with a hammer and a barrel	—	STEPHEN KENT HAGGER	1017
Hand with a pawn . . .	—	JOHN DONNE	488
Hand with a slipped rose . .	b.p.	BOURCHIER CLEEVE	951
Hand with a weight or a book .	—	WILLIAM HANDY	884
Hand with battle-axe . . .	s.b.c.	JOHN CARPENTER	587
Hand with cup	p.l.	BASILL GRAHAM	560
Hand with dagger on a shield .	—	GEORGE PEISLEY	709
Hand with gillyflower . . .	—	WILLIAM PHILLIPS	841
Hand with gillyflower or pink .	—	WILLIAM PHILLIPS	949
Hand with gillyflower or pink .	—	THOMAS PHILLIPS	1073
Hand with globe and star or sun .	—	THOMAS STEVENS	757

ANALYTICAL INDEX

ANALYTICAL INDEX

CHATS ON OLD PEWTER

CHATS ON OLD PEWTER

			No.
Monument and 78	l.p.o.	JOSEPH SMITH	522
Moon and 7 stars	p.l.	JOHN JOHNSON	237
Mullet in base of a heart	b.c.	BENJN. COTTERELL (or COTTON)	382
Mullets	b.o.	WM. KENRICK	291
Muskets, 2, in saltire and a powder-flask	—	W. FARMER	1014
Negro's head	s.b.c.	T. H.	216
Neptune	—	GEORGE TAYLOR	745
Neptune with trident	—	GEORGE TAYLOR	758
Neptune with trident on a seahorse	s.b.c.	HENRY NAPTON	159
Nutmegs (?), 3, and 76	p.l.	RALPH BENTON	274
Oak leaves and acorn	s.b.c.	H. D.	360
Old Parr	—	ROBT. PARR	352
Ostrich	p.o. / p.l.	GILBERT CORNHILL	164
Ostrich	—	ROBT. & THO. PORTEUS	999
Owl	p.o. / p.l.	I. H.	130
Ox, with an open book, 1700	—	JOHN JONES, Sr.	553
Padlock, 1678	p.l.c.	ROB. LOCK	303
Palmer, a	—	WILLM. HALL	447
Palm-tree	—	E. LANE	198
Partridges, 3, and large mitre	—	RICHARD PARTRIDGE	700
Peacock	p.l.c.	WILL. HURST	278
Peacock in his pride	—	RICHARD WRIGHT	737
Peacock, 68	v.s.b.c.	B. B.	108
Pear	b.c.	W. P. (? WM. PEARCE)	139
Pear	—	JAMES TIDMARSH	852
Pear (?) with a heart, 1706	—	JOHN SPICER	631
Pear with 04	s.b.c.	JAMES TIDMARSH, Jr.	615
Pears, 3	b.c.	H. B. (? HENRY BRETTELL)	54
Pears, 3, and 3 roundels	p.l.	JAMES BRETTELL	477
Pegasus	b.c.	W. B.	66
Pegasus volant with star above	—	JOHN BROWN	1063
Pegasus winged	b.c.	WM. GREEN	313
Pelican in her piety	b.c.	F. P. (? FRANCIS PARSONS)	138
Pelican in her piety	—	JO. GRAY / JA. KING	711
Pelican in her piety, crowned	p.l.	THOMAS RIDDING	233
Pelican in her piety, 164–	—	W. (?)	77

ANALYTICAL INDEX

CHATS ON OLD PEWTER

				No.
Scales	. . .	s.b.c.	JOHN WAITE	224
Scallop shell	. . .	s.b.c.	PAUL MITCHELL	766
Scallop shell	. . . .	—	HENRY JOSEPH	906
Scallop shell	. . . .	—	HENRY & RICHARD JOSEPH	1054
Scallop shell	. . . .	—	J. STANTON	1089
Scallop shell and 5 pellets	.	p.l.	JAMES TREW	227
Scorpion stinging itself	. .	p.l.	WILLIAM MORS[E]	308
Sea-horse	. . . .	p.l.	SAMUEL SEATON	387
Seal, and fish	. . . .	o.⁄p.l.	FRA. DURNFORD	234
Sheep	. . . .	p. shield	WOOD & HILL	1067
Sheep and dog	. . . .	—	JONATHAN BONKIN	722
Sheep and 171–	shaped punch	JOHN MERRIWEATHER	720
Sheep (2) with long tails	. .	—	RICHARD HESLOPP	641
Shepherd and crook	. . .	b.c.	WM. RICHARDS	193
Shepherd, crook, and dog	. .	—	HUMPHREY HYATT	241
Shepherd, crook and sheep . .	s.c.	SAML. SHEPPARD	419
Shepherd with crook and dog	.	—	RICHARD HANDS	834
Shepherd, with sheep, piping to a shepherdess	—	THOMAS SHEPPARD	654
Shield with arms of Spencer, 1702	—	THOS. SPENCER	600
Shield with arms of the Cinque Ports	—	NATHANIEL BESSANT	603
Shield, with 5 bars ermine, 1702 .	—	JOHN KIRTON	597
Ship and anchor	b.o.	CATESBY CHAPMAN	756
Ship in full sail	. . . .	b.o.	I. C.	153
Ship in full sail	. . . .	p.l.	JOHN COOPER, LONDON	465
Ship in full sail	. . . .	—	JOHN TIDMARSH	697
Ship in full sail, 1775 . . .	—	THOMAS DODSON	1027
Skull and crossbones and porcupine	b.c.	F. L. (? FRANCIS LARKIN)	309
Skull, cloven, and porcupine	.	—	ROBERT MORSE	283
Skull, crowned	. . . .	o.	RALPH BROWN	160
Skull and an eye	s.b.c.	WM. WAYLETT	609
Snail and ducal coronet	. .	p.l.	WILLIAM BRAINE	356
Snake, a, coiled (?)	. . .	b.c.	THOS. COOPER, Jr.	326
Snake, a, nowed	p.l.c.	RICHD. MEDDOM	212
Snake, coiled, 1732	. . .	—	T.D., N.M. (THOS. DARLING, N. MEAKIN)	843
Snakes, 3, coiled on a shield	.	—	DANIEL WILSON	481
Soldier	. . . . .	—	WILLM. GIBBS	1077
Soldier, mounted, with drawn sword and D.C.	—	WILLIAM HOWARD	920

232

ANALYTICAL INDEX

233

			No.
Stork	b.p.	JOHN KENRICK	885
Stork with wings displayed . .	p.c.	JOHN STRICKLAND	703
Strake, 1663	b.c.	I. H.	99
Sugar-loaf and 76 . . .	s.b.c.	M. C.	358
Sun	o.	SAML. TURNER	1075
Sun-crowned . . .	p.o. / p.l.	WILLIAM PAXTON	168
Sun in splendour	—	THOMAS SAUNDERS	404
Sun in splendour and a snake .	—	SAMUEL GRIGG	879
Sun in splendour and a wheatsheaf	b.p.	SAMUEL MILES	776
Sun in splendour and a wheatsheaf	—	IOHN BLENMAN	797
Sun in splendour and a wheatsheaf	b.p.	ABRAHAM FORD	717
Sun in splendour, crowned .	—	H. BRASTED	534
Sun in splendour on an anchor .	b.c.	JERE. LOADER	156
Sun in splendour rising from clouds	b.c.	JOSEPH COLSON	179
Sun in splendour, with dove and olive branch	b.p.	THOMAS RHODES	734
Sun in splendour, with thistle and crown	—	THOMAS THOMPSON	1004
Sun in splendour, 1698 . .	p.l.	ROBERT ATTERSON	501
Sun, moon, and 7 stars . .	—	JOHN BRUMFIELD	919
Sun (or star), 1663 . . .	s.b.c.	T. S.	119
Sun shining on a marigold . .	—	JOHN PAXTON	769
Sun shining on a rose . . .	—	HENRY MAXTED	861
Sun shining on wheatsheaf .	b.p.	MARK CRIPPS	786
Sun, with wheatsheaf and a cock .	—	SAMUEL SPATEMAN	825
Swan swimming	l.s.	CHARLES LOADER	1050
Swan with collar and chain .	—	ALEXANDER LANCASTER	750
Swan with wings addossed .	p.l.	THOMAS COWDEROY	473
Swan with wings raised .	b.c.	CHAS. HALIFAX	141
Sword	v.s.b.c.	W. W. (? WM. WHITE)	72
Sword and pistol in saltire, with star	s.b.c.	WM. RAVES	559
Sword, crowned	s.b.c.	E. H.	62
Sword-hilt and crown . .	—	ABRAHAM WIGGIN	651
Sword, point downwards . .	—	WILLIAM GILLAM	550
Swords, crossed	p.l.	WILLIAM CROOK[E]	351
Swords, crossed, with crown and fleur-de-lis	—	THOMAS WEBB	701
Syringe and worm . . .	b.c.	WM. COLMAN	502
Talbot	—	BROWNE & SWANSON (THOMAS SWANSON)	991

234

			No.
Unicorn rampant . . .	—	JOSEPH FOSTER	1047
Unicorn rampant and arms of City of London	—	ROBERT DAKEN	555
Unicorn rampant, with collar and chain	—	THOMAS BARNES	835
Univorn sejant on a torse and a star	—	ROBERT SKINNER	889
Unicorn supporting a headpiece .	—	IOHN SELLON	935
Unicorn's head, erased . .	p.l.c.	WILL. ADAMS	280
Unicorn's head, erased . .	p.l.	JOSEPH ROOKER	367
Vase of flowers	b.o.	JOHN LAUGHTON	480
Vase of flowers	—	THOMAS LANGFORD	969
Venus on a shell	b.c.	FRANCIS CLIFFE	476
Wheatsheaf	b.c.	RALPH MARSH	37
Wheatsheaf and a plough . .	—	EDWARD TOMS	912
Wheatsheaf and a rose . . .	—	JOHN WYATT	739
Wheatsheaf and a sun . . .	b.p.	WILLIAM MILES	706
Wheatsheaf and dove . . .	—	EDWD. LOCKWOOD	1055
Wheatsheaf, crowned . . .	p.l.c.	J. GRIMSTED	324
Wheatsheaf in a crown . .	s.c.	I. W.	455
Wheatsheaf, 63	p.c.	I. H.	136
Wheel	s.b.c.	STEPHEN BRIDGES	527
Wheel, crowned, 1723 . . .	p.l.	JOHN CARR	752
Wheel of Fortune . . .	b.o.	EDWD. QUICK	451
Wheel, 1697	s.b.c.	JOHN CARR	537
Windlass and well . . .	b.c.	RICHD. JACOBS	166
Windmill	b.c.	WM. GREEN	313
Windmill, 1640	oct.	NATHANIEL MILLS	47
Winged figure	b.c.	THOS. PORTER	394
Woman in gown, standing . .	—	ROBERT WALLER	1046
Wood, with sun shining . .	—	JOHN WOODESON	690
Woolsack	—	WILLIAM WALKER	1079
Woolsack (?) and 63 . . .	b.c.	I. R.	117
Woolsack crowned . . .	b.c.	DAVID BROCK	604
Worm of a still	s.c.	E. A.	418
Worm of a still	s.c.	RICHD. SPOONER	764
Worm of a still	b.c.	JOHN COWLEY	838
Worm of a still crowned . .	b.c.	NATH. MEAKIN, Jr.	1000
Wreath of flowers . . .	—	FRANCIS LITCHFIELD	571
Wrench and 76	b.c.	OBEDIENCE ROBINS	260
Wyvern above a star of 8 points within a crescent	—	WILLIAM COOCH	844

BIBLIOGRAPHY

A complete bibliography of the various books consulted by the writer when engaged on *Pewter Plate*, first published in 1904, and revised and enlarged in the second edition published in 1910, is there given. The following lists are classified according to the countries:—

ENGLISH, SCOTTISH, AND WELSH

Church Plate of Caermarthenshire. Rev. J. T. Evans.
Church Plate of the County of Dorset. Rev. J. E. Nightingale.
Church Plate of the County of Rutland. R. C. Hope.
Church Plate of Gloucestershire. Rev. J. T. Evans.
Church Plate of the County of Herefordshire. The Hon. B. S. Stanhope and H. C. Moffatt.
Church Plate of Pembrokeshire. Rev. J. T. Evans.
Church Plate of Radnorshire. Rev. J. T. Evans.
Church Plate in Yorkshire (East Riding). J. M. Fallow.
Church Plate of the Diocese of Carlisle, with the Makers and Marks. R. S. Ferguson.
Church Plate of Leicestershire, An Inventory of. Rev. A. Trollope.
Church Plate of the County of Wiltshire. Rev. J. E. Nightingale.
"Church Plate in Somerset, An Inventory of," in *Proceedings of the Somerset Archæological Society*, vols. xliii–xlix.
Memorials of the Goldsmiths' Company. Sir Walter S. Prideaux.
History of the Pewterers' Company (2 vols.). Charles Welch.
Memorials of London and London Life. H. T. Riley.
Livery Companies of the City of London. W. Hazlitt.
Old Base-metal Spoons. F. G. Hilton Price.
Archæologia, vol. liii, for article on "The Spoon and its History," by C. J. Jackson.
Old Scottish Communion Plate. Rev. T. Burns.
Pewter Plate. 1st edition, 1904. 2nd edition, 1910. (This edition contains facsimiles of the five Touch-plates still preserved by the Pewterers' Company.)
Scottish Pewter Ware and Pewterers. L. Ingleby Wood.
Pewter and the Amateur Collector. (Dealing chiefly with American pewter.) E. J. Gale.

FRENCH PEWTER

Catalogue du Musée de Cluny.
Études sur l'Étain. Germain Bapst.

CHATS ON OLD PEWTER

Dictionnaire de l'Ameublement. Havard. Under *Estaimier* and *Étain.* (This work
    is accessible in an English translation.)
Les Arts du Moyen Age. V. du Sommerard.
Dictionnaire du Mobilier français. Viollet-le-Duc. Under the headings of
    Assiette, Bénitier, Cuiller, Ecuelle, Fourchette.
Dictionnaire Raisonné Universel des Arts et Métiers. Lyon, 1801.
Encyclopédie Roret—Le Potier d'Étain.

GERMAN PEWTER

A very full bibliography of German works on pewter is to be found in the
    monumental volume by Herr Demiani, of Leipzig. It is in the main
    concerned with the Edelzinn, of which he has been such an indefatig-
    able collector, but in the works referred to by him there will be found
    much of general interest.

Zink, Zinn und Blei. Karl Richter.

SWISS PEWTER

Nos anciens et leurs œuvres. Published in Geneva.
Bossard, Dr. Gustav. "Schweizer Zinnkannen Kulturgeschichte" (*Jahrbuch
    des Schweizer Alpenklubs.* 43 Jahr).

SUPPLEMENTARY LIST OF BOOKS CONSULTED BY THE EDITOR (1949)

BRITISH

Old Pewter, its Makers and Marks. Howard H. Cotterell. London, 1929.
Pewter Craft. F. J. Glass. London, 1927.
Causeries on English Pewter. A. F. de Navarro. London, 1911.

GERMAN

Nürnberger Zinn. Erwin Hintze. Leipzig, 1921.

AMERICAN

American Pewter. J. B. Kerfoot, Boston, 1924.
Pewter in America. Ledlie I. Laughlin, Boston, 1940.

GENERAL

National Types of Old Pewter. H. H. Cotterell. Boston, 1925.
Pewter down the Ages. H. H. Cotterell. London, 1932.

GLOSSARY

Acorn-knopped. Spoons with an acorn at the end of the stem.

Aiken's metal. A variety of plate metal, but containing no bismuth.

Alliage (Fr.) } An intimate mixture of two or more metals effected by fusion.
Alloy

Ampulla (Fr. *ampoule*). A small vessel for incense or for the oil for extreme unction.

Apostle spoons. Spoons with knops intended for figures of the Apostles. They are very rare in pewter.

Appliqué. A piece of metal cut out and fastened to another is said to be applied or appliqué.

Ashberry metal. A hard alloy, containing nearly 25 per cent. of antimony, which gave very sharp castings. It was used for forks, spoons, teapots, etc.

Badges. Pewter or leaden signs worn on the outer garment by beggars, pilgrims, porters.

Ball and Wedge. In its earliest form this type of thumb-piece was used in England on baluster measures of the seventeenth century and earlier. A later and variant form was used in Scotland for adorning baluster measures of the late eighteenth and early nineteenth centuries.

Ball-knopped. Spoons with a small ball at the end of the stem.

Baluster-knops. A type of knops on spoons with a tiny button on the end of the baluster. They are found on sixteenth-century spoons.

Beaker. A drinking-vessel, with sides tapering outwards from the base.

Bénitiers. Vessels for containing holy water. Usually surmounted by a crucifix or a figure of the Blessed Virgin Mary. Made either to hang on the wall or to stand, or sometimes both.

Bimbelotier. A toy-maker.

Bismuth. A metal sometimes called tinglass, added to pewter to make it harder.

Black metal. An alloy consisting of tin with 40 per cent. of lead.

Bleeding-dishes } Bowls to contain blood. They are often graduated so as to
Blood-porringers } show in ounces the quantity taken.

Booge (Fr. *bouge*). The curved part of a plate between the rim and the bottom.

Britannia metal. An alloy of tin, antimony, and copper.

Broc. A large measure or vessel for wine.

Bud or *Bud and Wedge.* A type of thumb-piece found on English baluster measures of the late seventeenth and early eighteenth centuries.

Burettes. Pewter cruets or small bottles for sacramental wine, or for water.

Burning-on. A method of joining two pieces of lead or pewter. Hot metal is poured on the join till the temperature is raised enough for the pieces to fuse and unite.

Burnisher (Fr. *brunissoir*). A tool for giving a fine, smooth surface free from scratches. They are made of agate, silex, or bloodstone. Steel also may be used.

Candle-box. A wall-box to contain candles.

Canette. A measure.

Cardinals' Hats. A name given to dishes resembling these formal hats.

Cassolette. A vessel or box for perfumes, with a perforated cover to allow the diffusion of the scent.

Chalice (Latin *calix*). A sacramental cup.

Chapnet ⎫
Chapnut ⎭ A name applied to a certain kind of salt-container.

Chopines ⎫
Choppines ⎬ Synonyms for cruet.
Choppineaux ⎭

Chopin (Fr. *chopine*). A Scottish measure containing 6 gills.

Chrismatories. Vessels for consecrated oils.

Cistils. Little boxes, generally square or oblong.

Cloff ⎫
Cluff ⎭ Scrap-metal.

Coffin. A mould for containing the paste of a pie.

Costrel. A harvest or pilgrim's bottle, generally of wood or earthenware.

Counterpane. A plate of pewter on which the York pewterers stamped their touches.

Cri. The name given to the crackling sound emitted by tin, and by good pewter, when bent.

Cruet. Small sacramental vessels on feet, with lids, usually found in pairs, one marked A. for *Aqua*, the other V. for *Vinum*.

Cymaise ⎫ Pewter vessels used for presentation purposes, usually with swing
Cymarre ⎭ handles.

Danske pots. Danish pots. They may have been pots perfectly cylindrical in shape, like the Norwegian tankards, but no details of them are known to the writer.

Diamond-pointed knop. A name given to an early type (fifteenth century) of spoon.

Double Volute. The name given to a type of thumb-piece which bears a resemblance to the Ionic Volute capital in architecture.

Ear-dishes. Shallow dishes with flat projecting handles like ears.

Ecuelles or *Escuelles.* The French name for porringers.

Embryo shell. A type of thumb-piece in the form of a cockle-shell, but without the radiating ridges on its upper surface.

GLOSSARY

Equisetum hiemale. Pewter-wort. A plant which used to serve as a means of scouring pewter.

Esquelles. *Cf.* Squillery. Vide *Ecuelles*.

Estaimier. A pewterer. The word comes from the O.Fr. *estaim*. The modern French for "to tin" is *étamer*.

Estain. The French for pewter of the best quality.

Étain aigre. Second-quality tin.

Étain commun. Tin mixed with 15 per cent. of lead.

Étain doux. Pure tin, and 6 per cent. of brass.

Étain mort. Pewter of poor quality containing a large percentage of lead.

Étain plané. English tin, with 3 per cent. of copper added, and a small quantity of bismuth.

Étain sonnant. Hard and sonorous pewter, but inferior to *étain plané*.

Ewer (Fr. *aiguière*). A jug.

Fine. The name of standard pewter in England.

Flagon. The name usually given to large tankards with lids.

Florentine dishes. Dishes used for serving up meat where no crust was used.

Gadroon or *Godroon*. A geometric ornament consisting of curved lines radiating from a centre, the space between them being *repoussé* as a rule.

Galena. A lead ore, a native sulphide, which sometimes contains a small percentage of silver.

Galley dish ⎫
Galley saucer ⎬ Articles of which the shape is now unknown.

Garnish. A complete set of pewter vessels, consisting of 12 platters, 12 dishes or cups, and 12 saucers, or small flat plates.

Goddard (Fr. *godet*). A drinking-cup.

Grate (Fr. *gratter*). To scrape.

Grater. A scraping tool.

Gut (Fr. *gut*). Vessels for holding wine.

Hammerhead. The name given to a type of thumb-piece which, as its name implies, is in the form of a hammerhead, laid sideways on a wedge-shaped section on the lids of baluster measures of seventeenth century and possibly earlier.

Hanap (O.H.G. *hnapf*; A.S. *hnæpp*). Properly a goblet, especially the vessel from which the chief guest was served.

Hawksbill. A large ewer.

Heart-case. A case usually of lead, sometimes of pewter, in which a heart was embalmed and preserved for easier transmission for burial in a distant place.

Hexagonal knops. A common type of knop found on sixteenth-century spoons.

Hollow-ware. The name given to large pots, measures, tankards, and flagons.

Horned head-dress. A type of fifteenth-century spoon.

Horse-hoof knop. A rare type found on sixteenth-century spoons.

Kaiserteller. An ornamental platter with representations of one or more emperors.

CHATS ON OLD PEWTER

Latten (Fr. *laiton*). A brass alloy.

Lay
Lea } Tin mixed with lead, and thus allayed or alloyed.
Ley

Lay-men }Men who worked in lay-metal.
Ley-men

Limbeck. A still.

Lion knop. A form found in sixteenth-century spoons. The lion is represented sejant.

Loggerheads. Circular inkstands made of pewter, usually with a flat platter-like base, and a hinged cover for the ink-well.

Maidenhead. A form of knop found on fifteenth- and sixteenth-century spoons.

Maîtres de forge. Pewterers whose qualification was their ability to make a bowl and a dish with a hammer.

Maîtrise (Fr.)} A piece of work executed as a test-piece to qualify the
Masterpiece } executant as a "Master."

Monk's head. A type of knop found on early sixteenth-century spoons.

Monstrance. A shrine in which the consecrated Host is presented for the adoration of the people, either during the celebration of the Mass, or in a procession.

Mutchkin. A Scottish measure containing 3 English gills.

Peak. Is presumed, from the contexts in which it is found, to be lead.

Pechkrüge. Wooden tankards, with pewter inlaid work, waterproofed with pitch.

Pale. A name given to solder.

Pane. That part of the hammer which gives the blow on the object.

Peg-tankard. A tankard with pegs to mark divisions at regular intervals on the inside, usually near the handle.

Planish. To condense, smooth, and toughen a plate of metal by blows of a hammer.

Pied-de-biche. A seventeenth-century type of spoon, so called because the end is doubly split.

Pitcher. A vessel with a handle and an open spout.

Plate-metal. Metal of good quality used for making plates.

Platter. An absolutely flat disk of metal with a rim.

Pointillé. Ornament done by pricking the pewter with a sharp-pointed tool.

Porringer. A porridge dish; hence, a small deep vessel with upright sides, a nearly flat bottom, and one or two ears or handles.

Potiers d'Étain. Pewterers.

Potiers de rond. Pewterers whose qualification was the making a vase with the body in one piece.

Potiers menuisiers. Makers of rings, toys, pilgrims' badges, and other small articles.

GLOSSARY

Pricket. A candlestick with a pointed spike upon which the candle was forced down when required for use.

Quaich \ A shallow circular drinking vessel, somewhat like a deep saucer.
Quaigh / (Scottish.)

Rape (Fr. *râper*). To reduce by means of a rasp.

Ravensbill. A ewer.

Repoussé. Worked by blows directed on the under side of a piece of metal by means of hammers and suitable punches.

Sadware. Heavy, flat articles, such as plates, dishes, chargers, and trenchers.

Saler (Fr. *salière*). A salt.

Sand-box. A box for fine sand, with a perforated lid, by means of which the sand was sprinkled on freshly-written documents so as to dry them quickly.

Scouring. The technical name for the cleaning of pewter.

Seal tops. A type of knop on spoons, resembling a seal.

Silvorum. A sham-silver alloy.

Slipped in the stalk. A variety of stump spoons, the "cut off" being slanting (sixteenth century).

Solder (Fr. *soudure*). An alloy of low melting-point used for joining two or more pieces of other metal.

Spear-grater. A tool used by pewterers for turning pewter.

Spinning. A lathe process by which a thin plate of metal, rotating rapidly, is forced to take the shape of a wooden core.

Spout-pot. A jug for beer.

Squillery. Scullery.

Stippled. Marked all over the surface with dots.

Stump-end. A rare type of sixteenth-century spoon.

Swage. A shaped anvil or stake upon which large dishes, such as well-dishes, were fashioned.

Tappit-hen. A Scottish vessel, originally of three Imperial pints capacity. The term is now applied to all sizes of the same type of vessel.

Temper. The name given to copper when alloyed with tin.

Thumb-piece. The name given to the lever by pressing on which, with the thumb, the lever is raised.

Thurndell (thirdendales or thriddendales). A pot with a capacity of about three pints.

Tokens. Small coin-like disks of metal formerly issued in France and in Scotland to intending communicants.

Touch. A stamp-mark impressed on ware by the maker.

Touch-plates. Plates of pewter on which the touches of pewterers were stamped, and so recorded.

Treen. Articles made of wood, such as plates, bowls, etc.

Trellis. The circular grid-like disk in which pewter was cast for the greater convenience in cutting up into smaller quantities.

Trifle. Pewter of common quality.

CHATS ON OLD PEWTER

Triflers. Men who made spoons, forks, buckles, buttons, and toys.
Wedge. A thumb-piece somewhat similar to the English "Ball and Wedge," but made without the ball, or from which the ball has been removed.
Wriggled. A decorative pattern produced by rocking the tool regularly is called "wriggled-work".
Writhen-knop. A rare form of knop found on sixteenth-century spoons.
Zinn (German). The equivalent for pewter.
Zinn-stahl. Modern pewter reinforced with steel wire where required, as in the stem and prongs of forks, and in the stem of spoons and ladles.

ABBREVIATIONS

M.M.	Makers' Marks.
H.M.	Hall-marks, or rather the marks in the small punches.
T.P.	Touch-plate.
L.T.P.	London Touch-plate.
E.T.P.	Edinburgh Touch-plate.
L.	Date of taking up Livery.
Y.	Date of joining Yeomanry.
H.	Height.
D.	Diameter at top.
d.	diameter at bottom.
de.	depth.

All in inches.

b.c.	beaded circle.
s.b.c.	small beaded circle.
b.o.	beaded oval.
s.b.o.	small beaded oval.
p.l.	palm leaves occur in the touch.
b.p.l.	between palm leaves.
p.l.c.	palm leaves crossed.
p.l.c.t.	palm leaves crossed and tied.
b.p.	between pillars.
l.h.	leopard's head.
l.h.c.	leopard's head crowned.
l.p.	lion passant.
l.r.	lion rampant.
b.s.	beaded shield.
p.s.	plain shield.
s.c.	small circle.
s.s.	small shield.
s.p.s.	small pointed shield.
di.	diamond.
s.di.	small diamond.
t.h.	talbot head.

AMERICAN PEWTER
IN THE EIGHTEENTH
AND NINETEENTH CENTURIES

by

HENRY J. KAUFFMAN

A1   PLATE

Maker: William Will, Philadelphia, 1764–1798. Shallow form, smooth wide rim. Diameter $5\frac{11}{16}''$. Said to be smallest known American smooth-rimmed plate. Mark on rim: "Wm Wll"

(Courtesy, Henry Francis du Pont Winterthur Museum)

CHAPTER FOURTEEN

A SURVEY OF AMERICAN PEWTER FORMS

IT is interesting to note that for about three hundred years before 1800, there was little if any change in the composition of pewter or the mode of manufacturing pewter objects. Before learning to roll any metals into sheets, craftsmen discovered that molten pewter (consisting of lead, tin and possibly a little antimony) could be poured into bronze molds for shaping parts of vessels or complete objects. The round parts were assembled by soldering, after which they were turned on a lathe to remove burrs and to condition the surface for final polishing. Finally, parts such as spouts and handles were attached, and the object was complete.

Production of pewter objects by casting was a satisfactory procedure in an era of hand craftsmanship, but it did have certain drawbacks. Alloys were soft, and although the vessels were smooth and bright when they were new, they soon became dented and dull. Production methods were slow and laborious. And, finally, since bronze molds were expensive, they were used for a long time, some being handed down from master to apprentice. Continued use of expensive molds produced a rigid inflexibility in style.

Despite all these drawbacks, the product of the pewterer in the eighteenth century had considerable charm and sometimes a bit of originality, and it withstood the wear and tear of the average household for many years. If it were damaged beyond use, the piece could be taken to a pewterer, who simply recast the damaged vessel into a new product.

Before embarking on a discussion of American pewter, it is important to recognize the fact that the earliest pewter objects (like the earliest silver, copper, brass and iron objects) were derived stylistically from contemporary European objects, particularly those from Holland, Germany and England. The dominant influence came from England, since most of the colonists came from there and not only brought English objects with them but also recreated objects in the style they had known in their homeland.

Collectors of American pewter are very fortunate in the English ancestry of their pewter forms, for pewter-making reached its zenith in England in the seventeenth and eighteenth centuries. The early years of the industrial revolution brought into existence a more affluent middle class, especially in England, and thus increased the demand for objects made of pewter with simple designs well suited for use and display in the home, the inn and the church. While German barons were drinking from ornamented tankards and eating from engraved plates, the English country folk were using simple functional pieces designed with a minimum of ornamentation, but beautifully proportioned to fit their intended use. Large dishes with flat broad rims were used for serving food on the table, while smaller plates were shared by two or three individuals. When not in use, the various utensils were displayed in cupboards and on mantels. The soft accents of color and polished brilliance of the pewter pieces reflected light from candles or from the fireplace, creating a contrast in light and shadow which was both rich and satisfying. These utensils with their simple forms were also well suited to the first substantial homes built in

Massachusetts and Virginia, and many were passed down from one generation to another before being stored in the attic or melted for bullets.

By far the greatest popular interest today is in pewter objects made for use in the home, although these objects are not necessarily the most expensive or the most sought after by advanced collectors. Among the objects made for the home one finds dishes, plates, basins, spoons, dippers, porringers, beakers, coffee and teapots, sugar bowls, salts, funnels, inkstands and miscellaneous articles such as sun dials, drawer pulls, buckles, hunting horns and fifes.

The standard terminology used for flatware (low objects made in one piece) is that adopted by Ledlie Laughlin (in his definitive book *Pewter in America*) from the great English authority on pewter, Howard Cotterell. It is Cotterell's belief that flat vessels over 10 inches in diameter should be called dishes and that similar objects 10 inches or less in diameter should be called plates (see Plate A1). Plates $6\frac{1}{2}$ inches or less in diameter were often used as butter plates, although a few were used as Communion patens. The same terminology applies to semi-deep plates and dishes. Deep bowls, called basins in old inventories, were used for serving soups and stews, not for washing one's hands and face. Basins range in size from 4 to 11 inches in diameter, and most of them have a narrow rim with a rounded reed on the outer edge.

Other than a range in diameter from 5 to 18 inches, American plates offer relatively little variety. The few examples having smooth rims are considered very desirable because they generally date from the eighteenth or early nineteenth century. Usually the most important factor in buying a plate or a dish is the mark (sometimes called a touch-mark) of the maker. Many of these marks are difficult to distinguish because they were poorly struck in the first place or have been worn away. It should also be noted that some unscrupulous merchants sell plates with forged marks of some highly desirable makers. The very large and unusually small sizes always demand premium prices.

One oval dish has been identified as an American product, and any subsequent finds in this category must be regarded as great rarities and desirable additions to any collection. No American examples are known to have an octagonal shape or the so-called Chippendale edge frequently found on flatware made in Europe.

The condition of a plate or dish (or any piece of pewter) is also a very important factor in determining its value. A plate with a uniform coating of oxidation is preferred to one that is pitted or one which has been harshly cleaned and buffed. Dents can be removed and holes repaired by craftsmen who specialize in this type of work.

As the gamut of American forms of pewter is examined, it becomes clear that one of the most attractive is the porringer. Incidentally, American porringers are more plentiful than their English counterparts. Most of the American examples have a bulbous bowl to which is attached a handle pierced with a variety of designs (Plate A2). Makers' marks are frequently struck on the top or bottom of the handle, while many porringers without marks can be attributed to American makers because of their similarity to marked specimens. A style with a basin type of bowl and a solid handle with only a simple hole for hanging was made in Newport, R.I., and in Pennsylvania. Very few of the Pennsylvania type were marked by the makers; outstanding exceptions are those made by Elisha Kirk at Yorktown (Plate A3). Although the mode of construction is not known for the bulbous type, a complete mold rather recently discovered proves that the basin type was cast in one piece. Small variations on the basin type are

A2

PORRINGER

Maker: Samuel Hamlin, Providence, R.I., 1771–1801. Diameter of bowl 5⅜″, depth 2″

(*Kauffman Collection*)

A3

PORRINGER

Diameter 5⅜″, depth 2⅛″. The maker of this porringer is unknown, but its size and shape suggest that it was made by Elisha Kirk at "Yorktown," Pa.

(*Kauffman Collection*)

A4

TEAPOT

Maker: William Will, Philadelphia, 1764–1798. Pear-shaped body with spout slightly curved; high domed lid; spool-shaped finial with graduated, stepped top; S-curved wooden handle with scrolled spur at top. Marked, inside bottom, "X" over "Wm Will" in serrated rectangle. Over-all height 6½", over-all width 8"

(Courtesy, Henry Francis du Pont Winterthur Museum)

A5

COFFEEPOT

Maker: William Will, Philadelphia, c. 1785. Circular foot on square base; incurving shaft above; urn-shaped body with elongated neck; high domed lid; black wooden handle formed of one large reverse curve and small C-curve, spur at top; long, slender spout with leaf decoration; rows of beading on foot, at midpoint of body, on lid and on finial. Height 16"

(Courtesy, Henry Francis du Pont Winterthur Museum)

attributed to procedures used in trimming and finishing them on a lathe. Late in the eighteenth or early in the nineteenth century, many porringers, called "initial" porringers, were made in New England. This name was applied to them because many have two initials cast into the bottom surface of the handle, presumably the initials of the maker. A few porringers have two handles and at least one is known with four.

The rich European heritage of American pewter led to the production of some fine beakers, although most American examples lack the cyma curve found in the base of European examples. Some of the early American beakers are as tall as $6\frac{1}{2}$ inches, with a base diameter of 4 inches. Pairs of decorative lines were often cut into the outer surface as the beakers were finished on the lathe. Later beakers generally became much shorter; many of these lack any decorative details, and only a few of them are signed.

American pewterers were advertising teapots as early as the middle of the eighteenth century, but most of the surviving examples were made late in the century. One of the finest forms in American pewter is the Queen Anne style teapot, which is often described as "pear-shaped" (Plate A4). Some examples of this type had feet (to keep the hot bottom of the pot away from the top of the tea table), a wooden handle and an insert of wood in the finial of the lid. The style continued into the nineteenth century but in a less attractive form and with a handle of metal which was frequently painted black. In the Federal period, some drum-shaped pewter teapots were copies of contemporary silver forms. Some of this latter type also have handles of wood; however, only a few have inserts of wood in the finial. Present knowledge indicates that William Will of Philadelphia made the only important American pewter coffeepots of the eighteenth century

(Plate A5). His product appears to be an elongated form of the Queen Anne teapot resting on a square base to disseminate heat and give the pot stability. Its wooden handle and beaded edges combine with the rich form to make it very attractive.

Only a few forms of sugar containers are known, the most attractive examples being made by William Will and Johann Christopher Heyne (Plate A6). Early pewter creamers followed silver forms, but the fragile handles and feet are less attractive in pewter than in silver.

Because of space limitations and the rarity of examples, we can do little more than mention such miscellaneous objects as spoons, boxes, funnels, dippers, etc. Unsigned examples of such objects are not uncommon, but signed examples are extremely rare. The large quantity of spoon molds available in the past indicates that thousands of spoons were made by pewterers and traveling tinkers (Plate A7). The life span of a spoon was very short, so the same metal was probably recast many times before such spoons lost their popularity and usefulness in the American home. It is important to note that the oldest piece of American pewter extant is the spoon made by Joseph Copeland, who lived in Virginia late in the seventeenth century. Souvenir reproductions of this spoon are sold at Jamestown today. A few attractive ladles have survived, some being marked by Lee, Weeks or Thomas Boardman. The most famous maker of ladles was William Will, who signed a number of his products.

Churches have always been loath to part with the pewter objects they own, so ecclesiastical pewter has always been a scarce commodity on the market. Again, many of the early examples were inspired by European prototypes. Flagons have tall, tapering sides with massive handles, domed lids and a molded base which makes them attractive and stable. The *pièce de résistance* for many collectors is any

A6   SUGAR BOWL
Height $4\frac{1}{2}''$, diameter $4\frac{3}{8}''$. A number of similar bowls were made in Pennsylvania in the last half of the eighteenth century
(*Kauffman Collection*)

A7   SPOON MOLD
English or American, 1650–1690. Brass; for making pewter spoons; extremely rare. Length $7''$
(*Courtesy, Henry Francis du Pont Winterthur Museum*)

A8   COMMUNION FLAGON

Maker: Johann Christopher Heyne, Lancaster, Pa., 1754–1780. This important vessel has an interesting admixture of English and Germanic styles. The thumbpiece and feet are Germanic and the handle is a typical English form used on tankards of the eighteenth century. Height $12\frac{1}{2}''$, top diameter $3\frac{1}{2}''$, bottom diameter $6\frac{1}{8}''$

ecclesiastical product of Johann Christopher Heyne, a German pewterer who worked in Lancaster, Pa. Heyne's flagons had a different flare at the bottom from those of the English style, and instead of having the usual molded base they were mounted on three cherub heads in the typical continental manner (Plate A8). The continental fashion was also continued in their thumbpiece, which is a round knob. The bottoms of the flagons are made of 6-inch plates, most of which have the imprint "I C H, Lancaster" (compare Plate A12). The design of Heyne's chalices was also in the continental manner. A large and attractive ball design used in the center of the stems is unlike any other design used by American craftsmen. Some distinguished chalices were made by Peter Young of Albany, N.Y.; however, fine specimens by any maker are rare, and the designs deteriorated in the nineteenth century. Some fine Communion cups, christening bowls and patens have survived, but they are very rare and the original use of some of these vessels is debatable.

The remaining American pewter objects in this survey might be regarded as belonging to the commercial world and the inn. They consist of tankards, pots (often called mugs) and measures. There seems little doubt that the most sought-after piece of American pewter is the tankard. This halo doubtless surrounds tankards because they are regarded as remnants of aristocratic living in the past and because they have a very imposing appearance (Plates A9 and A10). The earliest type had straight sides with a molded base and a domed or flat lid. A few examples have a lid with a serrated edge opposite the handle known as a crenate lid. Late in the eighteenth century the tankard with the "tulip" shape and the double-C handle was made in America, but it never achieved the popularity of the earlier style. Tankards range in size from a pint to $3\frac{1}{2}$ pints, with the quart size being the most numerous.

Very few tankards were made in the nineteenth century.

The pewter pot or mug follows the lines of the tankard and was essentially the same vessel without a lid. The earliest examples had straight sides with a molded base; a few had solid strap handles instead of hollow handles, and most of them contained either a pint or a quart (Plate A11). Occasionally an exceptional shape is found, such as the barrel-shaped mug made by Parks Boyd of Philadelphia. In the nineteenth century some small mugs were made by placing a handle on the common beaker form.

One of the real rarities in American pewter is the open-topped measure, commonly called a baluster measure. Quart and pint sizes are known to have been made by Timothy Boardman. The Boardman pattern closely resembles the English pattern, and unless the measure bears the maker's mark it is virtually impossible to determine whether it was made in England or in America.

Another vessel used exclusively for drinking was the liquor flask. It is a well-known fact that liquor was issued to the soldiers of the American Revolution, and they naturally had to have containers for their liquor. The most famous supplier of liquor flasks was the German pewterer in Lancaster, Johann Christopher Heyne (Plate A12). These flasks, also called dram bottles, have an unusually high prestige in collecting circles.

In most cases it is difficult to distinguish American pewter forms from contemporary English forms. Many experts can quickly and easily distinguish between the two because they are familiar with the minute details and subtle differences, but the only resource for the amateur is to examine the mark struck by the maker on his product. However, since the early American marks look like English marks, much practice and familiarity are necessary for making positive identifications. Several available

A9   QUART TANKARD

Maker: Henry Will, New York, 1761–1775. Height 6¾″, diameter at base 5″

(Kauffman Collection)

A10   TANKARD

Maker: William Will, Philadelphia, 1764–1798. Circular body
with incurving upper section, flaring lower section; circular
molded footed base; flattened domed lid; S-curve handle with
upstanding thumbpiece decorated with heart cut-out; narrow
decorative band applied to widest part of body. Height 8″

(Courtesy, Henry Francis du Pont Winterthur Museum)

A11   QUART MUG

Maker: Thomas Danforth III, Stepheny, Conn. and Philadelphia, Pa., 1777–1818. Height 6″, diameter at base 4¾″, diameter at top 4″. The generous handle is an outstanding feature of this fine mug

(*Kauffman Collection*)

A12   FLASK

Maker: Johann Christopher Heyne, Lancaster, Pa., 1754–1780.
Flat-sided circular bottle; thin flat oval base; molded ring on
each side; cylindrical neck and cap with threads. Also illustrated is the mark on the base: "I C H" in a scalloped
rectangle over "LANCASTER" in a rectangle. Height $5\frac{3}{8}''$,
width $4\frac{3}{4}''$, depth $2''$

(*Courtesy, Henry Francis du Pont Winterthur Museum*)

books include biographical sketches of American makers and reproductions of their marks.

The facts in this survey of American pewter have been accumulated from a long experience in collecting, attending lectures on the subject and discussing the various problems with other collectors. The student of pewter will quickly discern, however, that I have leaned heavily on the above-mentioned bible for pewter collectors, *Pewter in America*, by Ledlie Laughlin. All of us are indebted to Mr. Laughlin for his magnificent contribution to the field of pewter collecting, and I gratefully acknowledge my use of this resource in the preparation of this survey.

CHAPTER FIFTEEN

THE BRITANNIA PERIOD

IT is obvious that vessels made of pewter were a great improvement over the wooden ones they had replaced, but the onrushing industrial revolution was bringing into competition with pewter new objects made of pottery, glass and china. The pewterer had to meet the new challenge to survive, and the first step was to improve the metal.

A new alloy called Britannia was developed in Sheffield, England about 1770 by two men named Jessop and Handcock. The metal consisted of tin, copper, brass and antimony, the major portion being tin. It was formed by melting tin in an iron vat and raising it to a red heat. Next, molten copper, brass and antimony were stirred into the tin until the mixture was complete and perfect. The alloy was then poured into cast-iron casting boxes which formed slabs of metal 15 inches long, 6 inches wide and 1 inch thick. These slabs could then be recast in bronze molds to produce vessels similar to those made in the eighteenth century, or it could be rolled into sheets from which objects could be formed by stamping and spinning.

Before discussing the production of Britannia ware in America, a word is in order about its qualities. The elimination of lead and the addition of other metals to the tin resulted in a metal that was tough, long-wearing and more lustrous than pewter. This improved metal allowed a decrease in the thickness of the walls of vessels and thus a substantial reduction in the weight of the objects. The lighter objects must have delighted the housewife of the period, whose arms must have often become very weary lifting and moving heavy pieces of pewter. The new metal was also more resistant to denting and distortion than pewter. The metal in some of the old objects was so soft that they sagged out of shape from ordinary use on the table, and plates became bowed from standing on edge in a cupboard for a long time. The greatest gain in the new metal, however, was a brilliant luster which charmed the buyers into believing that Britannia compared favorably with sterling silver. When Britannia was polished, it was almost impossible for an expert to distinguish between the two metals by sight.

There always was a certain technological lag between Europe and America in the eighteenth and early nineteenth centuries, so several decades passed before the new metal was used here. Extensive experimentation was required, or craftsmen and technicians had to be smuggled out of England to start American production. By the turn of the nineteenth century objects were being cast in the new metal in America.

The introduction of the new metal in America did not bring a dramatic change to the forms and modes of the older pewter production. Many of the earlier forms continued to be produced in the nineteenth century, for people accustomed to them were not eager to discard them for new Britannia forms. A few Britannia craftsmen preferred to be called pewterers, and as late as the 1860's Benjamin Buckley and Edwin Curtis were called pewterers in a business directory of Meriden, Conn. The survival of this old trade in Meriden is particularly interesting because this town was one of the most important early centers of Britannia production in America. A quotation from the book *A Century of Meriden* indicates the trend of events there at the beginning of the nineteenth century:

The business [Britannia] was begun in this town [Meriden] about the year 1808, by Ashabel Griswold, or Squire Griswold, as he was familiarly known. He learned the trade from Captain Danforth of Rocky Hill, this state, together with Mr. Boardman who settled at Haddam, and Charles and Hiram Yale, who located in Wallingford. Mr. Griswold built the house, 50 Griswold street, now occupied by Mrs. Charles Collins. His shop stood south of the house, separated from it by a garden. As there is no stream at this point, he must have used, at the start, either hand or horse power. Here for a number of years he made Britannia pots and tea and tablespoons. The pots were cast in two pieces and then soldered together and the spouts and handles added in the same way. The pots after soldering were placed on a lathe and turned and polished, and a very good finish was given to the articles.

The articles formed by casting were susceptible of high polish and presented quite an attractive appearance if properly cared for by the purchaser. Table and teaspoons were cast then scraped and burnished by hand if for table use, or sold rough for cooking purposes.

The output of such a factory as that of Mr. Griswold could not have been very large. In 1830 he employed not more than ten or twelve men, and in examining his sales at that time it is found that total sales of one month did not exceed $2,500. The power was furnished by an old blind horse traveling around a beam which communicated with the floor above. Among the articles disposed of by him were cloth of different kinds, glass tumblers, stockings, whips, and yarns. These goods were undoubtedly taken by Mr. Griswold in exchange for his wares. His merchandise was sold mainly by peddlers, who penetrated all parts of New England and frequently journeyed South. We learn of one such itinerant who returned with nothing but goose feathers in exchange for the wares he had taken out; but feathers were a valuable commodity in those days and undoubtedly the exchange was a profitable one for the peddler. Barter was the usual method of dealing, and as one early manufacturer expressed it recently, "Money was a mighty scarce article." As there were no railroads until 1838, if any shipments were made direct to purchasers at a distance, it was necessary to cart them to Middletown or New Haven and ship by boat.

This interesting account of Mr. Griswold's business activities at the beginning of the Britannia period indicates that although a new metal had been developed, its full potential could not be realized by using the manufacturing methods of the eighteenth century. A new method of stamping parts between dies was tried, particularly to produce bases for candlesticks and bodies for teapots which were not round. The cost of dies and the inflexibility of designs limited the use of the stamping method, but much ingenuity was used in combining parts made by different techniques. By combining the techniques of casting and stamping a variety of forms was achieved, but the charm of the eighteenth-century ware was lost.

About 1825 a dramatic new method of production called metal spinning was accomplished on the lathe. This technique was used late in the eighteenth century in England, where a number of metals were spun, but Britannia was particularly well suited to the new production procedure. On the lathe was mounted a wooden chuck. This chuck was a model of the object or the part of the object to be produced. A disc of sheet metal (Britannia) was pinched into the lathe and as the disc rotated, a workman deftly applied pressure to it and caused it to conform to the shape of the chuck. Only spherical objects could be easily spun. Usually halves of objects were spun on one chuck, but several chucks might be used to form completely one part of a vessel. It should be noted that plates and dishes were never spun in the Britannia period.

The new process brought many changes to the Britannia business. The old-time craftsman who worked at his bench with only a few apprentices helping him was now faced with the modern concept of standardized parts and the specialization of trades. A man no longer made a complete vessel and stamped his name on it; instead, workers specialized in spinning, engraving, soldering, etc. After the vessel was finished, a company name like that of the Taunton Britannia Manufacturing Company was stamped on it, and all the individuality of the craftsman was lost. For a while some very attractive eagle designs were used in conjunction with the names of the manufacturers (Plate A13), but eventually a plain stamp with block letters in a rectangular cartouche identified the maker.

The new process of spinning not only brought a vast increase in the production of goods but also led to new designs. The top and bottom halves of teapots became duplicate parts which required only one chuck, and the design of many parts was influenced more by the manufacturing process than by the function of the vessel (Plate A14). On the other hand, the thin walls of objects manufactured by spinning were one of the definite gains made at that time.

It should also be noted that the industrial revolution was bringing more money into the pockets of the middle class, most of whom seemed to want a teapot, or possibly a tea service, of Britannia metal.

Pewter makers like Griswold, Dunham and Gleason seem to have swung with the times, and slowly changed from making objects of pewter by hand methods to manufacturing objects of Britannia by machinery. Some new companies also appeared on the horizon, such as the one owned by Messrs. Babbit and Crossman in Taunton, Mass. From a very humble start in the mid-1820's, this company grew into one of the biggest producers of Britannia ware. For about five years in the early 1830's it was known as the Taunton Britannia Manufacturing Company; later the company label was Leonard, Reed & Barton, and finally only Reed & Barton.

A13   MARK OF THOMAS DANFORTH III

Within a circle, an eagle with outspread wings facing right; body partly covered by shield; feet grasping olive branch (at left) and arrows (right); above eagle's head, in roman capitals, the initials "T. D"

(Courtesy, Henry Francis du Pont Winterthur Museum)

A14   TEAPOT

Maker: William McQuilkin, Philadelphia, 1840–1853. Height 8″, diameter 6″. This teapot, made of Britannia metal, was formed by spinning. Other craftsmen produced a similar form

(Kauffman Collection)

CANDLESTICKS

A16

Maker: Taunton Britannia Manufacturing Company, Taunton, Mass., 1830–1835. Height 6½", diameter of base 3½"

(Kauffman Collection)

LAMP

A15

Maker: Taunton Britannia Manufacturing Company, Taunton, Mass., 1830–1835. Height 8", diameter of base 4¾". Shares a common stem form with the two candlesticks in Plate A16, made by the same firm

(Kauffman Collection)

THE BRITANNIA PERIOD

Another famous producer of Britannia ware was Sellew & Co. of Cincinnati, Ohio. This company was organized in 1832 by Enos and Osman Sellew, who were joined in 1836 by a third brother named William. In their earliest years the Sellews manufactured forms typical of the earlier pewter era. In the Britannia period they produced a large number of candlesticks, for which they are famous today. In 1841 the company employed eight workmen, the value of their annual output was $12,840, and they shipped their products to many parts of the midwest.

There is yet another area, which must have been the capital of the Britannia business: Meriden, Conn. The work in that metal was so popular there that a street was named Britannia Street, and dozens of workmen were in some way connected with the production of objects from this bright new metal. An official listing of Meriden manufacturers in 1845 includes the information about eight Britannia firms shown in Table 1.

TABLE 1 *

Names of Manufacturers	Number of Hands	Capital Invested	Amount of Goods Manufactured
Bull, Lyman & Couch	7	$3,000	$9,000
James A. Frary	8	4,000	15,000
De Witt Kimberly	3	1,500	4,400
Enos H. Curtis	2	1,000	1,500
Edwin E. Curtis	2	600	1,000
Lemuel J. Curtis	2	1,200	3,200
Thomas R. Holt	8	5,000	10,000
Isaac C. Lewis	5	3,000	5,000

* Table 1 is based on information in *A Century of Meriden* (see Bibliography), used by kind permission of the Journal Publishing Company, Meriden.

Thus, thirty-seven men were employed by the several companies making Britannia ware in Meriden. In an earlier era they would all have been pewterers, but they had now become specialized as metal spinners, burnishers, engravers, Britannia workers, Britannia turners and Britannia fitters. Later most of these people worked for the Meriden Britannia Company, which was organized in 1852.

When considering objects made in the Britannia period, the reader must remember that vast quantities were manufactured in the 1830's, 40's and 50's. Because of this larger production and the shorter lapse of time, many more of these Britannia objects have survived than have pewter pieces from the eighteenth and early nineteenth centuries. Thus, Britannia pieces are less costly than the earlier, rarer and more charming pewter pieces.

From Table 2, which gives information on the output of the factory in Taunton (owned by Crossman, West & Leonard in 1830, by the Taunton Britannia Manufacturing Company in 1834), and from Table 3, dating from the ownership of the factory by Leonard, Reed & Barton in 1838, it is evident that the long-standing stability of the earlier pewter period had completely disappeared. The whims of fashion were raising and diminishing demand then just as now. For example, no caster frames were reported among the products of Crossman, West & Leonard in 1830, but 410 were reported in 1834 by their successors, the Taunton Manufacturing Company; 7,416 were reported in 1838. It is very obvious that in 1830 a fashionable table setting did not include a caster set, whereas by 1838 such a set was probably a "must" on every table on the eastern seaboard.

The absence of coffin plates in the report of 1834 and the production of 298 dozen in 1838 indicates that another new social custom had started, one which survives until today. When they were an innovation, it was said that no respectable citizen of New England could be buried without one.

THE BRITANNIA PERIOD

TABLE 2 *

Items	Number Shipped	
	1830	1834
Teapots	2,429	787
Lamps (pairs)	1,395	2,861
Sugar and cream sets	870	129
Coffeepots	760	62
Slop bowls	345	123
Looking-glass frames	143	20
Urns	64	43
Glasses	42	—
Tumblers	8	—
Caster frames	—	410
Tea sets	—	328
Candlesticks	—	77
Church cups	—	12
Church plates	—	42
Church tankards	—	31
Fruit dishes	—	24
Ladles (dozen)	—	21

* Tables 2 and 3 are based on information in *The Whitesmiths of Taunton* (see Bibliography), used by kind permission of the Harvard University Press.

TABLE 3

Items	Shipped
	1838
Caster frames (without bottles)	7,416
Tea sets	706
Teapots	2,749
Urns	143
Sugars and creamers	710
Coffeepots	359
Coffin plates (dozen)	298
Lamps	736
Slop bowls	74
Plates	82
Cups	60
Tankards	18
Bowls	12
Shaving boxes (gross)	2
Pepper caps (gross)	12

The large number of lamps reported in these tables calls for some comment. It seems that the great impetus for American lamp production came with the marketing of whale oil, a fine replacement for the fats and greases used in earlier lamps. Unlike the archetypal open lamp with wick of reed or rope, dating from antiquity, the type made of Britannia metal was closed and had one or a number of wicks inserted in tubes in the top to draw fluid upward by capillary action. The plate into which the tubes were soldered was attached to the oil container by threads, and could easily be removed when the lamp needed to be refilled.

The lamps consist of a base, a stem and a bowl to contain the oil. The bowls are bulbous, conical, cylindrical, urn-, lemon- or acorn-shaped. Most of the bases are convex, with attractive bands and ridges which provide a resistance to the sagging that could otherwise occur after many years of use. The stems vary in designs from very attractive to very unattractive. Some were cast and turned on a lathe and then fitted to spun or cast bowls and bases. The lamp illustrated in Plate A15, made by the Taunton Britannia Manufacturing Company, was produced in the finest tradition of the old pewterers. Many lamps were not marked by their makers because they were more difficult to mark than objects with big flat areas.

The annual reports of Britannia manufacturers also indicate that a fair number of candlesticks were made. As a matter of fact, some lamps were made to fit into candlesticks (this type of lamp was also made of metal or glass). Lamps and candlesticks also sometimes shared a common stem design (Plate A16). At least one instance is known in which identical stems were used in lamps and candlesticks; however, the stem in one was inverted for the stem in the other. Britannia candlesticks range in quality from the very attractive ones made by the Taunton Britannia Manufacturing Company to some very poorly designed ones by other makers. There is little evidence of influence from earlier fine sticks made in Europe and imported into America.

Of the remaining products of the Taunton Company and of Leonard, Reed & Barton, the most impressive are their tea services. Various components of a tea service, particularly the teapot, sugar bowl and creamer, were made in earlier times, but rarely, if ever, in sets. The social prestige attached in the nineteenth century to the possession of a complete tea service easily explains the great number of sets made by the various manufacturers. One tea service style made at Taunton was based on the urn shape (with handle, spout and lid attached). This set consisted of a teapot, coffeepot, sugar bowl, and cream pitcher. The handles were made of metal, and on the two pots they were painted black to simulate the wooden handles used on earlier pots. This style must have been very popular, for in the 1840's it was produced by more than one factory. A less attractive style, but one more costly to produce, was based on an urn shape with flat, faceted sides. This pattern could not be spun; the parts had to be stamped and then cleverly assembled so the joints could not be seen.

Another object of considerable interest is the coffee urn, which was made by a number of manufacturers. The capacity of the coffee urn was several times that of the coffeepot. It was a very important part of the social life of the period. The urn form was mounted on a flaring base, and coffee was dispensed through a faucet on which was mounted a handle which was both decorative and functional (Plate A17).

Britannia Communion sets consisting of a flagon, paten and two chalices were produced of fine metal, but were inferior in style to the ones produced in the pewter era. An exception to this poor styling were the attractive flagons made by Boardman and Company in the 1820's.

Among other interesting Britannia items are the attractive "lighthouse" coffeepots made and engraved by Israel Trask (Plate A18). These pots with tapering straight sides were not spun but fabricated from sheet stock, with a long joint under the handle or under the spout. This joint can usually be detected by examining the inside of the pot. In addition, some interesting shaving boxes were made by Ashbil Griswold, and a large number of coffeepots were made by Bailey & Putnam, Boardman & Hart (Plate A19), J. Danforth, J. B. Woodbury and others. The coffeepots made by these manufacturers were tall and bulbous, many measuring ten to twelve inches in height.

The pitchers made in great quantity by McQuilkin (Plate A20, page 272), Gleason, Boardman (with the Boardman lion mark), F. Porter and others deserve special mention. They range in size from $5\frac{1}{2}$ inches to 12 inches in over-all height. These vessels were made with or without lids. J. B. Kerfoot, in his book *American Pewter*, called the largest of the Gleason products a "magnificent" water pitcher, a compliment which is entirely justified from the present writer's point of view. Although these pitchers are not rare examples of grace, they are attractive, distinctively American, and functionally satisfactory.

Another vessel of the Britannia period much admired by Mr. Kerfoot is a sugar bowl made by G. Richardson. Kerfoot used a photograph of this bowl as the frontispiece of his book and lavished praise on it. He characterized it as a "plebeian" sugar bowl of the 1830's which stands with considerable grace among the "aristocratic rarities of the pre-Revolutionary period."

It is the opinion of most experts that there was a marked deterioration in style in the Britannia period, but from Mr. Kerfoot's point of view the cause of quality was not entirely lost. I agree.

A17   COFFEE URN
Maker: Roswell Gleason, Dorchester, Mass., 1822–1871.
Height 14″

(Courtesy, the Brooklyn Museum Collection)

COFFEEPOT

A18

Maker: Israel Trask, Beverly, Mass., 1825–1856. Height 12″. Trask was one of the few makers of Britannia to engrave his products

(William G. Himmelreich Collection)

COFFEEPOT

A19

Maker: Boardman & Hart, New York, 1827–1850. Height 11¼″, diameter 6″

(Himmelreich Collection)

CHAPTER SIXTEEN

AMERICAN PEWTER MAKERS

THIS list appeared in *American Pewter*, by John Meredith Graham II, and is reprinted by kind permission of the Brooklyn Museum.

Name of maker or firm	*Location*	*Approximate Working Dates*
BOSTON		
Austin, Nathaniel	Charlestown, Mass.	1763–1807
Austin, Richard	Boston, Mass.	1793–1817
Badger, Thomas	Boston, Mass.	1787–1815
Carnes, John	Boston, Mass.	1723–1760
Gleason, Roswell	Dorchester, Mass.	1822–1871
Green, Samuel	Boston, Mass.	1779–1828
Morey & Smith	Boston, Mass.	1857–1860
(D. B. Morey and Thomas Smith)		and later
Richardson, George	Boston, Mass.	1818–1828
Skinner, John	Boston, Mass.	1760–1790
Smith & Company	Boston, Mass.	1847–1849
(Thomas Smith, D. B. Morey, Henry White)		
Smith, Eben	Beverly, Mass.	1841–1856
Taunton Britannia Mfg. Co.	Taunton, Mass.	1830–1835
RHODE ISLAND		
Belcher, Joseph or	Newport, R.I.	1769–1776
Belcher, Joseph Jr.	Newport, R.I.	1776–1784
	New London, Conn.	after 1784
Billings, William	Providence, R.I.	1791–1806

Calder, William	Providence, R.I.	1817–1856
Day, Benjamin	Newport, R.I.	1744–1757
Hamlin, Samuel	Providence, R.I.	1771–1801
Jones, Gershom	Providence, R.I.	1774–1809
Melville, David	Newport, R.I.	1776–1793
Melville, Thomas	Newport, R.I.	1793–1796
Melville, Thomas 2nd	Newport, R.I.	1796–1824

THE CONNECTICUT VALLEY

Barns, Stephen	Probably Middletown or Wallingford, Conn.	1791–1800
Boardman, Thomas Danforth	Hartford, Conn.	1805–1850
Boardman, Thomas Danforth & Sherman	Hartford, Conn.	1810–1850
Boardman, Timothy & Company (sales agents for T. D. and S. Boardman)	New York, N. Y.	1822–1825
Boardman & Hart (sales agents for T. D. & S. Boardman	New York, N. Y.	1827–1850
Danforth, Edward	Middletown and	1788–1790
	Hartford, Conn.	1790–1794
Danforth, John	Norwich, Conn.	1773–1793
Danforth, Joseph	Middletown, Conn.	1780–1788
Danforth, Joseph, I and	Middletown, Conn.	1780–1788
Danforth, William	Middletown, Conn.	1792–1820
Danforth, Josiah	Middletown, Conn.	1825–1837
Danforth, Samuel	Norwich, Conn.	1793–1802
Danforth, Samuel	Hartford, Conn.	1795–1816
Danforth, Thomas, II	Middletown, Conn.	1755–1782
Danforth, Thomas, III	Stepney, Conn.	1777–1818
	Philadelphia, Pa.	1807–1813
Danforth, William	Middletown, Conn.	1792–1820
Fuller & Smith	Poquonock Bridge, Conn.	1849–1851
Griswold, Ashbil	Meriden, Conn.	1807–1835
Lee, Richard	Grafton, N.H.	1788–1790
	Ashfield, Mass.	1791–1793
	Lanesborough, Mass.	1794–1802
	Springfield, Vt.	1802–1820
or		
Lee, Richard, Jr.	Springfield, Vt.	1795–1816
Pierce, Samuel	Greenfield, Mass.	1792–1831
Southmayd, Ebenezer	Castleton, Vt.	1802–1820
Treadway, Amos	Middletown, Conn.	1760–1790
Whitmore, Jacob	Middletown, Conn.	1758–1790

AMERICAN PEWTER MAKERS

Bassett, Francis	New York, N.Y.	1718–1758
or		
Bassett, Francis, II	New York, N.Y.	1754–1799
Bassett, Frederick	New York, N.Y.	1761–1780
		and
		1785–1800
	Hartford, Conn.	1780–1785
Bassett, John	New York, N.Y.	1720–1761
Bradford, Cornelius	New York, N.Y.	1752–1753
		and
		1770–1785
	Philadelphia, Pa.	1753–1770
Brigden, Timothy	Albany, N.Y.	1816–1819
Capen & Molineux	New York, N.Y.	1848–1854
(Ephraim Capen and		
George Molineux)		
Elsworth, William J.	New York, N.Y.	1767–1798
Endicott & Sumner	New York, N.Y.	1846–1851
(Edmund Endicott and		
William F. Sumner)		
Hopper, Henry	New York, N.Y.	1842–1847
Kirby, William	New York, N.Y.	1760–1793
Leddell, Joseph	New York, N.Y.	1712–1753
or		
Leddell, Joseph Jr.	New York, N.Y.	1740–1754
Stafford, Spencer	Albany, N.Y.	1794–1830
Weekes, James	Poughkeepsie, N.Y.	1833–1835
Will, Henry	New York, N.Y.	1761–1775
		&
		1783–1793
	Albany, N.Y.	1775–1783
Will, John	New York, N.Y.	1752–1763
Yale & Curtis	New York, N.Y.	1858–1867
(Henry Yale and		
Stephen Curtis)		
Young, Peter	Albany, N.Y.	1785–1795
	New York, N.Y.	1775

Barns, Blak(e)slee	Philadelphia, Pa.	1812–1817
Boyd, Parks	Philadelphia, Pa.	1795–1819
Brunstrom, John Andrew	Philadelphia, Pa.	1783–1793
Harbeson, Benjamin Jr. and		
Harbeson, Joseph	Philadelphia, Pa.	1800

Heyne, Johann Christopher	Lancaster, Pa.	1754–1780
Palethorp, John H.	Philadelphia, Pa.	1820–1845
Palethorp, Robert Jr.	Philadelphia, Pa.	1817–1821
Will, William	Philadelphia, Pa.	1764–1798

MARYLAND

Kilbourn, Samuel	Baltimore, Md.	1814–1839
Lightner, George	Baltimore, Md.	1806–1815
Porter, James	Baltimore, Md.	1803

NORTH CAROLINA

Eggleston, Jacob	Middletown, Conn.	1795–1807
	Fayetteville, N.C.	1807–1813
Johnson, Jehiel	Middletown, Conn.	1815–1825
	Fayetteville, N.C.	1818–1819

VIRGINIA

| Danforth Joseph Jr. | Richmond, Va. | 1807–1812 |

Unidentified marks

"T.S." (*1760–1780*)
"R.B." Boston or Newport (*about 1760*)
"T.L." with anchor (*probably late 18th century*)
"I.H." (*18th century*)
J.M. Ufen
Eagle mark, only known example, about 1805
Kerfoot's eagle touch No. 1 (*possibly Gershom Jones, Providence 1774–1809*)
Four lion hall-marks and crowned X (*Pennsylvania, 18th century*)
Horse with raised foreleg (*early or mid 19th century*)
Rose-and-crown (*probably Pennsylvania, 18th century*)
"Semper Eadem" with rose-and-crown & London (*Boston, 18th century*)
Love, with crown and two birds (*Pennsylvania, late 18th or early 19th century*)

Initialed porringers

"E.G." (*probably 18th century*)
"I.G." (*probably 18th century*)
"W.N." (*probably 18th century*)
"R " (*probably 18th century*)
"R.G." (*probably 18th century*)

AMERICAN PEWTER MAKERS

BIBLIOGRAPHY

A Century of Meriden. Meriden: Journal Publishing Company, 1906.

Gibb, George Sweet, *The Whitesmiths of Taunton*. Cambridge: Harvard University Press, 1943.

Graham, John Meredith, II, *American Pewter*. Brooklyn Museum, 1949.

Jacobs, Carl, *Guide to American Pewter*. New York: The McBride Company, Inc., 1957.

Kerfoot, J. B., *American Pewter*. Boston and New York: Houghton Mifflin Company, 1924.

Lardner, Rev. Dionysius, *The Cabinet Cyclopedia*. London: Longman, Rees, Orme, Brown, Green & Longman, 1834.

Laughlin, Ledlie I., *Pewter in America*. Boston: Houghton Mifflin Company, 1940.

A20   PITCHER
Maker: William McQuilkin, Philadelphia, 1840–1853. Height
7½″, diameter 6″

(*Kauffman Collection*)

INDEX

(Page references in heavy type indicate illustrations.)

273

CHATS ON OLD PEWTER

INDEX

CHATS ON OLD PEWTER

INDEX TO THE AMERICAN SECTION

4714